# Journey to Dyatlov Pass

AN EXPLANATION OF THE MYSTERY

2nd edition

Keith McCloskey

Cover Photograph; Mikhail Petrov
Frontispiece Photo: *The Mountain of the Nine* Valentin Yakimenko

Journey to Dyatlov Pass / Keith McCloskey
ISBN: 979-8657792676

# Contents

Kian Michael McCloskey
22 November 2013

*In memory of my Grandson who had
one brief day of life*

# Introduction

This book is a slightly revised and updated edition of the same title that was published in 2016. For anyone who has purchased the first edition, I say do not buy this one because there are not enough changes to justify it. There have been a couple of developments in the Dyatlov story in the past few years which I cover towards the end of the book. In addition, I have added more photos and looked at aspects of the missile/rocket theory as well as the Mansi theory. On the analysis of the missile/ rocket theory I have included some excellent research by Hungarian Dyatlov theorist SZTALKER (his online 'handle'). This book also assumes that the reader already knows the Dyatlov story. This is not an introduction to the story, but rather a follow on from my first book *Mountain of the Dead* published by the History Press. There is plenty of material on the internet and several other books to get acquainted with the story. I want to mention that there was some criticism of the first edition of this book, saying that the 'journey' element was some kind of padding. In fact, the opposite is true. There are enough books out now to cover the full Dyatlov story and I didn't want to add to the pile. What I wanted to do is to give people an idea of what it was like to travel there and describe the location first hand. Nevertheless, as I said, I have tried to expand the military theory here and I have also added some research on the Mansi to back up why they may have been involved in the deaths of the group. I have also included a section on Intuitive Communication from a Dyatlov researcher. I had hoped to be able to include another report on an Intuitive Communication session from a lady who has helped police forces in the USA but is unable to spare the time at present. I hope to be able to include her findings on my website at a later stage. Towards the end, I explain the machinations behind getting the Dyatlov case reopened in Russia.

I also wanted to add a little comment here on the circular loop many of us seem to have got into with investigating this story. The Dyatlov Incident is a mystery but it is also primarily a police investigation and I give two police case analogies in the book. The first here concerns an incident from over 30 years ago. At the time, a book came out about "Cop Stories" in the USA. One of the most horrific involved a head-on car collision on a rural road which killed everyone in both cars. One of the cars was an open top coupe and had contained a family with a baby and the rescuers could not find the baby in the wreckage. The emergency services immediately started pulling the wreckage of the car to pieces to find the missing child, but there was no sign of it. A search then began in the vicinity to see if it could be found. When this search failed to turn up anything, a more organized search was begun and this too, was to no avail. Further police were called in and along with volunteers they formed a concentric ring at the crash site and worked their way slowly outwards. They went out several hundred feet to a point where nothing could have reached it from the crash site. However, they still had not found the child. It was getting dark by now and the perplexed volunteers had gathered back at the scene of the crash wondering where the child was. As much out of boredom as anything else, one of the searchers slowly panned his flashlight up into the overhanging trees directly above the crash site and there was the body of the baby. It had been impaled on the branch of a tree having been catapulted directly upwards by the force of the crash.

For me, this dreadful story symbolises what the Dyatlov story has now become. A large number of people constantly searching for evidence that must be there and going around in circles, but despite their best efforts, constantly drawing a blank. If you take a figure out of the air, say 25,000 people worldwide for arguments sake, and from that figure, say half of them have studied the Dyatlov Incident in depth, not one person has yet come up with a satisfactory and plausible scenario which answers all the questions as to what happened to the group. I have read some people in forums who say they have the answer to the mystery, give their theory and then announce their qualifications to back it up and that is an end to the matter. Against this, I have spoken to distinguished experts in various fields including a professor of chemistry, pathologists of many years' experience in different countries, professors of ethnography and the former Chief of a NATO armed forces group among many others and none can come up with definitive proof that answers all the questions. If you consider that hundreds, if not thousands, of people have mulled over this story, nobody seems to be able to come up with a conclusion that satisfies everyone.

At least, in the story above regarding the crash, there was a tragic but firm conclusion. I also feel that once someone settles on 'their' theory, nothing will dislodge them from it. To those who claim to know the story inside out and stick to their theory, I would say:- Imagine you are in court appearing as defence for your theory in front of a highly critical prosecutor and sceptical jury. The theory usually holds well until you reach the awkward parts and the prosecutor starts to dismantle the weaker parts of the theory. My view is that one should keep an open mind and pull your own theory to pieces for the flaws. My favoured military theory of an exercise gone wrong is the same. It has a number of flaws but I base it partially on the reaction of the authorities at the time. Urakov arrives from Moscow and in one day shuts the whole investigation down – why? Why were tests for the presence of radiation carried out for people who had died in the mountains on a hiking trip? The refusal by the authorities to issue permits for travel in the area for four years is also strange. Health and safety matters never particularly concerned the Soviets, so again – why? Ski Tourism didn't stop anywhere else in the USSR and the landscape in the Dyatlov Pass area didn't change in four years unless it was to remove or tidy up something, which is what I believe happened. However, I fully accept the flaws in the theory I support and there are plenty. Perhaps the main argument I have against my own military theory is the lack of information concerning military exercises in that area of the Urals. Equally the lack of confirmation of military exercises in that area of the Urals does not mean it didn't happen, but that is not proof that stands up.

The other element is that many who come to this story try to solve it by going on the internet and reading books and watching TV. Ask yourself, would a detective investigating a murder just try to do it by looking on the internet, watching shows on TV and reading books? Wouldn't he/she at least visit the scene of the crime to get a feel for it? The answer to the mystery lies not in the scrutiny of every single word written about the incident online or in books or the translated case files (which I think mislead), but probably lies in either or both of two places. Firstly, the memory of someone from that time and that person, if they are still alive, will be very close to the end of their life now. Alternatively, a file in an archive, as yet unseen, has the information which will unlock the answer to this mystery. The key for me would be to find that file in the archive and find that person with the memory.

I refer to the two police cases for comparison with this story because I feel that the Dyatlov case is no different as there were no immediate obvious answers and the Dyatlov case was subject to, what some might say, was a less than rigorous police investigation.

In the introduction to the first edition of this book, I finished by saying that getting a satisfactory answer to the Dyatlov mystery is not easy, but that I believed the incredible work carried out by Valentin Gerasimovich Yakimenko and the revelations in Evgeny Fyodorovich Okishev's interviews firmly point us in a particular direction. However, I still try to keep an open mind and am always open to discuss any new theory or variation on current theory.

In the final chapter I describe briefly the efforts made in getting the case reopened or more correctly, re-investigated. I started a GoFundMe account to raise the balance of funds in the West to cover the legal fees and travel costs for the Dyatlov Foundation and Leonid Proshkin to make the petition. I would like to thank all who contributed and a list of those who kindly contributed is at the rear of the book.

Keith McCloskey
June 2020

## Notes on the text

The various names and meanings of the mountains involved are well discussed elsewhere. I refer to the mountain the group died on as Kholat Syakhl. As a matter of interest, Russian Dyatlov theorists have now started referring to Kholat Syakhl as *The Mountain of the Nine* as an allusion to the nine hikers who died there.

In my first book, a number of readers said they had difficulty getting to grips with the Russian names. What I have done to try and make it slightly easier is to try and reduce some of the names of the Dyatlov group as follows:

- Lyudmila Dubinina — Luda
- Zinaida Kolmogorova — Zina
- Igor Dyatlov — Igor Dyatlov
- Semyon Zolotarev — Zolotarev
- Georgy Krivonischenko — Krivoy
- Yury Doroshenko — Doroshenko
- Alexandr Kolevatov — Kolevatov
- Nicolai Thibault-Brignoles — Thibo
- Yury Yudin — Yury Yudin

Yury is a common Russian forename and the Yury most commonly mentioned in the text is my good friend Yury Kuntsevich of the Dyatlov Foundation who I refer to as Yury K.

I also wish to apologise for the image quality in Appendix VII as these were all that were available and they are scans of scans, not originals.

# Chapter 1

In early 2015 I was in touch with Yury Kuntsevich (Yury K) from the Dyatlov Foundation in Ekaterinburg, Russia. Yury K runs the Foundation to keep alive the memory of the nine hikers who tragically died at what came to be known as the Dyatlov Pass, and also acts as a conduit for ideas and theories as to what may have happened to the Dyatlov group on the night of 1/2 February 1959. He was discussing the planning of his trip in the summer from Ekaterinburg up to the Dyatlov Pass, over 400 miles (644km) in the northern Ural Mountains. It is a trip he makes every year with different groups and individuals each time. Since my first visit and the publication of my book in 2012 on the Dyatlov Incident, we had kept in regular contact and discussed various theories and any additions to those theories that cropped up from various quarters. What he had to say on this occasion certainly piqued my interest as there were two separate points which had cropped up which related directly to my own theory of what had happened to the group that fateful night. The two points actually concerned the Chistop Massif, which is a mountainous area, the westernmost edge of which lay approximately 40 kilometres (25 miles) to the east and slightly to the south of Kholat Syakhl, where the bodies of the Dyatlov group were found. I was very keen to be involved in this particular trip. The problem though was would there be enough time to combine a visit to the Chistop Massif as well as a visit to Kholat Syakhl where the members of the Dyatlov group died? Whilst there were several miles between the two locations, we would be on foot and going through trails in thick forest. There are trails for all-terrain vehicles in the area but once it rains, you can walk as fast as an all-terrain vehicle can slowly grind its way through the sea of mud that the trails become.

There was also another problem that I had not expected. With the fighting in Ukraine and the sanctions imposed on Russia by the EU and USA, getting a visa was not quite as easy as it had been on my trip a couple of years previously. Even without the trouble in Ukraine, relations between Russia and the West seemed to be declining over the past few years. We had enjoyed friendly visits by all types of Russian military aircraft to air shows in the UK in the 1990s but now were seeing a return to something more akin to the Cold War years with Russian bombers approaching the UK causing RAF aircraft to be scrambled to intercept them and cat and mouse games being played in the Baltic between Russian and NATO ships and aircraft. A friend of mine in Russia remarked to me "it looks like the Iron Curtain is slowly starting to descend once again". On my first visit to Ekaterinburg, I only had to send my passport in by post for my visa with the accompanying paperwork. This time I now had to go in person to the outsourced company that processes Russian visas and have my fingerprints taken. I had problems as my original application was rejected due to voucher issues. My Dyatlov friends and colleagues were perplexed at the trouble I was having getting a visa issued and one of my Russian friends had said that he had been refused a visa for Switzerland recently. I had more or less given up on the trip because of the visa issues and fully expected the application to be declined, but barely two weeks before I was due to leave, it came through. I was going to the Dyatlov Pass!

# Chapter 2

During the early summer of 2015, reading comments on news forums in the West, many of them stated that Russia was tottering on its feet as a result of Western sanctions on the country's economy. While that may have been true to some extent, it certainly wasn't apparent on my drive into Ekaterinburg from the airport in August 2015. There were plenty of new cars on the roads, tower cranes worked on several new multi-storey buildings which were in the process of going up, and when we reached the city, a large team of workmen were resurfacing a road. If the country was verging on collapse, as alleged by some, there was certainly no sign of it on the surface.

After checking into the hotel, I had wanted to conduct at least one interview, but with only twenty four hours before we were due to leave for the Dyatlov Pass, there was not enough time as, not only did I need to help with the packing for the journey, but I also had to go to the main post office and register with the police and Ministry of Emergency Situations. I went over to the Dyatlov Foundation to see Yury K with my translator, Marina. The Foundation is located on Pervomayskaya Street, just to the west of the centre of Ekaterinburg. The name Pervomayskaya relates to the May Day holiday, and is not a street of convicted sex offenders which the name may sound to Western ears. By the time we had been to the main post office with Yury K and Marina and completed the formalities, there was only time to go back to the Foundation and prepare for the trip.

There were many people, including foreigners, travelling both north and south up to that area of the Ural Mountains from Ekaterinburg. I had been told that many foreigners who make the trip don't bother to register, but I was anxious for as little as possible to go wrong from officialdom's point of view. On my last trip I had made the mistake of applying to the Ministry of Foreign Affairs in Moscow through the British Consulate in Ekaterinburg for permission to travel up to the area of the Dyatlov Pass. This was six months before we were due to travel and after being asked for our passport details, the application went backwards and forwards with requests from the Consulate to the Ministry about what was happening, with the response from the Ministry always that they were still "looking at the request". Eventually we ran out of time and nothing had happened. I thought it best not to travel in case there was any issue and it turned out we were not given permission to travel by the Ministry. It would have looked bad if we had been stopped and found that we had made the trip after applying for permission and then travelling without it being granted. I knew of some foreigners who had made the trip and also people who had come from the opposite side of the Urals (the Perm Krai/Komi Republic or western side, to the eastern, Sverdlovsk Oblast, side and then south to Ekaterinburg). This time I thought I decided to register with the police and the Ministry of Emergency Situations, so I had some official backing and then just go and see what happened. There are two large areas closed to foreigners in the near 400 miles between Ekaterinburg and Ivdel but I figured that staying on the railway should not create any problems.

There are always people coming and going at the Foundation and after registering at the post office, a number of people were there. I was not sure how many of us were going up to the Pass as I had assumed it would be just myself and Yury K plus two guides Sergey Fadeev and Alexander (Sasha) Alekseenkov, who were both present at the Foundation when we arrived. It turned out there was going to be a much larger number making the journey but we were to meet them at the main Ekaterinburg Railway Station. Some of them were coming from as far away as Moscow, Kazan and Saint Petersburg.

Yury K sorted out the large quantity of food that we needed to take and divide among us. Space and weight was at a premium. The collapsible and comfortable chair I was looking forward to spending my evenings on was an early casualty. For seating, we were to use a thin piece of foam with slits cut at the sides and through which a length of fabric was used to thread through and tie at the front at our lower stomach area, so in effect the foam was permanently on our backsides while we were trekking, the idea being we could just collapse on a log or the ground when we took a break.

I spoke to Sergey Fadeev about the work he had done on the locations of the bodies of the Dyatlov group when they were found. Contrary to what some people may think the locations are not beyond dispute. Sergey and Yury K showed me the pictures and calculations that Sergey had made using the photos taken by the search parties in 1959. He used these photos from 1959 to transpose onto pictures taken through the years right up to date to show the changes in the topography. Clearly, he had spent months, if not years, working on them. Sergey travels up to the Dyatlov Pass at least twice a year and spends most of his time there working on the different locations. We examined the cedar tree photos where the first bodies (Doroshenko and Krivoy) were found by the burnt-out fire. The actual cedar tree itself is one of the most hotly disputed locations among Dyatlov theorists. Sergey showed me first the photo of the bodies as they were found in February 1959. The picture was taken from roughly a couple of metres behind the tree to the right of it, with the bodies lying in the snow just beyond the tree. A couple of metres beyond the bodies are two stumps in a "V" shape. He then showed me a picture he had taken the previous year (2014). It seemed to be virtually the same except he pointed out that within the "V" shaped stump of two trees in the background, there was another tree stump crossing over the other two stumps. He felt that this cast some doubt over the location. Despite this though, it was highly unlikely, impossible even, that in over 50 years, the location would be relatively unchanged. Nevertheless, I had to admit that the photos he showed me were pretty conclusive that this was the correct location. To support his view that this was the cedar tree, he showed me more photos which were taken at different times of the year, including February (the same month as the deaths) to track the angles of the shadows. He had drawn grid lines on the newer photos to show the shadows were following the same tracks of the shadows from the trees as that from the 1959 search party photos. Sergey then pulled out another set of photos. These were all taken from the ground upwards and showed the trunk of the cedar tree with a number of broken branches at different heights. Again, there was the same painstaking work with grid lines drawn on the photos to show the direction of the shadows along with close-ups of where the branches were broken. Some of the complete breaks of branches were of quite thick branches and very close to the trunk which made me think they would have been impossible for members of the Dyatlov group to have broken for their fire in 1959 as it would have required considerable strength to have taken them down because of the sheer size of them. While it would be amazing to stand at the cedar Tree and look up at the broken branches imagining the members of the Dyatlov party desperately breaking off branches in their bid to build the fire up to stay alive, the truth is that it was unlikely the tree would have remained totally untouched in that time. I would think that some of the numerous visitors to the Pass every year would probably shin up the tree to break off souvenirs of their own. And again, this is assuming that this cedar tree is the same one where Doroshenko and Krivoy were found. As I said though, Sergey's arguments and work looked convincing to me and I looked forward to seeing it for myself.

Two female twenty-year-old architecture students, Lisa Kuzmina and Nastya Golovachova, were assisting in the preparations for the trip and were coming to Kholat Syakhl with us. They were very pleasant and with beautiful manners. Both of them spoke good English and wanted to practice their English with me. I asked them to help me learn Russian and I cursed myself for my inadequate preparation with a bare smattering of a few words and basic greetings. Lisa would teach me a word that sounded to my ears like ARM-CHAIR-RI-KA-REEBOK and she would tell me the meaning and ten minutes later I would forget it. I found it a hard language to get my tongue around. I had become lazy by relying on my translator, Marina, to do all the talking and explaining and this had kept me in my comfort zone, but Marina was not coming to Kholat Syakhl with us, so it stung me out of my lethargy into trying to get involved in the language.

There was also a woman (Helga) and her son (Victor Venedeev) helping us pack and prepare. They were not coming with us either but they lived in Ekaterinburg and were very keen "Dyatlov enthusiasts". The son, Victor, said his mother would like to speak to me and he would translate. We got a cup of tea and sat down as I was always interested to hear other peoples' views, particularly people from Russia. Helga explained her theory as to what had happened to the group and it was one I had come across before. She asked if I had heard of the balloons that had been launched by the West over the Soviet Union in the mid to late 1950s. I said I had heard of the United States' and probable NATO use of them.

The balloon project seemed to me to be a bit of a cack-handed attempt for them to be used for photo reconnaissance over the Soviet Union, but such was the demand for intelligence on the Soviet military capabilities at the time that anything was worth trying. Helga then asked if I had heard of the Japanese use of similar balloons with explosives (*Fu-Go* or Fire Balloons) during the Second World War against the USA, which I had. She mentioned the only deaths caused by these Japanese balloon bombs were in Oregon when a woman, 26-year-old Elsie Mitchell, and five of her students aged from 11 to 14 were picnicking when she saw one of the balloons lying on the ground. They had approached the strange balloon as they were intrigued as to what it might be. When she attempted to open the casing carried by the balloon, it exploded and killed them all. Thus, Elsie Mitchell and her five Sunday School students had gained the unfortunate distinction of being the only Americans killed by enemy action on US soil during World War Two.

Helga's theory was that the Americans had placed explosive charges in these balloons and that one of the balloons had come down close to the Dyatlov party on the night of 1/2 February 1959. It could explain what appeared to be a large white object in some of the photos taken from the group's cameras. On seeing the balloon and the casing underneath it, some of the group approached the balloon and tried to grab the casing underneath it when it exploded, seriously injuring them. Hearing the screams of the injured and fearing something dreadful, the remaining members of the group cut their way out of the tent and taking the injured members of the group with them, made their way to the treeline at the bottom of Kholat Syakhl to get out of harm's way fearing more explosions were about to happen. She said that, relieved of the weight of the explosives, the balloon lifted back into the air again and was then carried completely away from the area. I said to her that I certainly accepted it was a possibility, which it was. The *Project Genetrix* programme, as the NATO/USA programme of balloon flights was known, had stopped almost as soon as it had started in 1956, but balloons continued to overfly the Soviet Union for many years afterwards despite the use of spy satellites and the start of U-2 spy flights. The first U-2 flights over the Soviet Union started in late 1956. The balloons were launched mainly from Norway and were carried towards Yakutsk and then onto Japan. Aside from the risk of injuring Soviet civilians, in the event of a balloon coming down, it seemed like a big risk to take. The U-2 flown by Gary Powers, which was shot down near Sverdlovsk (Ekaterinburg), carried explosives to destroy the aircraft in the event of it coming down in enemy territory. However, Powers had failed to arm the explosives prior to his baling out of the stricken aircraft after it was hit. The result was that the Soviets were able to recover most of the aircraft despite the damage from the crash. So, it was possible according to Helga's theory that had a balloon come down near the group, it may have contained explosives which were designed to destroy the photo reconnaissance equipment it carried. Not realising the danger, Zolotarev and Luda may have been the closest to it when it went off, with the others who had suffered lesser injuries standing further away. It could account for the fact that some members of the group had cameras with them and also could account for the panic to get away from the immediate area if they thought there were more balloons around.

I said to her that it was certainly all possible, as with so many of the Dyatlov theories. She then asked me about my idea of a Soviet military accident. I explained that this was the reason for my visit as I wanted to talk to Yury K and also interview some people who I felt could help with this theory. I told her about the testimony from the crewman of one of the two Tu 95M *Bear* bombers from the Ukraine, that had flown over the area that night and may have dropped either parachute mines or explosives of some kind in which pressure rather than shrapnel may have killed the group. She asked me where they would have been heading from a base so far away in the Ukraine. I replied that it would not have been necessary for them to have had a destination planned, the bombing area may just have been in the northern Ural Mountains, but I said that 600 miles to the north of the Dyatlov Pass was Vorkuta and that they may have been heading there to land before going back to their base. Vorkuta lies on the northern edge of Russia in the Polar Urals and is one of approximately half a dozen "bounce" aerodromes built during the Cold War by the Soviets. These "bounce" aerodromes had very long runways for the bombers and were intended to be the last stop on the way out for Soviet bombers attacking the USA to refuel and the first stop on the way back, assuming they made it back, and also assuming that there was anything left to return to. For a Tu 95M *Bear,* the journey to Vorkuta from flying over Kholat Syakhl would be around about an hour and twenty minutes. Helga did not think that Vorkuta would have been a likely destination but as I said, it was a theory and at this point not the military theory that was foremost in my mind.

A number of people arrived at the Foundation whilst I was talking to Helga and her son and I asked her, as well as any of the older people who would like to comment on it, about the reaction of the Soviet authorities at the time. It is always tricky talking about politics in many places and I was aware that a number of people present had lived through the Soviet era and I neither wanted to offend nor end up getting a good kicking. What I said was (and I genuinely believed it) that the impression I had from talking to people and reading about the Soviet times was that the Communist Party was in control and that they liked to present an image to the people that they were in control and knew what they were doing. They had an answer for everything and that if anything went wrong it could always be blamed on enemies of the state, capitalists, saboteurs etc. I said that with the Dyatlov story, the conclusion reached after the investigation was that nobody in authority knew what had happened and that this conclusion of an "unknown compelling force" being responsible seemed strange for an atheist, hard-nosed government because there was a hint of the supernatural or UFO involvement in the conclusion. I said that here was a government which was planning missions to the moon, building a mighty military and throwing up housing for the population as fast as it could. It presented itself as a government and way of life that was superior to any other on the planet and yet it seemed stumped by the deaths of the nine hikers. It just did not ring true to me.

Helga responded to this by saying her view was that the cause of the deaths was so strange that the authorities' reaction to it was that they were as puzzled as everyone else and that they had no answers. I didn't agree with her view but like everything else in the Dyatlov story, it was always plausible because there was nothing to prove or disprove it.

In the middle of all the preparations and packing, Yury K sat down with me and Marina to talk about the journey. One of the two reasons for my own trip to Russia this time had unfortunately evaporated into thin air. It was a massive disappointment to put it mildly. Earlier in the year Yury K had told me that the wreckage of the Yak 12 observation aircraft which had been flown by Gennady Patrushev, and in which he had been killed when it crashed in 1963, had been located on the Chistop Massif. This was of great interest to me because Patrushev had allegedly flown over the Dyatlov group's tent on Kholat Syakhl the day before it was discovered and radioed in the position. He had seen two bodies by the tent. At the time, Patrushev was 26 years old and although he lived in Sverdlovsk (Ekaterinburg), he was regularly posted out to outlying airfields such as Ivdel to carry out observation duties in designated areas. He had actually been posted out to Ivdel in early 1959 and had met the Dyatlov group when they had got off the train from Serov and were waiting for a bus to take them to Vizhay on their way to Mount Otorten. At their meeting Patrushev had warned Igor Dyatlov to be careful on their trip. This may be poetic licence as the group had arrived late at night and spent the night at Ivdel railway station before taking the bus to Vizhay the following morning. Ivdel is not a large place, so news of the arrival of a group at the station would have spread fairly quickly, so it is quite possible they did meet up. In any event, Patrushev knew Igor Dyatlov from Sverdlovsk beforehand. Gennady Patrushev therefore had a personal interest in finding his friend and the other members of the group when the word came to Ivdel for him to commence searching the route that they had taken and locate them. In the aftermath of the discovery of the bodies, Patrushev felt deeply uneasy about the circumstances surrounding the whole story. He was to be killed in 1963 when his aircraft crashed less than 30 miles (48km) from the Dyatlov Pass and just a few years after the deaths of the Dyatlov group. I will elaborate on the circumstances regarding Patrushev later.

For me personally, though I had a great interest in aviation and wanted to view the wreckage myself to see what could be deduced from it. Joining us on the journey north was an aviation specialist from Kazan who was also very keen to have a look through the wreckage. Patrushev's body had been recovered from the wreckage at the time of the accident, but the majority of the aircraft had been left where it had come down. What had happened was that a hunter had recently come across the wreckage on the Chistop Massif. This news had reached the Dyatlov Foundation and the intention was that, although our destination on the journey would be Kholat Syakhl, a few of us would either divert from the route to Kholat Syakhl and go south to the crash site and then make our way over to catch up with the others at the base camp on Kholat Syakhl or set up at Kholat Syakhl and make our way to the crash site from there. Yury K said that it was unlikely there would be enough time to do it all but I was hopeful that we could. In the event, the decision was made for us. The hunter who supposedly had discovered the wreckage of the Yak 12 now refused to give the co-ordinates of the location. It seemed odd that the hunter would give out the information that he had found the wreckage and then afterwards refuse to give any details of the location. As Patrushev's body had long been removed from it, it could not have been out of any respect for the dead, but it made me wonder if this particular hunter had really found the wreckage. Either way we were stymied. The area of the Chistop Massif is huge, so it was not a search we could undertake ourselves. It was a disappointment we had to swallow and hopefully Patrushev's aircraft would eventually be found another time.

Gennady Patrushev with a Yak 9 fighter (Gamatina)

We were going to make the trip in the first two weeks of August and fortunately it was out of the season to be bitten by Siberian ticks which could give you Lyme Disease. However, the one thing that concerned me about the trip was the presence of bears in the northern Urals. I am basically a coward and always have been. I had assumed at first that the bears were quite small and resembled the cuddly smiling *Mischa* of the Moscow Olympics who looked ready to leap into your arms and lick your face. However, looking at pictures of Russian bears in a book and on the internet, it seemed that, not only were some of them extremely large, but many of them looked as if they were dealing with unresolved anger issues. Before I left the UK, I was talking to the wife of my best friend and mentioned my almost irrational fear of bears. She replied, quite seriously, that would it not be better to be torn apart in a bear attack than to end your days senile and dribbling in a care home? She worked in such a care home and saw this for herself. I wasn't quite so sure but I have to say it was a slightly more positive take on the whole thing that I hadn't really considered before.

Both Yury K and Marina scoffed at my fears. Yury said that the bears were well fed in the summer and the time we were going. Although they ate carrion and mammals, their diet in the summer consisted of berries, roots, grasses and insects which were plentiful. He said that they didn't like metallic sounds and when they heard groups of people carrying tins or metallic objects making a clattering noise, they would move away. The only time to be concerned about them was in the fall (autumn) when they were trying to eat as much as possible before they hibernated. Yury K had studied bears and said that an interesting thing about them was when they awoke from hibernation, the way they cleared their systems (bowels) was to find an ants' nest and disturb it with their front paws and snout. The furious ants would crawl all over the bear, biting it wherever they could. The resulting mini shocks to the bear's system would cause it to have a good dump and clear its system out so it could go and start eating afresh.

Yury K said that the only animal to be concerned about was not bears or wolves but wolverines. It seems that many people assume wolverine was a superhero in the cinema. I had heard of wolverines, but reading up about them, it was odd to see a fairly small, almost comical looking animal that resembled a raccoon or chipmunk on steroids. However, they possess an aggression and ferocity out of all proportion to their size. They are highly territorial and have no fear of any animal larger than itself. They regularly attack bears, and Wikipedia gives an account of a wolverine that was seen to kill a Polar bear by seizing the throat of the bear with its teeth and hanging on until the bear had suffocated.

Despite what the others in the group said regarding my concerns about bears, I was not entirely convinced. I grew up in Africa and have developed a very healthy respect for large wild animals that can eat you. They are highly unpredictable and I don't belong to the Timothy Treadwell school of thinking. As if to add fuel to my paranoia, the night before I left for Russia, I had watched a programme on TV about a South African named Marius Els who had raised a hippo from five months old in South Africa. The hippo had matured to full size and despite ominous signs and the concerns of his friends and colleagues about the danger the animal presented, he told them it was like a son to him and there was no danger, only for him to be killed by it one day.

Despite all the scoffing and teasing from the others about my irrational bear fear, as it turned out, I was later to have the last laugh at Kholat Syakhl.

# Chapter 3

In the late afternoon, we assembled outside the Foundation for photos before we set off on our trip on the overnight train to Ivdel. My rucksack weighed about 25 kilos (55lbs). I had spent some time training for the trip but I was unprepared for what lay before me. Walking a few steps outside a corridor into a parking area is not quite the same as hiking in the forest and mountains with a heavy rucksack. Helga and her son, who I had earlier been speaking to about the *Project Genetrix* balloons, had been to the Dyatlov Pass before, but were not going on this occasion. She had her car though, and did us a great favour by taking our rucksacks to the main railway station in Ekaterinburg whilst the rest of us made our way there separately in one of the trolley buses that criss-cross the city. There was a great air of expectation and excitement, even though we were two to three days travelling time away from reaching the base of Kholat Syakhl. There were several other people at the station to meet us. Our portion of the group who had travelled from the Foundation numbered eight and we met up with a much larger number that swelled the group to 24 people in all, including Yury K and the two guides.

Buying a train ticket in Russia is not quite the same as buying a train ticket in Europe. Yury K had booked my return ticket to Ivdel for me online which required my passport details and when we got on the platform a woman was checking each passenger against a list. She took issue with the translation of my surname into Cyrillic for some reason and said it had not been done correctly. Eventually she agreed to let me on and I made my way to my allotted berth. We had booked ourselves into a sleeper carriage which was full of people with not a spare berth. Despite the fact it was full, with no privacy, people seemed generally more respectful of the body space of others and seeing I was a foreigner, people went out of their way to help me. There were pillows already on each berth and a uniformed woman came around to each passenger and gave us a plastic bag which contained sheets and a towel which we had to sign for. It struck me as a very civilised way of doing things. Once I had stowed my rucksack away in the locker under the seat, Yury K said to come down to the other end of the carriage for something to eat and to meet people. Trains in the West usually have a buffet or restaurant car; on our train there was a small room at the end of our carriage in which sat a woman with some bars of *Snickers* and bottles of mineral water laid out on top of a cupboard. It was basic, but it worked for me.

Lisa Kuzmina, the 'Spirit of the Forest' (Mikhail Petrov)

Alexey the Officer who runs the RUSFORS project in the Urals (Mikhail Petrov)

The carriage had sections of four berths facing each other down one side with two below and two above. Some of the group were sitting on the lower berths of the end section with Yury K. There were the two guides who I had already met at the Foundation: Sergey and Alexander Alekseenkov (Sasha) along with Lisa Kuzmina and Alexey Martin (Alexey the Officer). I sat down on the lower berth and said hello to everyone. Sasha was a real live wire who looked lean and fit. It came as no surprise to me that he made the trip north to the Dyatlov Pass three to four times a year from Ekaterinburg, including at least one trip in the middle of winter to keep his hand in by making the journey in the most difficult conditions as faced by the Dyatlov group. Alexey the Officer spoke very good English and had served in the Russian army as a *Starshiy Letenant* (Senior Lieutenant). He had left the army and now ran his own online media business in Ekaterinburg. He was also the Urals co-ordinator for RUFORS (the Urals UFO group). Alexey the Officer said something which I felt was quite insightful. He said that as a young man he was crazy about war and would have gone anywhere just to be able to fight in one. However, after he joined the army and being involved in a real war (the second Chechnyan campaign), he said that having taken part in a genuine war, it no longer had any appeal for him. When we spoke about the Dyatlov deaths, he told me he was a big supporter of the Yury Yakimov light-set theory which included aspects of possible extra-terrestrial/UFO involvement. I explained that people were either strongly for Yury Yakimov's theory, or strongly against it if they did not believe in UFOs. It was perhaps one of the most contentious theories on account of this because people were so strongly divided on it. The whole UFO involvement idea has people either believing it or saying that it is preposterous nonsense. As I always do when I discuss it, I say that I have my own ideas but that I am completely open to suggestions and will consider any new theory. What every single theory lacks is definitive proof, and as far as I was concerned, until proof is produced to support a theory, then each one as is valid as the next.

I wanted to meet Yury Yakimov who had come up with the light-set theory and I had been told in Ekaterinburg that he was joining our group when we arrived at Ivdel railway station. However, Alexey the Officer me that he had received a message from Yury Yakimov just before he (Alexey) left, in which Yury Yakimov explained that he was ill on account of a sore back and would not be able to make the journey to the Dyatlov Pass with us. Alexey said it was strange how in the Dyatlov group there were to be "two Yurys" and how one of them (Yury Yudin) had had to turn back because of illness and he said now here is our group going to the Pass, which should also have "two Yurys" (Yury Kuntsevich and Yury Yakimov) and how one of them has had to turn back because of a sore back. I replied that I hoped that would be the only similarity and that our trip would have a happier ending.

The two girls, Nastya and Lisa, who had travelled with us from the Dyatlov Foundation intrigued me. They were both from the closed city of Chelyabinsk but were living in Ekaterinburg and studying Architecture at the Ural State University of Architecture and Art, under the well-known (in architecture circles - both inside and outside Russia) lecturer Mikhail Gavrilovich Matveev. They both spoke good English and reiterated what they said to me at the Dyatlov Foundation; that in return for me speaking English with them for practice, said they would look out for me – an offer I couldn't refuse. The blond girl, Lisa told me she was a child of the forest. Since the age of eight, her grandfather took her hunting in the forests for extended periods and as a young girl probably spent more time in the forest than she did in a town or city. As her grandfather grew older and unable to hunt, her father would then take her hunting in the forests. She said that when she spent any time in a city, she felt trapped and would have to go out to the forest for a while just to escape from the claustrophobia. It was no idle boast. To see her later in the forest, everything she did, whether it was observing animal tracks, preparing food over a campfire or cutting trees came as naturally to her as walking along a street in a town looking at shop windows. Quite simply it was obvious she was totally at ease in the forest and could deal with any problem that arose. She impressed me far more than any of the "personalities" in the survival-in–the-wild type programmes I have seen on TV. She was the forest and the forest was her. She lived and breathed it. I asked her why she had chosen to come on the trip to the Dyatlov Pass and she told me that her grandmother had attended the funerals of the seven members of the Dyatlov group (these were Dyatlov, Doroshenko, Thibo, Kolevatov, Rustem and the two girls – Zina and Luda) who had been buried at the Mikhailovskoe (*St. Michael the Archangel*) cemetery in Sverdlovsk. She said that she had later met Yury K who sometimes lectures at the university, through her architecture lecturer and through him became more interested in the Dyatlov story and wanted to make the journey to see the Pass for herself.

Her friend Nastya was quite deep and introspective. I asked her about her reasons for the trip and what she thought about what had happened to the Dyatlov group. She said that she had known about the Dyatlov story for a long time and she viewed the trip as a chance to indulge her love of the outdoors and also look at the Dyatlov story afresh after seeing the location. She explained that she had read up on all the theories and that her view of what happened to them coincided with Sergey's, one of our guides. I asked her what her and Sergey's view was and she said that in her view the following happened;

*The Dyatlov group had made their way up to the outlying rocks heading towards Otorten via the Kholat Syakhl spur. Kolevatov who was carrying the tent injures his leg and with this complication, it makes more sense to pitch the tent for the night and to continue on their way in the morning. The location for the tent is in some ways an ideal test of their abilities as the conditions and terrain are harsh and Igor Dyatlov feels it would fit into their plan to push themselves as hard as they can. While they cleared the area on the slope, Zina bandaged Kolevatov's leg. Once the tent is set up, they go inside and start to eat but without setting up the stove. Zolotarev and Thibault go outside to answer a call of nature when suddenly a luminous object appears in the sky (possibly a rocket or a UFO). Zolotarev takes a quick picture of it. Krivonischenko also takes a picture with his camera through a hole in the tent. Rustem Slobodin decides to go outside and puts his boots on. The object flies right over the tent leaving a trail of vapours/gases. The fumes make it very difficult to breathe and Zolotarev and Thibault make some cuts on the tent before running away from it. Those inside the tent start to panic and tear the tent to shreds to get out. A couple of big incisions are made which enable them to get out and run after Zolotarev and Thibault. Igor Dyatlov is one of the last to run as the group leader, but out of the group, he inhales the most of the fumes. Slobodin runs but falls and hits his head and is unconscious for some time. He is very cold and starts to move again sluggishly before stopping and freezing to death. Group leader Igor Dyatlov, becomes exhausted and cannot reach the cedar tree 300 metres (985ft) away and soon dies in a sitting position before his body lowers with his hands remaining on his chest. The other seven in the group reach the cedar tree and start to make a fire. Zina is one of the best dressed against the cold and she goes in search of Dyatlov and Slobodin to find them both dead. She decides to go to the tent but changes her mind and in order to save her energy turns to return to the fire at the cedar tree. About 800 metres (2,625ft) from the cedar tree she is exhausted, falls down and freezes to death. The others by the cedar tree realise the extreme seriousness of their situation and that nothing short of a miracle is going to save them. They split up and Zolotarev and Thibault, being warmly dressed, start digging the flooring for the shelter whilst Dubinina stays at the fire. Kolevatov also goes over to help with digging the shelter. Doroshenko and Krivonischenko climb up the cedar tree and start breaking branches off and throwing them into the fire. There are also rotten birches lying around but they are not as good for catching alight as the cedar boughs. Both Doroshenko and Krivonischenko lose consciousness, with one falling from the cedar tree, and they both freeze to death. Dubinina is also beginning to lose consciousness, but she manages to cut the clothing from the corpses of Doroshenko and Krivonischenko and distributes the clothing to the ones in most need. The fire has by now long gone out and Dubinina makes her way over to the shelter which has four seats with some flooring created by twigs. They deepen the shelter by two metres. Eventually the cold kills all of them. Zolotarev is the last to die, and realising the hopelessness of the situation, he pulls a notebook and pencil out of his pocket to make a note telling whoever finds them what happened. He dies before writing anything. The snow continues to fall and eventually the weight of the snow buries all four of them, breaking the ribs of two of them and damaging Thibault's skull. Kolevatov is lying further up from the others and suffers no real injuries but suffocates under the weight of snow. The entire group are now dead. A few days later the military appear on skis. They inspect the tent, find the bodies and inspect them as well as checking their pockets. They turn some of the bodies over, including Doroshenko. They report the finding and on 6 February the official case is opened. The authorities realise that a missile test has caused the deaths and decide to shut down all enquiries. They set a target date of 14 February to start moving things and eventually get aircraft, helicopters and search parties organised with the tent eventually being found on 26 February and the first bodies on 27 February.*

As a theory it was very plausible, although as I will later elaborate on, I had my own take on the likelihood of a rocket or missile test firing.

The two guides Sergey and Sasha invited me to share their food with them. We tucked into the food on the table between us as the endless Russian landscape rolled past the train window. The distance we had to travel was the same as London to Edinburgh and yet to look at the distance on a map of Russia looked like a short commute between two points. Sasha told me about his regular trips up to the Pass each year and his obsession with the Dyatlov story. The aviation specialist Shamil, pointed out of the window as we passed a row of self-propelled guns which looked like Sprut-SDs covered with tarpaulins on flat railway wagons. Their barrels poked upwards out from under the tarpaulins like some kind of prehistoric animals sniffing the air. As if to underline the military nature of the whole region we were passing through, the first stop for the train was Verkh-Neyvinsk. The town is built around a large lake and we could see people on jet-skis on the far side throwing up plumes of water as they twisted and turned in the late evening sunlight. Unlike many stations we were to pass through, Verkh-Neyvinsk was modern and clean looking. The buildings we could see were also clean and modern in appearance. Alexey the Officer told me that it was a closed city and that security here was so tight that even an invisible alien would have a job getting in. Everyone laughed when it was said that what they did there was not to be discussed but it was something to do with Centrifuges. A bit of internet digging later showed that security at Verkh-Neyvinsk was so tight because it was a diffusion plant for Plutonium U-235.

It is a place that was a mystery to the CIA and other Western Intelligence agencies for a number of years after the war. Both the USA and the Soviet Union had a number of captured German scientists working on their respective atomic weapons programmes. The German scientists were subject to the strictest security by their Soviet captors and allowed to occasionally write the occasional innocuous letter back to their families in Germany. These letters were closely examined by Western Intelligence for clues as to where the Soviet atomic research facilities might be located, as the Soviets would not allow any reference to either their work or where they were based. They looked at the comments made in the letters which spoke about the time taken on train journeys from Moscow and the weather on different days. Using weather reports and train timetables along with very brief descriptions of "large towns" etc they were able to pinpoint some of the locations such as Kyshtym, near Chelyabinsk but one location which was regularly visited by the POW German Scientists was unknown by name and the Western Intelligence services were unable to identify it. It was known and referred to by the German scientists only as "Kefirstadt" because of the soft drink available there which was "Kefir", the fermented milk of the Caucasus. After some of the scientists returned to East Germany, a number of them defected to the West and were debriefed after they had defected. "Kefirstadt" was finally identified as Verkh-Neyvinsk.

After we had eaten, people began to settle down for the night journey to Ivdel. As I mentioned, there was no privacy. A woman on the opposite of the corridor and I assumed her daughter and son aged around 15 and 20 years respectively, started to get ready for sleep. They held a sheet across the lower bunk for the daughter to give her privacy and the rest of us made up our bunks. The 20 year old male who had held the sheet for his sister was in the upper bunk opposite to me and he pulled himself up and slid effortlessly into it. I looked at my upper bunk and realised it was not going to be quite so easy for me. I slowly hauled myself up at the bottom end of the bunk from the corridor and climbed onto the bunk on my knees, getting myself wedged with my back on the roof and looking for all the world, like a geriatric chameleon. I gazed enviously at the lower bunks whilst pushing hard to free my back off the roof. Once I lay down on the bunk and pulled the sheet up it was actually quite pleasant. I checked the photos I had taken on the camera and settled down for the night listening to the clackety-clack of the train on the rails; the motion of the train soon sending everyone to sleep.

One difference between our journey and the railway journey undertaken by the Dyatlov party was that we did not have to change trains at Serov. Our train had left Ekaterinburg's main station at 8pm and although we did not have to change, it stopped at Serov just after midnight. I thought about the military aspect of the region again because less than 50 miles (80km) west of Serov lay Kosvinski Mountain on the eastern edge of the Ural Mountains. This contains a deep underground facility, like Cheyenne Mountain in the USA. This is a command and control centre for the Russian strategic rocket forces in the event of a nuclear war. I had been reading about the defence system known as "Dead Hand" which was officially known as "Perimeter". It is a system of sensors around Russia, which react to pressure and light and it is controlled from Kosvinski Mountain. The idea being that if there was a nuclear first strike on Russia which wiped out the leadership, a retaliatory nuclear response could be launched without human intervention, hence the name "Dead

Hand". In the event of a nuclear explosion which would trigger the sensors, a signal would be automatically activated. If this signal is not responded to within a given time (*ie* because the leadership had been knocked out by the nuclear strike), then an algorithm would automatically start which could not be stopped or reversed, which would send a signal out to automatically launch every missile in Russia's nuclear arsenal (including submarines). It was, or should I say is, a frightening prospect. It also obviously troubled the Russian leadership because there is always the possibility of a large meteor hitting the country which actually happened in the Ekaterinburg / Chelyabinsk area in February 2013. The Tunguska event in 1908 had the same effect as a nuclear weapon in terms of pressure and light. It was decided to place human intermediaries in the link rather than rely solely on machines. I wondered if the human intermediaries sitting over in Kosvinski Mountain thought about the jobs they had to do. The facility at Kosvinski Mountain was in the process of being replaced by an even larger and deeper underground facility at Yamantau Mountain in the southern Ural Mountains.

With the arrival of daylight, we all started to prepare ourselves. I wanted a good wash and brush up before we arrived in Ivdel because it was to be the last opportunity for a decent wash for the next ten days before returning to Ekaterinburg. The toilets on the train were not the vision from hell that I expected but were actually very clean. They were cleaner, in fact, than the First Great Western trains I regularly travelled on at home, although I suppose that is not much of a yardstick to judge by. I had folded up my sheets to give back to the lady who had doled them out and I heaved my rucksack on as we pulled into Ivdel. It was the same station building that the Dyatlov party had stayed in when they arrived in January 1959, before they took a bus to Vizhay the following morning. The outside of the station building had the year of construction on the front – 1940, which was the year before the Nazis had invaded Russia. We all walked up the side of the building into a car park where two large vehicles awaited us. The heavy-duty trucks had monster tyres which I could later see were the only way to travel other than by foot in the mountains. The one we were handing our rucksacks up into for storage at the back looked as if it had been customised from a KAMAZ truck. Basically it was a driver's cab at the front and at the back a basic box with seats which had been welded or fixed on for passengers. This was to be our carriage for the next eight hours. I had seen pictures of luxurious custom-built vehicles used for tourists to view Polar Bears in Alaska and Canada where they had an open area at the rear for easier viewing. The truck we were in was as basic as it gets with seats that would have made an Edinburgh Corporation bus of the 1950s seem like unashamed luxury. Despite the hardness of the seat I had a window seat and I was too interested in what I was seeing to be over-bothered about the lack of suspension or the hard seat. I can honestly say that I was entranced for the whole of the eight hours at the world beyond the window. Not everyone was so fortunate, as one of our guides, Sasha, had lost out in the rush for seats and had plonked himself down in the narrow corridor on top of his rucksack and remained there for the whole journey. What I liked about the Russians in general is their stoic take on life. They may grumble occasionally, but they just get on with it. Things break down in Russia just as they do everywhere else, but they just fix it without too much drama and carry on.

In the seat in front of me was a woman, Svetlana Zeitullaeva and her daughter Elnara. Elnara's husband Sasha sat on the seat opposite. They were from Saint Petersburg and Elnara and Sasha spoke excellent English. Svetlana, the mother was out of her seat constantly recording out of the upper open window with her video camera. Despite the swaying of the vehicle and bumping around, she hung on with one hand whilst using the other to record the passing scenery and say what she was seeing for the recorder. I thought she was going to be flung to the other side of the cabin at one or two points when we descended suddenly into giant potholes. At first I thought she was recording every part of the journey just for the sake of it but it turned out that she was a Video blogger (Vlogger) who was always looking for new stories and the Dyatlov Incident was on her list. She had been to Chernobyl to record the deserted place for her Video blog (Vlog). Many of her Vlogs are on Youtube and she always looked for a new angle on each story.

The KAMAZ lorry stopped for the first of many smoking and comfort breaks by a couple of small wooden houses on the road from Ivdel to Vizhay. To call it a proper road would be too grand a term, rather it was a dirt track more than wide enough for two large lorries to pass each other and being the main road north into the mountains, it was well used. A law had been passed in Russia that forbade smoking indoors in public places and I expected that this would be roundly ignored but I was quite surprised to see that everybody took heed of it and not just in the city. I always thought Russians had a long-running love affair with their cigarettes and would protest or ignore the new law completely, but everywhere I went I would see small knots of people smoking outside buildings just the same as back in the UK. I welcomed the regular stops as it gave my battered backside a chance to recuperate from the bone-shaking ride. I noticed on the road out of Ivdel, a sign pointing the way to the airport which was used as the base for the helicopters and Antonov An 2 aircraft back in 1959 when the search commenced for the missing Dyatlov party. The airport was basically just a grass strip with just a rickety old wooden building and control tower on top. I had seen up to date pictures of it and it did not look any different to what it was like in 1959. I regretted that we could not take a quick detour to see it and take some photos but I doubted that anyone would want to indulge my interest in aviation and from the point of view of the Dyatlov story, the airfield played only a minor role.

After our first roadside stop for a break, our next stop was in what appeared to be a mining village. The road was still basically a dirt track but there was a sizeable mining operation located to the left of the road. This was the village of Pruchunoye and it was the last place before we went into the mountains where we could buy anything from a shop. Everyone piled out of the KAMAZ truck and into the shop which was built from wood but was extremely well stocked with food, fresh fruit, booze and bottled mineral water. There were half a dozen assistants serving and they were busy as other vehicles were stopping besides ourselves. While we were waiting to be served, Lisa and Nastya pointed out a large electronic calculator on the counter which was right next to an abacus. The assistant who served us counted up the cost of our purchases on the abacus, ignoring the calculator. Her hands moved the wooden beads on the abacus faster than I could keep pace with the actual movement. One of our group asked if I could buy him a bottle of mineral water for the journey ahead which I was happy to oblige. However he was furious when I bought him a large bottle as he had wanted a small one, which he had failed to tell me. I resolved to try and find a way to give my money away and please the recipient at the same time in future.

As we stood just outside the store, Lisa pointed out a wooden building on the other side of the road and said that it had been built by German prisoners of war, as had a number of other wooden buildings nearby. She said it was possible to differentiate them from other wooden buildings because the Germans built their houses in a style which had three windows together and the tops of the windows were finished with curved half-moon tops rather than just straight across. The German prisoners of war were housed in the gulags around the Ivdel area, although the majority were eventually released by 1956 under an agreement reached between Konrad Adenauer and Kruschev.

We climbed aboard for the next haul and the rain which had started shortly after we left Ivdel was coming down constantly and heavier. From this point onwards, night and day, it seemed to rain almost non-stop for almost a week which was going to make things very difficult. As we approached the end of the road from Ivdel, we came to the small village of Vizhay. It seemed like a long haul from Ivdel, it looked close to Ivdel on the map, in relation to the journey from Ekaterinburg, but we were making fairly slow progress along with the constant stops. I was also surprised to see Vizhay with some new wooden houses, probably half a dozen as the whole village of Vizhay had been burned down in a raging forest fire only a few years previously. The houses which were now standing there, were brand new and a couple more were in the process of being built. Vizhay is where the Dyatlov group had arrived on the bus from Ivdel back in 1959 and then took a lorry to the wood cutters settlement on 26 January 1959.

After leaving Vizhay we crossed a bridge over the Vizhay river which at this point was fairly wide but shallow. Once we reached the other side of the Vizhay river, we came across a sea of blackened trees on both sides of the trail. This sea of blackened tree stumps continued for a few kilometres and were then interspersed with normal forest trees which had been unaffected by the fires before the carbonised trees started again. Forest fires are a major hazard in the region in the summer and the one which engulfed Vizhay in 2010 was a big one, with firefighters and volunteers coming in from all around the region to help fight the blazes. As I looked at the blackened trees, Alexey told me that Yury Yakimov had travelled up from his home near Ivdel to volunteer his services when he heard about the fires closing in on Vizhay. He knew the area well from his mining days in the region and stayed until the fires had been beaten down, but unfortunately not before Vizhay had been razed to the ground.

The deeper we went into the forest, the worse the state of the trail became. The truck's massive tyres ploughed through deep holes filled with mud as the rain hammered down. Several times the engine cut out straining to come out of some holes and I wondered if it would start again, but it always did. After driving over a number of rivers, we arrived at the Mansi village of Ushma. Ushma was 35 Kilometres (22 miles) from our destination at the base of Kholat Sykhal. There were a number of wooden houses, all well-spaced from each other and they appeared to be spread over three sides of the confluence of the rivers Ushma and Lozva. The place seemed to be deserted but given the damp weather I didn't blame anyone for wanting to stay in and I suspect the Mansi were probably fed up with being objects of curiosity to everyone who passed through who was not connected with forestry work. The truck drove over to the other side of the River Ushma where there were a few Mansi dwellings. At this point there seemed to be some kind of an altercation. Sasha, one of our guides, who had been sitting on his rucksack for the whole journey got up and spoke through an intercom to the drivers cab at the front. The driver came around to the door of the passenger cabin. There seemed to be a discussion going on over the route the driver wanted to take and the route Sasha wanted him to take. The driver seemed disgruntled but it appeared to me that Sasha won the argument, much to everyone's amusement. The lorry started up and went back over the River Ushma from where we had just come and followed a route which ran alongside the River itself. The other River (Lozva) went north from Ushma towards our eventual destination, but we were taking a different route. As we left Ushma I saw three of the Mansi standing outside, two men and a woman, all looked to be in their twenties. They were talking amongst themselves and were dressed in jeans and ordinary looking clothes. They would not have looked out of place on any city street.

We were now going much slower, not much more than walking pace in fact, but it beat walking. The trees and undergrowth had closed right in around the lorry, some of the branches hit the windows so hard that I thought the glass would break. After another hour or so of driving, Alexey the Officer, turned to me and said that we were only about a kilometre and a half away. I thought to myself "great stuff", because if we were that close to the base camp area then our hike was not going to be too much trouble. How wrong I was! What Alexey meant was that at that point we were only a kilometre and a half away from where we were going to be dropped off to begin our trek of 32 kilometres (20 miles). I had been told that a certain level of fitness would be required for the hike and for five months previously, I had built up to an hour and twenty minutes of cardio training in the gym each day. As it turned out, I was woefully underprepared. We all climbed out of the KAMAZ truck and dutifully hauled our rucksacks onto our backs eager to get cracking on the hike. The rain was now a constant drizzle. The trail through the forest was easy enough to start with as it resembled a Sunday walk in my local nature reserve, but within a very short space of time, it started turning into an assault course that had been designed by a deranged and sadistic Special Forces Instructor. The ski pole that I had been given by Sergey the guide, I had assumed would be a useful prop for photos, turned out to be a lifesaver I could not have done without. The constant rain had turned the trail into a quagmire in parts. As we went along at a fairly fast pace, I found that the best way to tackle what was nothing less than an obstacle course, was to keep to the sides of the path when the mud looked particularly deep. With one hand I would use a branch to hold on to and with the other hand, push the ski pole into solid ground on the other side of the mud to maintain my balance. Even when I tried to walk around the obstacle in front of me I would find that the mud in the undergrowth was worse than the mud on the trail itself. This worked well where the trail was narrow, but in other parts a sea of mud awaited me which was anything up to twenty feet across, and mud which resembled quicksand. I lost count of the times I sank into the mud which came over the tops of my wellington boots and into the boot soaking my socks. I stopped bothering about my mud soaked socks only pausing to empty the mud out of my boots. On one occasion, my left leg stuck fast and I could not free it.

My leg sank right into the mud and although I was holding onto a branch I was stuck fast. Sasha, the guide, saw my plight and came and dug my leg out. Even when the trail seemed like a normal path in a forest, a large tree would have fallen, crossing the trail with regular monotony and we would either have to climb over it or crawl underneath it (not easy with a 25 kilo rucksack on your back), or walk around it if it was too big. The gap between the fittest and the least fittest (me) widened considerably and I found that by the time I arrived at a place where we were stopping for a break, the ones who had arrived first (*ie* the fittest) had already had their ten or fifteen minutes and were putting on their rucksacks to continue the journey. Not knowing the way, I didn't want to be left too far behind in the forest. However, as the journey wore on and my mangy carcass screamed in agony at the exertion it was being subjected to, I literally didn't give the proverbial toss and just went along at my own pace. I also took as long as I needed to get my energy back.

We covered about one third of the total distance and the sun was going down so we stopped to pitch our tents for the night. The rain had been constant and my trousers and jumper were sodden. Two fires had been started, around which everyone was hanging their sodden and muddy clothes. The result of that was that although the fire had dried my clothes eventually, they literally reeked of smoke. We all had changes of clothes but I found I was changing them frequently as everything got wet and muddy as soon as you put them on. I figured that as everyone's clothes stank of wood smoke it wouldn't matter.

On that first day we had trekked 10 to 12 kilometres (6.2 to 7.5 miles). The following day we set off again for the main part of the trek to get to the base of Kholat Syakhl. Again, it had poured with rain overnight, hammering on the tents, without stopping. This ensured that any few areas of dry ground ahead of us would be well and truly swamp-like. We were all up early and ate a good breakfast. I particularly liked the *Maleyna* tea which was tea made with raspberry leaves. Two large metal tins were boiled up over the fires with the leaves thrown in when the water boiled. It had a nice tang and was a refreshing drink. After breakfast, we limbered up for the main phase of the journey. As we made our way on this second day, I hit a brick wall with my energy levels and really struggled to keep up. By the time I reached the break points for a rest, instead of taking my rucksack and then my jacket off, I literally collapsed onto my back and just lay on my rucksack, exhausted and past caring.

On their journey to Kholat Syakhl, Zina had written in her diary how signs of the Mansi were everywhere on their trip through the forest. Just before reaching one rest point, Yury K showed me a tree with ten horizontal marks down the trunk. It looked as if someone had taken an axe and had ten goes at chopping the tree down and given up. The incisions were all the same size though and evenly spaced, one above the other. Yury K explained that a Mansi hunter will take one tree to record his hunting kills and this tree showed that the hunter who had made the mark had killed ten Wolverines. One thing that I found interesting about the Mansi was that they spoke four different dialects which were so different that the speaker of one dialect could not fully understand the speaker of one of the other dialects. About 15 years ago the Western dialect was considered more or less extinct and the number of dialects has now reduced to three with only around 900+ speakers left in the whole area. There are around 3,000 Mansi speakers left in the whole of Russia.

The River Auspiya (Mikhail Petrov)

We followed the River Auspia most of the way on this final stretch which mirrored the route the Dyatlov group had taken, although for the most part, they had actually made their way along the frozen surface of the Auspia. Sasha the guide explained to me that travelling along on top of the river in winter was not as easy as it sounds because the surface was uneven due to the amount of rocks, even though it was covered in ice and snow at that time. As we neared the base camp location, I staggered along the edge of the path and put my foot onto what I thought was fairly firm ground only for the boot to disappear into the mud and as I lost my balance, the weight of the rucksack twisted my body around and wrenched my knee. I managed to walk on and fortunately it was not much further to go, but it was not a good omen. By this point I found a literal fellow traveller in Shamil, the aviation expert from Kazan. Shamil was his own man and he was travelling at roughly the same pace as me and had long ago decided that he was going to travel at his own pace and nobody else's. We passed an open area which contained large wooden carvings of a giant fork, knife and spoon, which feature in many tourists photos of the area. From here we only had about half a kilometre to go to the area where we set up our base camp at the foot of Kholat Syakhl. The final destination was, of course, the mountain itself with the location of the tent and where the bodies were found, but it was better to be camped in the forest at the base right by the Auspia river for cooking and washing. We were still a good kilometre (0.6 miles) from the nearest point of interest which was the Dyatlov memorial rock.

# Chapter 4

I was exhausted by the time we reached the area where we set up Base Camp. The forest obscured the view of the mountain itself, but it was exciting to be so close to our final destination. The sun was close to going down and we had covered the best part of 20 kilometres (12.5 miles) to reach the location. As this was to be our home for the next week or so, we had plenty of work to do. This involved not just setting up the tents but also creating a central area where we could cook and which would serve as a place where we could sit and talk as well as the now familiar routine of drying our soaked and mud-stained clothes. Four large logs were rolled into position, two large fires were started and tarpaulin was draped over the whole area to keep off the incessant rain. After dark we ate our first meal at the site which was something that looked like mincemeat with white tubes sticking out of it. I didn't dare ask what it was, so I held my breath, closed my eyes and got it down me. I was starving. We weren't making a Jamie Oliver documentary in the Urals and the food was basic and intended to give us the energy we needed as we had a lot of hiking and climbing to do over the following days. There was plenty of food and we all made sure we had our fill. In addition, everybody carried some form of biscuits or energy tablets with them for a quick energy boost when we were up on the mountain.

Yury K told me that the location we were camped on was where the well-known picture was taken in the forest, of the Dyatlov tent with the chimney sticking out of it. The picture can be seen on many Dyatlov related websites. I was glad to lie down and go to sleep that night and slept from sheer exhaustion. Part of me felt I wanted to go straight up to the mountain when we arrived with a torch to look at the sites and the other, more knackered part of me, just wanted to collapse in a heap. I was one of the first up just after sunrise the following morning and walked down for a wash in the freezing cold water of the River Auspia. The cold took your breath away and although it was foolish, I filled up my water bottle from the fresh mountain water. The bacteria in water was always a concern, but one of the guides said that we should always boil the water even though this water in the Auspia was fast flowing and close to its source; but he said he never bothered to boil it. I started getting ready for the trip up onto the mountain. I had notebooks, two cameras and photos of the various scenes from 1959 that I wanted to use to compare the scenes from then to how it looked today.

As I walked back to the tent after washing, I noticed a single fresh paw print in a small area of mud in the grass about ten feet from our tent. I assumed it wasn't a one legged animal of some kind and I showed it to Nastya, who after looking at it said it was most likely a wolf. The other prints weren't visible in the grass. Strangely enough despite my fear of bears, I was not so troubled by wolves, maybe because I held the thought that if I was surrounded by a pack of wolves I could always throw a stick for them and make my escape. Against that vain hope I had also watched a programme on TV about a pack of starving wolves trying to distract a huge grizzly bear to get at her cub. The mother grizzly was in a rage, and despite the fact that one blow from her paw could kill a wolf by breaking its back, they were not deterred from trying (unsuccessfully as it transpired) to get at her cub.

After an hour or so, everyone was up and we quickly had our breakfast. Not everyone wanted to go up to the mountain immediately. Sasha, our medical man and his wife had made the trip before and they were going to go up later. I breathed a sigh of relief that we didn't have to take our rucksacks. We were on the forested lower slope of the mountain and the going uphill was fairly steep. Once again, it had rained all night and the trail we followed up the mountain was the usual mudbath we had encountered on the hike, but despite being steeper, it was easier to negotiate because we didn't have our rucksacks this time. An air of expectation built up for me as the trees thinned out to fledgling trees and bushes and then onto open ground going up. I did not want to look until I was closer. I walked up with Alexey the Officer and when I lifted my head up from looking at the path in front of me, there was the memorial stone with the memorial on top. Behind the memorial stone and towering above it was Kholat Syakhl. It was an incredible moment for me and I just stopped to take it all in. Kholat Syakhl is not a large mountain, but the top was shrouded in mist and it looked impressive.

I had seen many photos of the rock where the memorial plaque is seen fixed in place, along with the metal framed memorial on top of the rock itself. These metal framed memorials are called 'Pyramidka' (pyramid) and are common in Russian graveyards because they are cheaper and easier to make than stone memorials. A 'Pyramidka' was used on top of the memorial rock instead of stone to save on weight and hauling it there. The story of the memorial is that after the obelisk memorial with photos was placed at the seven graves at the Mikhailovskoye (*St. Michael the Archangel*) cemetery in 1962, Valentin Yakimenko decided that a memorial should be placed at the Pass as well. While the search was going on for the remaining four bodies in April 1959, a small metal "Pyramidka" with a star was flown up to the Pass by helicopter. It was placed in the middle of the Pass, but it was too small and was practically lost between the boulders there on the stone belt ridge. Valentin Yakimenko felt duty-bound to make a proper memorial. He saw it as a large plaque with the profile of an austere looking man and the words "They were nine" with an inscription in smaller letters reading "To the memory of the past and departed we have named this Pass after the Dyatlov group". Surprisingly, Yakimenko did not meet any obstacles in what he was doing. He did not coordinate the naming of the Pass as the *Dyatlov Pass* with the authorities and the name is now generally accepted and referred to in maps. Furthermore, the group encountered no problems in being granted a permit to travel up to the Pass to work on the memorial at the end of July 1963. There was no official lifting of restrictions on travel as such but the area was generally open (with permits) from that time onwards for groups wishing to go up there. There was a surprising amount of goodwill towards the project, for instance the architect's design and the casting of the plaque from duralumin were made practically for free and, just as important, they received help in taking the heavy plaque and concrete mix to the Pass by a helicopter that was then engaged in fighting forest fires in the area. The group arrived at the Pass on 30 July and working in two groups they chose the large rock where the memorial is now for the location. Working over two days, with one group preparing the mortar and the other cutting a flat area in the rock, they had everything finished on 1 August 1963. Working there with the group and Valentin Yakimenko was Yury Yudin. The weather over the three days was terrible with the constant rain and wind which seems to be a feature of the summer there. When it was finished, they were rightly proud of the memorial to their lost friends.

On the opposite side of the rock from the memorial plaque were three further plaques, surrounded by plastic flowers. These were placed there in 1989 to commemorate thirty years of the tragedy. There were other messages left along with flowers in various crevices. A joker had left a small piece of aluminium on which he had inscribed the following message in Russian;

"LET ME SLEEP

SIGNED

THE YETI"

The rock was part of a large outcrop of rocks at the edge of the spur forming the Dyatlov Pass before the land fell away down to the tree line. Some of the more agile members of our group climbed the approximately thirty feet to the top of the rock for photos beside the memorial at the top. Some thoughtful soul had also brought two bags of wine up as well for people to slake their thirst.

In many ways, the mountain has had an unfair press because of its name Kholat Syakhl, which translated means *Dead Mountain* from the Mansi language. *Dead Mountain* is a Mansi descriptive term which is supposed to mean that nothing grows there and is therefore a waste of time for the herders to take their animals up there. However, to say that nothing grows there is not strictly true. When I looked at pictures of the mountain before I physically went there, it seemed that in the summer, the mountain was at least covered in grass with large areas of bare rock. When I got there and started to walk across and up the mountain, what at first looks like grass from a distance and in photos is, in fact, thick vegetation about a third of a metre deep (1ft). As you walk across it in boots, your feet sink into it like snow and, because the roots are thick, it is easy to catch your foot and trip. What at first looks like it would be a bit of a jaunt across a grassy area is actually pretty hard work after a while. There were many areas of bare rock which again from a distance, looked easy to walk across but it was all loose rock varying in size and many of them were unsafe. I had to test each rock before putting all my weight on it. Some people were nimbly leaping across them with the ease of mountain goats but a couple of people lost their balance on the loose rocks and fell.

We made our way across from the outcrop of rocks where the memorial plaque was, to the location of the Dyatlov tent. This, for many of us was the highlight of the trip. The tent location had been marked with two red flags by Yury K and was roughly 0.8km (half a mile) from the outcrop of rocks on the stone belt ridge and at a slightly higher level. It was an amazing feeling to stand on the spot or at least close to the spot where the Dyatlov tent stood. I closed my eyes and tried to imagine what it must have been like on that fateful February night in 1959 when they all left the tent and what must have been there to make them do it. I had brought my photos to compare the scene and our guide Sasha had also brought several photos with him, for members of the party to look at and compare. The most famous photo is Yury Koptelov crouched down surveying the scene with the collapsed tent in front of him and the backdrop of the slope to the tree line and the mountains in the distance. The precise location of the tent is strongly disputed by some theorists with some saying it was further over under Kholat Syakhl itself whereas the location of the tent we were standing at was under a ridge which runs to the west of the mountain. The simple truth is that nobody knows for sure. When I discussed it with Sasha the guide as we were standing there, he also said the same and he pointed to a ledge that was only about 20 feet (six metres) away and said that their tent could just as easily have been pitched in front of the ledge which had a drop of around two metres (six feet) for shelter. In the last photo taken of the group digging the snow to prepare to pitch the tent, it can be seen there is a ledge or build-up of snow behind them which could have been the ledge. In the famous photo of Yury Koptelov crouched down looking at the tent, the ledge would have been behind him. Sasha had a copy of the photo with him and compared it to the dip or ledge before us. Even leaving the ledge or dip aside and looking at the scenery in the distance, I reckoned I could have moved roughly 15 to18 metres (50 or 60 feet) to the left or right, backwards or forwards and it would not have made one iota of difference to the scenery in the distance. We were roughly in the right location but it was impossible to be certain because there were no frames of reference near enough to work out exactly where the tent was. Some people have tried to use the mountains in the distance as frames of reference, but it can only be very rough guesswork. I had seen the amount of painstaking work that Sergey Fadeev, the other guide, had put in to determining the exact cedar tree where the first two bodies were found and it made me think that it was a near pointless task to try and do the same with the tent location, even using photogrammetry, because the fixed points had changed in the intervening years. For historical photos the way photogrammetry works is; firstly to establish the features in the photographs taken of the tent on Kholat Syakhl that have not changed over the past 50+ years. Then, ideally, to take accurate GNSS (Global Navigation Satellite System of which GPS is one type) measurements at those positions. With that information it is possible to establish the focal length of the camera lens. If there is sufficient stereo-base between the photos it can be possible to calculate the position of the tent on the mountain. There are a number of powerful software tools to do this. Whilst it is not impossible, photogrammetry experts I have consulted, using the main photos showing the tent in 1959, say it is not possible to accurately work out where the tent would have stood.

The flag in the foreground shows the location of the tent. The top of the ridge to the left and the angle of the slope shows the unlikelihood of the conditions for an avalanche (Author's photo)

The treeline as seen from the location of the tent (Mikhail Petrov)

One thing I did do was to closely examine the ridge above where the tent was located and just the mere sight of it was enough to dismiss the avalanche theory; and this was the opinion of everyone there. Sasha quoted the often mentioned slope angle of 18 degrees which is below that where an avalanche can start. It looked greater than 18 degrees to me but I had no way of checking. The thing however was the fact that the top of the ridge was very close. It cannot have been more than a few hundred feet at the very most and nobody there thought there could have been enough snow build up for a supposed avalanche in the small area above where the tent stood and that applied right along the ridge to the left or the right if the tent location was further over either way from where we were. I took a sequence of photos from left to right of the ridge from below it to take home and examine. I wanted to get to the top of the ridge to look over the other side because there was an old airstrip there in the distance. One line of thought had it that it was built by the Nazis as a refuelling stop after they were attempting to bomb the mines at Pruchunoye. However, the Germans had never made it anywhere near as far as this. The strip had been built by German POWs as an emergency refuelling stop in the Urals for lend-lease aircraft being delivered from Alaska and the Soviet Far East. Despite my interest, I wanted to conserve my energy as there was still a fair amount of walking up and down slopes to do.

Another member of our group was Mikhail Petrov, a photo journalist from Moscow. An extremely likeable and highly educated young man in his early thirties with Hollywood film star looks and to top it all off, as fit as the proverbial fiddle. Again, his almost flawless English put my lack of Russian to shame. I found him very interesting to talk to and I wondered if he had any flaws as he was also very well mannered. As we looked at the ridge above where the tent had stood, I asked him about his interest in the Dyatlov story and what his view was, now that he had seen the location. He said that he had long been interested in the story and had read as much as he could on the subject. His first observation as he looked at the ridge was how unlikely the avalanche theory was now seeing the location of the tent and the slightly sloping ground above it which certainly was no more than a couple of hundred feet at the very most. Mikhail said that the ground was fairly flat and not big enough for any kind of an avalanche to cause the kind of injuries to members of the

Dyatlov group that have been suggested, nor even enough of an avalanche to seriously damage the tent. He ruled the avalanche out completely now that he had seen the site. He also said that he did not believe the footprints found at the site of the tent leading down to the treeline in February 1959 belonged to any of the Dyatlov group. He had spoken to numerous skiers and hikers who told him that footprints in the snow in these regions can disappear completely within a few days. He also said that the nature of the footprints, even if they were still the same ones from when the group died, belonged to people who had killed them. His view was that they were murdered, possibly as a result of having witnessed a military test and that they had possibly been killed by the intelligence services of the USSR. Also, he felt, that the rockets that many theorists refer to may have had something to do with what they had witnessed. The big issue for him was that if the military or intelligence services had been involved in the group's deaths, then surely enough time had elapsed for some information to be published or released about what had really happened to them. Mikhail's line of thinking was the same as a large body of the Dyatlov theorists, especially the Russian ones, that lurking in the background somewhere was military involvement.

One glaring fact stood out about the tent's location for me – why there? It made absolutely no sense whatsoever. They had to climb up the mountain with no definable path to get to where the tent was pitched. It cannot even be said that they got lost because once you came out of the tree line, the ground was sloping steeply upwards and it was obvious you were out of the forest. They had been following the river Auspia which was clearly defined and would have been like following a road, it was so clear. They came out of that to almost wander haphazardly up a mountain to the spur of the Pass and then again wander haphazardly to a point at which they decide to pitch the tent. It defied logic. Furthermore, Kolevatov was carrying the tent, so not a light load, and he had injured his knee. So why go up a mountain which was not on your planned route? It would have been harder for him with the injury as well as the extra work involved in carrying his load. If that is what they did, it was baffling.

If the location of the tent made no sense however, then the next stage made a great deal of sense, notwithstanding the comments made about the group's footprints. The treeline, the Pass itself and the ridge ran for miles it seemed in many directions whichever way you looked at it. On exiting the tent that night, the Dyatlov group had headed straight down to the treeline at its nearest point to the tent. On the face of it, that move made a great deal of sense to me. The trees offered shelter and some limited security from the open mountainside, and from where the bodies were found they had not deviated from a direct line. It does beg the question as to how did they know that was the nearest point of the treeline because it was dark and it was a full mile away (1.6km). They would not have seen it in the dark but it could be argued that they just followed the slope of the mountainside straight down. Either way it was a logical step.

Members of our group started to make their way down towards the treeline to the locations where the bodies were found. The two guides Sasha and Sergey led the way. For me I found the going downhill just as hard as coming up. The thick small bushes still caught your feet and the areas of loose rock had to be negotiated carefully. I was more worried about damaging my new camera through falling on the rocks than any possible damage to my head. One point about the topography has changed considerably. The tree line has moved up the mountain by at least a couple of hundred metres (very roughly around 500 to 600 feet). As we got closer, bushes and shrubs started to appear followed by young trees. In 1959 this area of two hundred odd metres (600 feet) would have been open ground on the lower slope of the mountain. This also highlighted the issue with regards to the location of the tent, and as we were shortly to see, the location of the bodies as well. People's memories are fallible, which is why nobody can pinpoint the exact location of the tent. Apart from having no direct reference point around the tent, there are enough people still alive (for instance Boris Slobtsov and Yury Koptelov who were there in 1959) who should be able to give an idea, and they, of course, can. However, in February 2016 it had been 57 years since the tent was discovered. Permits for travel into the area were not allowed until 1963 so in effect it was sealed off for four years afterwards. It meant nobody was able to venture up to the Pass to look around and possibly reinforce their memories. Memory plays tricks and events and places from such a long time ago can become distorted with the passing of the years. To give an example of this, at the 2013 Dyatlov Conference hosted at the Ural Federal University (UFU - formerly UPI) an argument broke out between original search party members Mikhail Sharavin and Yury Koptelov about the appearance of the tent when it was first found. They also argued about whether anything had been moved out of the tent and replaced. Both of them were there and had seen it and yet they strongly disagreed on what they had seen. On the face of it one was right and one was wrong but it is possible both were wrong. Nobody knows for sure.

As we came down to where the bushes and young trees began, Sasha the guide told us this was the area where Zina's body was found. Zina was the darling of the group; highly intelligent and very attractive with a warm outgoing personality that drew everyone she met towards her. The deaths of all of them were tragic but I felt Zina's to be especially poignant. She was the closest to the tent, although she was a good kilometre (0.60 mile) away from it. One the face of it she had attempted to get back to the tent but succumbed to the extreme cold long before getting anywhere near it. Compared to the rest of them she was reasonably warmly dressed, although nowhere near enough despite four pairs of socks, but she had no jacket or mittens. The photographs of her body after the snow had been dug away from her corpse when she was found, showed she had curled into a semi-foetal position as her life ebbed away. It was noted by Ivdel Prosecutor Vasily Tempalov that there was not a single tree within a radius of 70 metres (230ft) and the photos confirm her body was out in the open. In 2015 this had changed considerably as the tree line and shrubbery had overtaken the spot where she was found and advanced further up the slope. After taking photographs of the scene we moved on to the location of the next body which was Rustem's. In the rough sketches and drawings made by the search party, Rustem's body appeared to lie midway between Igor Dyatlov and Zina, with all three of them in a roughly straight line heading back up towards the tent. However, even allowing for the fact that the exact spot where the bodies were found could never be pinpointed now, it was quite apparent that Rustem was closer to Zina than he was to Igor Dyatlov. After we had seen the location of Igor Dyatlov's body, I estimated that Rustem was probably one third of the total distance from Igor nearer to Zina and that allowed for plenty of room for error in the calculations of distance. What was odd about the area where Rustem's body was found was a stream which ran down the mountainside and led into a large open area of shallow water which had a weird gigantic crust of ice across the top of it. It was not a single flat sheet of ice, rather it was a hexagonal, honeycomb type of texture. Each of the honeycomb shapes had dips in it which had a red colour in the middle of it. Alexey the Officer said to me that he was not sure what caused the red colour in the middle of the hexacomb shapes. The red had soaked into the ice and Alexey said it could be caused by the red berries that came down with the water while one or two people said it could have been caused by chemicals. It was obviously worth investigating because one of the many theories in relation to the deaths concerned the presence of dangerous chemicals in the area. Someone mentioned rocket fuel but it was not immediately apparent how it would have got on top of the ice and there was an awful lot of the red marking over the whole sheet of ice which measured roughly 18 to 21metres (60 to 70 feet) long and about 65 metres (20ft) across.

From the area where Rustem had died, we walked further into the tree line and came to the location where Igor Dyatlov had been found. In 1959 this location was where the forest started to thin out to shrubbery and then into the open area of the slope leading up to the mountain and the tent. Now it was well within the tree line, although the actual location itself was more shrubbery and fledgling trees. Igor Dyatlov's body had been found close to small trees and although it was said he was on his back, it is believed he had been turned over onto his back as rigor mortis had long set in and his left arm was rigid above his chest which would not have happened if he had been lying on his back at the time of his death. This area was pretty thick with shrubs and again we moved on after taking photos. At each point we stopped at, Sasha would explain the injuries to the bodies with the aid of photos from 1959.

The next location however, was to be a big surprise to me. When I first looked at the Dyatlov story I was puzzled as to why everyone should have been split up so far from each other. In particular, I could not understand why the most seriously injured of the group should have been placed so far away from the others (estimated in the searchers' drawings of the scenes at 70 metres (230ft). Even if the snow shelter was dug at the supposed best location and the cedar tree was the highest at the treeline, it would seem to make sense to stick together for safety's sake and also to keep an eye on the most seriously injured. Why build the fire so far away from the snow shelter if that provided the best shelter? Especially when there was plenty of other wood around to build a fire at the snow shelter and have the cover of the shelter, along with the fire just outside it. Furthermore, it was supposedly dark so it would be very difficult to communicate with each other if they were so far apart from each other in the dark. I found the forest a place where it would be an easy enough place to lose your way in brilliant August sunshine. However, when we came to where the bodies of Luda, Thibo, Zolotarev and Kolevatov were found, I was amazed to see that they were at a far lesser distance from the cedar tree than 70 metres (230ft). I estimated the distance to be no greater than around 20 metres (66ft), if that. Sasha showed us the rock in the stream that Luda's body had been found draped over with the bodies of Zolotarev, Thibo and Kolevatov close by. There was certainly no doubting the rock itself as the one where Luda was found as there was nothing else in the vicinity that matched it. The rock and stream were in a small ravine with reasonably gentle sloping sides, quite thick with trees and vegetation. From the rock up to the cedar tree itself was just a short journey of barely a minute or so. What this showed was that the group (excluding Zina, Igor Dyatlov and Rustem who appeared to be making their way back to the tent) were much closer than I first thought which would make much more sense from a safety point of view. This supposes that the cedar tree was the same one which the near-naked Doroshenko and Krivoy were found next to, with the remains of the burnt out fire. It certainly seemed to fit the bill. It was a mature tree and there were branches broken higher up the trunk although I doubted if these were the ones broken by the members of the Dyatlov group.

Mikhail Petrov stands at the base of the Cedar tree (Mikhail Petrov)

There was a smaller tree with a split trunk nearby and this was the one that Sergey had showed to me in the photos he had been working on back at the Dyatlov Foundation in Ekaterinburg. This smaller tree with the split trunk was present in the photos taken of the bodies of Doroshenko and Krivoy in 1959 and, although there were some differences, they weren't major and after fifty plus years it was understandable it would have changed in that time. Everyone in the group wanted their photo taken by the tree and I took several from different angles including one from the small tree with the split trunk facing towards the cedar tree. The space between the two trees was where the bodies of Doroshenko and Krivoy were found. I stood in quiet contemplation of how they met their end, freezing to death with the remains of the pitiful fire unable to heat them enough to keep them alive. From the cedar tree I looked back down towards the rock where Luda was found with the others nearby. Even in the dark, they were within distance to each other that they could have loudly all talked to each other without too much difficulty. I had to keep reminding myself that where we were standing was the original treeline then and we would have been standing at the edge of the forest with open mountainside right next to us. As it was, we were well inside the forest area.

At this point the other guide, Sergey Fadeev, took over from Sasha. We went down past Luda's rock where a few more photos were taken and then followed the stream for about 10 metres (33ft) where the stream ran into another stream coming down from our left. We went up this stream for a little way and then Sergey explained to us that it was his opinion that this is where the snow shelter was located. His opinion differed from the other guide's Sasha in that he believed the shelter was about 30 metres (98 feet) further away from where Sasha thought it was. Sergey explained his reasoning with the use of photos and comparing them to the area in front of us. The topography looked similar in the photos but I felt the ground before us looked much steeper. I wasn't entirely convinced but I had to say it was difficult to be sure. On the subject of distances, Alexey the Officer had brought a laser range finder with him but unfortunately it was playing up and would not work properly. It would have been ideal for measuring the distances correctly.

I spent the next few days looking over the various locations and trying to work through the different theories as to what happened and why. If you just looked at where the tent was and where their bodies were found, then on the face of it, they had run away from something – but what? Not one of the theories made any sense. The avalanche theory accounted best for their running down to the tree line at the base of the mountain. However, if you stand at the location of the tent and look up at the ridge, quite apart from the fairly low angle, there is absolutely no distance of any kind for an avalanche to build up and the group must have seen this when they arrived there. Even if there had been a panic at the beginning and they rushed away from the tent, on their way down the mountain to the tree line it must have occurred to at least some of them that they were heading towards certain death in the conditions. It took our group over well over half an hour to make our way down to the location where the bodies were found. By this I mean bypassing the locations of the bodies of Zina, Rustem and Igor Dyatlov, as it is assumed they had gone down and were on their way back up the mountain again. We made our way fairly leisurely and were stopping to talk and take photographs as well. With the depth of the snow, even with the hard crust on top, it would have taken the members of the group some considerable time to reach the tree line. In that time, one or two of the more sober heads may have considered that they were heading away from their only place of real safety, or at least a place where there were tools for their survival. I would have thought that if they were making their way down to get away from an avalanche, someone might have looked back and at least considered the possibility of returning to the tent to get footwear and jackets if they could not see anything coming towards them. Still following the avalanche theory, it may be that they had all decided to get to the tree line and wait for a few hours until they felt that the threat of the avalanche had passed and would then make their way back to the by now ruined tent to retrieve what they needed. In some ways the attempt by Zina, Rustem and Igor Dyatlov looked like this is exactly what they were doing. However, the question then has to be asked: Would a group of nine highly experienced ski tourists, knowing the deadly position they were in, have even put themselves so at risk in the first place? In temperatures of -27 degrees Celsius and a wind chill factor that would have lowered the temperature even further, the extreme cold would have attacked them immediately the initial rush of panic and adrenaline had worn off. The avalanche theory has its supporters but is also discounted by many who know the conditions in the northern Ural Mountains. While filming for a programme on the Dyatlov Incident a couple of years ago, I had met a survival expert in Lithuania who had been caught by an avalanche himself and survived. He told me that what had happened in his case was that an upper slab of snow had moved and caught him and carried him along. He described the feeling as similar to being caught by a large wave in the sea and not being able to fight against it. He said that it is possible a slab of snow had moved against the Dyatlov tent and this had started the panic. He was certain that it was some kind of avalanche that had caused the deaths by forcing them away from the tent in a hurry. It sounded good but I kept looking at the ridge area above the tent and I just could not imagine how any amount of snow could have built up in such a short space to have alarmed them so much.

Later on, down at our base camp, Lisa came up to me and warned me to stay away from the north of the camp as a bear had been seen barely a couple of hundred metres (a few hundred feet) away in the forest. She suggested that if I wanted to do my "business" I should go into the forest to the south of our camp. As we were talking, we were approached by Sasha (Elnara's husband) from St Petersburg. Sasha, like his wife Elnara, was very pleasant and genial and spoke perfect English. Lisa said to me "Here is Sasha, he is the one who saw the bear". Sasha then described to us that he estimated the bear stood around 1.8 to 1.9 metres at the shoulder. That is around six feet and slightly taller than I am. My hidden fears rose to the surface and it was not helped by speaking to Alexey the Officer later on who informed me that he had gone off to explore the tree line at the base of Kholat Syakhl and came across what looked like some kind of large den in the undergrowth. He said it looked as if a very large animal had been sleeping there and smelled strongly of some type of animal. He guessed it was probably a bear and he said he didn't want to hang around to find out. It may have belonged to the bear that Sasha had seen but it may well have been another one. So there were possibly two bears in the immediate vicinity and one of them a veritable giant.

After the information circulated among us to be careful of our new neighbour/s, I sat on the logs with a few people around the camp fire. Many of the group were constantly giving me berries and nuts to eat which were plentiful around the camp and I found them quite tasty but didn't have a clue as to what was edible and what wasn't.

Yury Kuntsevich in summer dress for the Urals (Mikhail Petrov)

As I ate, I watched Shamil the aviation specialist from Kazan. I liked him. He had a great sense of humour. Shamil had his tent set away in the bushes about 10 metres (33ft) away from us. I watched as he moved away from his tent to some bushes nearer to us at the camp fire and he let out a massive roar. I have to say it sounded convincing but as I had seen him do it, it made me laugh. However, the people I was with jumped up in great alarm to look in the direction the roar had come from as it sounded like a bear, or how I would imagine a bear would sound. The look on their faces was priceless. I will save their blushes and won't name them. I do have to say though that had I not seen Shamil do it, I too would have thought it was a bear and within seconds would have been at the top of one of the numerous trees around us, propelled there by a powerful rocket jet of diarrhoea.

That night Yury K asked for some volunteers to try and recreate the same conditions in the tent to see how the Dyatlov group managed their sleeping arrangements. The tent he and I were in was the same dimensions as the Dyatlov group's tent and was shared by Yury, myself and a young couple from Ekaterinburg, Aina and Anton, who slept at the other end. Five more people came in and we settled down like a row of sardines for the night. There was barely room to turn over, so the Dyatlov group may have altered their sleeping arrangements for everyone to get in a little more comfortably, but it was a tight squeeze whichever way you did it. Our tent was pitched on a slight slope and we were all in our sleeping bags. During the night Lisa had rolled towards me and pushed me towards Yury K so I woke up in the morning with my face in the back of Yury K's hair. This may sound erotic but it wasn't!

# Chapter 5

I spent a few days travelling up and down the mountain and working out how all the various locations related to each other. I was fairly tired as once again my lack of physical preparation started to tell on me. After a few days, it was getting dark one evening and I decided to gather my thoughts and put down what I had seen on paper. Aina, Lisa and Nastya worked feverishly to quickly prepare the food for the roaring fire. We all ate a good bucketful (almost literally) of pasta followed by biscuits and washed down with more herbal tea. I had bought a box of Twinings Golden Darjeeling tea bags which was the one luxury I enjoyed for no extra weight carried. After we had finished the meal, I stood up to go and wash my plate and cup when disaster struck. I slowly stood up from the log I had been sitting on when my right knee felt as if a red hot poker had been jabbed right into it. It was absolute agony and at first I thought maybe I had just stood up awkwardly and had twisted my knee so I tried to walk and when I put my weight onto my right leg, the pain in my knee was so bad I had to collapse back onto the log.

Our doctor, Sasha, looked at my knee and tried to yank my leg straight but that only served to make me howl in agony. He gave me some paracetamol and cream for the knee and put a tubular bandage around it. He recommended that I go straight to my tent to lie down and rest it and see how it was in the morning. I hobbled back over to my tent and duly went to sleep, but I was not hopeful of a speedy recovery.

The following day I woke to find my leg was no better. If anything, it was worse because the knee had seized up and any bending movement was very painful. It was extremely annoying because five members of our group were going to go with Sergey the guide to travel to the top of Mount Otorten, the destination of the Dyatlov group. It went without saying that it was a harder trek than we had undertaken beforehand, as it was higher than Kholat Syakhl and not such a well-travelled route. It would also take two days to get there and back. I could barely hobble to the camp fire so it was out of the question to consider going and it was a bitter blow to take. By way of compensation, Mikhail Petrov, the Moscow photo journalist said he would kindly take some photos for me there. It was not the same as being there but it was decent of him and I could at least get an idea of what the conditions were like up on the mountain. That left me with the problem of my knee and wondering how I was going to make the 30 kilometres (18 miles) trek back through the forest to the pick-up point for the KAMAZ truck to take us back to Ivdel for the train. Yury K said I still had a few days for it to get better and make the trek. I wanted to share his optimism but it was pretty obvious there was something seriously wrong with my knee and it was not going to sort itself out in 72 hours or so. I considered the possibility of starting back 24 hours ahead of everyone else but not knowing the route or wanting to be in the forest alone, I would need at least one person to go with me to carry my rucksack which although the food was now out of it, still weighed a good 15 or so kilos. There was also the strong possibility that despite using two ski poles to help get me along, I was going to have to move fast to cover the mileage in time before everyone caught up with me and neither could I expect them or the KAMAZ truck to wait once they had overtaken me. They all had trains and planes to catch once they arrived back in Ekaterinburg. If I missed the truck at the appointed pick-up time that meant around another 10 kilometres (6.2 miles) back to the Mansi village at Ushma where at least there was some semblance of civilisation. There was also the strong possibility that if I pushed myself too hard to try and get ahead of everyone else and by going as quickly as I could, I risked doing irreparable damage to my knee. Whichever way I looked at it, there weren't many options. Yury K discussed the problem with the guides and it was decided that the best solution was for me to get up onto Kholat

Syakhl and wait by the memorial stone. From the other side of the Dyatlov Pass, it was possible to get up to the memorial stone on Kholat Syakhl using all-terrain vehicles via a fairly        long-winded route. The idea was for me to wait there until a vehicle or vehicles passed and get a lift back with them. Yury K suggested that Rashid, one of our group, would wait with me and translate for me to anyone who came along. The idea was that if I could get to Ivdel I could then get a new train ticket and make my way back to Ekaterinburg. The other possibility was that if nobody was going to Ivdel, I could hopefully get them to at least take me to Ushma where I could pitch the small tent I had been given and wait for the group to meet up with me and then take the KAMAZ truck back with everybody. It was not going to be easy if I got to Ivdel trying to explain that I wanted a ticket back to Ekaterinburg and I couldn't imagine the Mansi in Ushma coming out of their homes in grass skirts to dance a welcome to a miserable, crippled stranger to their village.

This was all assuming a vehicle came along in the first place whose driver would be willing to take me.

There was no other decision to be made, so I packed my gear up into my rucksack and Rashid, along with two strapping lads in the form of Alexander and Paul were going to accompany and help me up the mountain to the memorial stone. To add to the misery, it had been raining again so the path up the steep slope was once again, a quagmire. It also occurred to me that the route we were taking to the memorial stone would bring us into the path of the giant bear. I asked Rashid nervously about the bear. He responded;

*"No problem. Bear come, we say here three big Russian man – Bear run."*

He said this with a dismissive wave of his arm to give the impression of the bear running for its life into the distance. It sounded good, I have to say, and he certainly seemed to mean what he said. On the other hand I didn't dwell on what it would be like to come face to face with a monster that was over six feet at the shoulder and weighed almost half a ton. In the event, we didn't run into it, mercifully. Paul and Alexander lifted me by my arms to start helping me up the slope. It was agonising as my bad leg dragged and kept catching on undergrowth. We had almost a quarter of a mile to go up the slope and I used two ski poles to hobble up, assisted by the others.

It took well over an hour to get up to the memorial stone as I had to keep stopping to rest my knee. After we reached the memorial stone which was the last in an outcrop of stones on the ridge next to Kholat Syakhl, I looked at two separate piles of rusting tins and rubbish nearby. It seemed such a shame that in this remote and beautiful spot in the mountains that people could not be bothered to clear up after themselves. I remembered on one of the numerous Dyatlov forums reading about someone who had been here and had complained that they were turning it into a rubbish dump.

We set up the small tent and waited and waited and waited. Within an hour of our arrival at the memorial, Paul and Alexander said their goodbyes and it was just myself and Rashid. Surprisingly, there was a fairly constant stream of people passing by the memorial including people from our group below in the Auspia valley going over to the area of the tent and further on. Some were hikers making their way through the mountains and going on to the seven standing stones of Manpupuner (the *seven strong men* rock formations of the Komi Republic). I had a large bottle of water and Svetlana, the lady Vlogger from St Petersburg, her daughter Elnara and Sasha passed by and gave me a large bag of peanuts. We took a few photos together and they said if they saw any vehicles they would inform them of my plight. There was a constant wind up on the Pass and I moved around the memorial stone for shelter. As I did so a man carrying a metal detector, came up to me and introduced himself. He could not speak any English and of course with my zilch Russian we could only grin at each other. Rashid with his broken English explained that the man was another Dyatlov Incident author named Evgeny Tamplon. Evgeny is a Fellow of the Russian Geographical Society and his book (in Russian) favours the R7 missile theory plus the possibility of another missile, the Lavochkin La 350 (named *Burya,* meaning *Storm*) Cruise Missile project as being responsible for the deaths of the Dyatlov group. He also stresses that chemicals carried by the rockets were primarily responsible rather than any explosion from the rockets themselves. Not long after this we heard some vehicles driving up the Pass towards the stones. Rashid ran over to speak to them. It raised my hopes slightly as he said it looked hopeful, but unfortunately they were going north towards the Polar Urals.

After another couple of hours of gazing over the mountains, a tall, powerful looking man in his thirties came around the memorial stone and introduced himself. His name was Roman and he spoke fluent English. He said he was with a group of people and they all had quad bikes. He asked what the problem was and I explained about my badly damaged knee. He replied that as far as he could see I had two options. The first was to get a forestry vehicle up from Ivdel to take me back which would cost around about a thousand dollars. I gulped slightly. It was not the end of the world cost-wise but it certainly was not cheap. But, he said, all the forestry vehicles have gone north and wouldn't be back for five days to a week. The other option, he continued, was for a helicopter to come and rescue me and take me out of here by air. I didn't ask the next obvious question, but he said it anyway. It would cost twenty thousand dollars. The figure seemed like a grotesque joke of some kind. A virtual deposit for a house or flat back in Britain! He said the nearest helicopter was six hundred kilometres away so it would take a little time. Roman obviously realising I was not some playboy billionaire asked if my travel insurance would cover it as he could make a satellite call. I had insurance and I could imagine how the phone call would go;

*Roman – Hello Keith McCloskey who is insured with you under reference xxx is stuck halfway up Kholat Syakhl with a badly damaged knee and needs twenty thousand dollars for a helicopter to fly him out.*

*Insurance Company – Sure! Where do we send the cheque?*

The helicopter seemed an unrealistic solution, but more and more I felt like Morrowbie Jukes, in the Kipling short story who falls down a slope into a leper colony in India and can't get out. I thought it best to just hang on and see what transpired, even though, with each passing hour, I was starting to feel more and more helpless. Nor had I forgotten the giant bear and his possible companion which were just along in the vicinity of the tree line, barely a hundred metres away (a few hundred feet) from where I was lying by the memorial stone. Roman said he would make a call to Marina, my translator, so she could let the British Consulate in

Ekaterinburg know of my predicament and my exact location. I figured that if I came to a grisly end they would at least know where to find my bones and camera. The parallels with the Dyatlov group felt familiar, especially with the memory card in my camera which had all the pictures of the trip. As he turned to go, Roman said that he had to go north but that if I was still there when he returned, he would take me back with him. I asked him how long he would be, thinking it might be four or five hours but he said a week, maybe ten days. I looked at my bottle of water and bag of peanuts and thought it might be an idea to try and increase my stocks somehow as it looked like I was going to be in for a bit of a wait. Despite giving me a few blunt truths, I had enjoyed Roman's brief company, as despite my grim circumstances, he was genuinely cheerful and friendly.

As I lay there looking out over the mountains towards the vastness of Siberia, it occurred to me how huge Russia really is and I wondered how Napoleon or Hitler could ever have thought that they could conquer Russia with conventional armies. Vladivostok, in a straight line lay 5,150 kilometres (3,200 miles) to the east from where I was sitting. I was already 1,850 kilometres (1,150 miles) inside Russia from the border with Belarus. Even Ivdel, which was roughly 130 kilometres (80 miles) away, was considered part of the local neighbourhood up here in the northern Urals. The sun was about to set and Rashid and Alexey the Officer came back up. We went over to some of the rocks which lay slighter higher than the memorial stone and we watched as the sun went down behind Kholat Syakhl. With the darkness, I thought it might be best to climb into my sleeping bag and wait to see what the new day brought. As I hobbled over to my tent, Rashid tapped my shoulder and said he could see the headlights of a group of vehicles approaching. I wasn't over hopeful as it seemed every man and his dog was heading north. After ten minutes in the dusk, Rashid walked around with a friendly looking man who was wearing jeans and a puffer jacket, a boy aged around 14 years and a glamourous looking blond woman. They were part of a larger group of four vehicles and most of the men in the group looked like military types. Alexey the Officer from our group had been further up the mountain and he came back to translate as his English was very good. He said that there was good news and bad news. The good news was that the group of hunters would take me back all the way to Ekaterinburg from the memorial stone here on Kholat Syakhl. The bad news was that they could only take me, not Rashid and also they wanted to go to Mount Chistop first which would take a couple of days more. I was not over fussed as I was so relieved. I was guided to one of the vehicles with two of the hunters in it. This was Artem and Zack. Both were wearing military combat fatigues and Artem was a human dynamo of energy. Zack was a giant bear of a man. They had a two seater all-terrain vehicle with a space for their gear behind the seats in the cab along with a large covered space at the rear for all their food, tent and equipment. I hauled myself in on top of the gear in the cab behind the seats with a great sense of relief. I said my farewells to Rashid and Alexey the Officer. They were going to go back to the group at the bottom of the mountain. They had another day left before they would start on the return trek to rendezvous with the KAMAZ truck and then make their way back to Ivdel to catch the train back to Ekaterinburg. I said I would hopefully catch up with them when they arrived back in Ekaterinburg. We drove away from the Dyatlov memorial and as I left the mountain, I looked over at Mount Otorten and considered that I had missed out on the trip there, but I had, at least, spent a night on Kholat Syakhl. However, we were not out of the forest yet, figuratively and literally. The track, which was about 5 metres (16 feet) wide as we drove away from the mountain, was made up of rocks laid into the ground. However, the rocks weren't flat, so as to ease the path of any vehicle crossing over them to avoid the mud. Most of them looked like large rugby balls which had been pushed into the earth with a sharp end sticking upwards to make it as awkward as possible for the tyres of any vehicle to go over them. We drove at a speed of barely ten miles an hour, slowly going up and over each rock. Some of them were so large, the underside of the vehicle, which was high, would bang down on them as we drove over them with a resounding thump. Our convoy had gone barely 200 metres (600 hundred or so feet) when we came down hard on one of the rocks. Artem was driving and he had two sets of gears on the truck. He tried moving one of the gear sticks slowly on one column and put his foot down on the accelerator. The engine noise grew in volume but nothing happened. Artem cursed and switched the engine off. I assumed it was a curse because I know I would have done in the same position. He leapt out of the truck followed by Zack to look underneath the vehicle.

The others all pulled up close by and a jury-rigged arc light was set up to run off a generator. It was completely dark by now. My door opened and the glamourous blond and her son opened my door and tried to talk to me in broken English. Their names were Natasha and Danil and they both had a cheerful manner, which lifted my spirits despite our predicament, broken down in the middle of the mountains. They were interested in what I was doing up on the mountain and someone explained that I had written a book about the Dyatlov Incident and I was now writing another one. In the meantime, Artem would fly out from under the vehicle and grab a spanner or tool from the cab before getting underneath again and cursed and banged away with a manic energy I don't think I have ever seen before in anyone. He didn't stop for a drink or anything to eat for exactly three hours. I was beginning to think that the vehicle was completely knackered and wondered what might happen because all the vehicles were full of people, and whilst one or two might squeeze in with the others, I felt I was too much baggage. I consoled myself with the fact that if the worst came to the worst and it was still dark, I could still hobble back to the Dyatlov memorial stone which I could just make out in the gloom. It would mean going back to the drawing board and waiting for someone else to come along, but I was getting fatalistic by this point.

Finally Artem and Zack got back into the truck and switched the engine on. Artem pushed the gear lever forward and slowly we moved a couple of feet with a great sigh of relief all around. They packed up and I said my goodbyes to Danil and Natasha. Our convoy set off and I closed my eyes as I could no longer watch as the headlights cutting through the darkness showed us going down the side of the mountain at angles at which I was convinced we would overturn and roll down the rest of the mountainside. Even with my eyes closed I could feel the precarious angles we were at. I felt another wave of relief when we reached the bottom of the mountain and the land levelled out. The trail had now gone from rocks shaped like rugby balls to a quagmire that was far worse than the trail we had originally hiked on to Kholat Syakhl. The incessant rain had created pools of water in giant potholes that looked as if they would submerge the vehicle once we started to drive into them. After about an hour of driving we pulled into area of grass to camp for the night. The group I was with wanted to have the Russian equivalent of a piss up whereas I was exhausted. It must have been around two in the morning. Artem gave me some cheese and chocolate together which actually tasted not too bad. It turned out that after seeing the state of my knee, one of their group who was a doctor said my knee really needed to be looked at sooner rather than later. I will say at that point that Artem and Zack had reaffirmed my faith in humanity as they said they would take me back immediately and cut their trip short. We needed rest first because it was 675 kilometres (420 miles) back to Ekaterinburg with a good part of that, about 95 kilometres (60 miles) driving through the worst conditions I have ever seen. After the tent was pitched I got my head down and slept like the proverbial log.

In the morning, we ate a quick breakfast and packed everything up. Danil came over to say goodbye as they were going straight to the Chistop Massif. We set off on the first part of our almost 17 hour trek back to the big city. To start with it was just a very rough trail through the forest with trees and thick undergrowth on both sides. Then the track seemed to turn into a more well-kept and well-travelled trail before turning back into an Indiana Jones type route. After a couple of hours there was a loud bang and we stopped the truck. We had been going fairly fast (fairly fast through this terrain meaning around 48kph ((30mph)) and one of the rear wheels had hit a rock so hard it had gouged the metal of the wheel. We got out to have a look at it and once again it occurred to me that it was not a place where I would want to be stranded as I had no idea where we were and up to that point had not seen another vehicle. The wall of the forest was very close on both sides and I found the silence quite unnerving. The rock had gone through the metal of the circular wheel edge and gouged it outwards. It reminded me of a large block of metal I had seen at the Tank Museum in Dorset which had been hit by a depleted uranium shell. The round had gone cleanly through the metal and the exit hole had a large flange area where the metal had been forced outwards. The wheel edge now looked the same, but the tyre itself was reasonably okay, or so we thought. For on-board maintenance, the truck had all mod cons including a high pressure air-line attached to a bottle of compressed air. After checking the tyre pressure a few times over several minutes it was losing small amounts of air, so the remainder of the journey involved us stopping to keep it constantly topped up. I gathered that a spare had already been fitted earlier so it was very much make do and mend from here on in.

The trip we made through the forest in the mountains was one of the weirdest I have undertaken. We were driving for mile after mile with only the sound of the truck and nothing but the forest on either side and then we would come across some sign of life. At one point we came across a red tracksuit top which had been draped by a branch at the side of the trail. There was nobody around. We slowed down for a look to see if anyone was there, but nothing. I wondered if it had fallen off a vehicle and someone passing later had picked it up and put it on the branch in case the owner returned to look for it, although why anyone would want to drive 40 or 50 miles just to find a tracksuit top in these conditions was beyond me. After about three hours of driving, we came across two women walking on the side of the trail ahead of us. I assumed they were Mansi, and were both middle aged. Artem slowed down to speak to them. They stood well back from us and seemed apprehensive and fearful. Artem asked if they were OK and if they needed anything. They quickly answered that they were fine and watched silently as we drove away. Six miles after this encounter we saw a wooden platform built high up in the trees, presumably for hunters and not far away from this, a wooden shack with a couple of outhouses. There was nobody here and maybe it was my morbid imagination but it reminded me of numerous horror films set in the backwoods of America. The shack had a wooden corral type of fence around it with a swing and slide in it so it seemed a family must live there, but nobody was home. About five or six miles after the wooden shack, we come across a hiker on the trail. He was heavily laden with camping gear. It seemed to me that in the mountains there was some kind of code whereby you stopped and asked everyone if they were OK and needed anything because once again, Artem slowed the truck to a stop beside the male hiker who looked to be in his early 20s. He seemed to be a genuine hiker as opposed to a Mansi and he too stood well back from us without smiling. Artem asked him if he was OK or needed anything and he just shook his head. Whatever effect this forest and mountains had on people, it certainly didn't make them effusive and voluble. I wondered why anyone would want to hike alone through this area with dangerous wild animals around, because if anything happened on your own, there was no way of summoning help as there was no satellite signal.

We started to come into areas where the forest was well managed, although at one point we came across a massive tree blocking the trail, lying on its side the trunk was wider than the height of the truck so there was no question of driving over it and it looked like it was impossible to drive around it. Looking towards the base of it which had branches reaching 6 metres (20 feet) in the air, we could see that someone had cut a gap for a vehicle to just squeeze through. It was difficult to see at first because of the angle the tree was lying at, but we literally just made it through with only inches to spare on each side. The journey through the mountains also took us through several rivers which we crossed without any problem despite the level of the water coming up to the lower part of the engine. Although we didn't see any bears or other animals, we turned a corner in the trail at one point and standing in front of us about 60 metres (about 200 feet) away was a weird looking bird in the middle of the track. It was quite large and seemed to have the head and body of a turkey and the neck of a giraffe. Artem stopped, switched the engine off and reached for his rifle. As we were on a slope leading down to the bird, he released the brake so we rolled slowly and silently towards it, closing the gap. We had closed the distance by about half and Artem put the brake on again and took aim out of the window. There was a loud crack and the bird went over in a flurry of feathers. He walked over to it and brought it back and told me it was a 'Gloo-Har' which I later learned was a Wood Grouse. In spring they are so busy courting and mating, they are oblivious to everything around them hence the name 'Gloo-Har' which means 'Deaf' in Russian.

After a journey that seemed it would have no end, just mile after mile of forest, we started passing the burnt out trees near Vizhay, which I recognised from the journey in on the KAMAZ truck. This meant we were now on the edge of the mountains and the road, although still rough and unpaved, was reasonably flat and we were able to pick up speed.

We left Vizhay behind and I noted there were numerous large trucks going back and forth. It occurred to me that had the Dyatlov group been making the journey today, they would have been able to get much closer to Kholat Syakhl in one hop from Ivdel in the same way we had done on the journey up. I also wondered how popular ski tourism was with students at the university in Ekaterinburg today compared to 1959. Many Russians seemed to enjoy hiking in the Urals in the summer but going up into the mountains in the depth of winter was a completely different proposition and I think younger Russians have other diversions or ways of enjoying themselves without undertaking such an extreme test of physical fitness. As we came out of the mountains, the first opportunity we had to get a satellite signal for our phones came as we approached the mining village of Pruchunoye. There is only one rough road heading through the village going south towards Ivdel and heading north to Vizhay. There was however one smaller, dirt track which led out of Pruchunoye to the east and then south. This road also goes to Ivdel but just outside Pruchunoye it goes north for about three Kilometres and ends at the Penal Colony No 62 known as the Black War Swan. It houses long term criminals who have been found guilty of serious crimes such as rape and murder. This was the original Ivdellag prison camp with numerous outlying sub-camps. Compared to their counterparts in the West, Russian prisons are places where you do hard time and I wondered what it must be like to serve your sentence in such a remote and inhospitable place. Although Ivdel was just over 30 kilometres (18 miles) away to the south with a small airport and good rail and road links south, the prison camp was surrounded by forest and nothing but wilderness to the north and east and forest and mountains to the west. One theory for the deaths of the Dyatlov Group was that they were killed by escaped prisoners. It seemed far-fetched and is a theory that is generally discounted because there appeared to be no injuries to any of the group that might have been caused in a violent death by such an attack by prisoners (if you discount the supposed hand injuries to Igor Dyatlov and Rustem which were supposed to be similar to hand injuries caused in fighting with fists, plus the fractures sustained by Luda, Zolotarev and Thibo). My own view was that though the camp was close to Pruchunoye it seemed improbable that prisoners would make their way 120 kilometres (75 miles) over to the Pass across such an inhospitable area. However, what I did not know to begin with is that the forest which covers the whole area north of the camp and over to the Pass was worked on by the prisoners so most of the ones engaged in forestry work would have become very familiar with the various trails and the terrain. The whole area is divided into Kvartals (quarters) and portioned off with fire breaks for ease of management, and many of the prisoners were used in logging and managing the forest, so they would have known their way around quite easily. The whole area is crisscrossed by rivers which also acted as a guide to where you were and there was a further guide of the Chistop Massif which ran as a barrier to the south of the route. So long as you kept that mountain area to your left as you were heading west or to your right if you were heading east, it was possible to navigate easily enough even if you lost the trail. Nevertheless, I never really considered the killing of the group by prisoners to be a possibility because of the items that the group had left behind, such as knives, axes and flashlights, which would have been useful to prisoners in the mountains. Despite this, after seeing the location of the prison camp and seeing the area of forest that the prisoners were working in, it would have been quite plausible for any escaped prisoners to have murdered the group in the right circumstances.

Back on our journey south, once we had left Ivdel, the road south to Ekaterinburg was a major route and the miles passed quickly. After one stop to blow up our slowly deflating tyre again we made real progress. There were numerous roadside cafes and truck stops to pull in at. I was so grateful for the help from Artem and Zack that I suggested we stop at one and offered to pay for a meal and drinks for all of us but Artem would not hear of me paying for anything and insisted on treating us all to a meal of several courses. The place we stopped at, which was not far from Serov, was fairly small with around a dozen tables and chairs and a TV showing some Russian chat show. It was clean though and the woman serving was pleasant and asked how our journey was. A man and two girls in their late teens or early twenties walked in and looked as if they had escaped from the cast of a 1950s American musical. The girls had *Bobby Sox* type clothes on and the man who looked to be late thirties or early forties, had his hair combed in a James Dean style and was wearing a *Teddy Boys* long jacket. Despite the gaiety of the outfits, they looked hard. I suspected they were there to provide entertainment to the passing truckers and I don't mean musical entertainment. Each time a truck or a vehicle pulled in, they rushed out and returned a few minutes later. It could of course be that they were on their way to Ekaterinburg to audition in a production of *Grease* and they were just trying to hitch a lift, so maybe I am being a bit too unkind.

Our final run into Ekaterinburg was just as the sun was coming up. We had driven from the Dyatlov Pass with just a few breaks in not much under 17 hours and Artem had driven all the way without a decent break other than at the truck stop. We drove around the outskirts of the city to where Artem lived to park the truck and offload the gear. His large house was in the style of an English manor house with well-tended gardens and lawns. My knee had virtually seized up completely by now and I could barely hobble with the aid of my ski pole. Artem asked me to come around the back of his house as he wanted to show me something. Behind the house was another house which Artem said was his guest house. It was almost as big as his house in front. I dragged my leg up the steps and went inside. There were a number of rooms leading off from the spacious entrance hall. There was a dining room, a sauna, a pool room and another room which looked like a study with various uniforms. I had previously said to Artem on our journey down, that I was interested in Soviet military history. He went into the room and came out with a leather Soviet officers despatch bag with an officer's cap from the Second World War (or the Great Patriotic War from 1941 to 1945 as it is known in Russia). He gave them to me and said it was a present to remind me of the trip. I was genuinely overwhelmed at his generosity. It was hard to accept it because both he and Zack had refused to take the money I offered them as payment for the petrol and the hassle I had caused them by having to bring me back immediately and cutting short their trip with their friends. Artem said Zack would drive me back to the hotel and that I should get my knee seen to as soon as possible. I said goodbye to him and Zack drove me over to the hotel. They were two of the most decent men I have ever met and to me they epitomised the expression "the kindness of strangers".

Once I reached the hotel I have never been so glad to see a comfy bed and have a nice hot bath. A doctor said that the ligaments in my right knee had been torn and would take at least three months to heal.

# Chapter 6

Although I had managed to get back to Ekaterinburg ahead of the group at the Dyatlov Pass, I had to kick my heels a bit in a manner of speaking as I needed to rest my knee. However, one person I was able to meet with was Yury Yakimov. My translator Marina brought him over to the hotel as he had recovered from the illness which had prevented him from coming with us to the Dyatlov Pass. When I reproduced Yury Yakimov's theory in my first book on the Dyatlov Incident, I came in for a certain amount of flak from some quarters with (some) people dismissing his story as nonsense. I keep a very open mind on all theories related to the Dyatlov group deaths for the simple reason that no matter what the theory is, nobody so far has been able to come up with a completely adequate and plausible explanation that answers all the questions. Until that day comes, in my view, one person's theory is as good as another's. Equally I do not feel that one person should dismiss another theory if they have no way of proving their own. What attracted me to Yury Yakimov's theory was the fact that he had experienced something strange in the northern Ural Mountains, not that far from where the members of the Dyatlov group had died. I felt at the very least that he was worth hearing out. The other reason that I felt Yury Yakimov was worth hearing first hand is because he had seen strange lights when he was in the Mountains and strange lights at night is a major part of the Dyatlov mystery.

71

Yury was much fitter and younger looking than I expected when he arrived with Marina. I knew he was retired but he explained that miners retired earlier than other workers in Russia because of the very trying conditions which they worked under. He was currently living just a few miles to the west of Ivdel and had travelled down on the train to meet me and also to meet up with Yury K and others from the group at the Dyatlov Foundation when they returned. He apologised for not being able to go up to the Pass when we travelled as he was too ill. I very much liked his manner. He was polite and spoke in a calm, rational way. Although I had studied his light theory before, I asked him to explain to me what exactly happened to him the first time he saw the lights. It took place at an open mine which was about 120 kilometres south (75 miles) from the Dyatlov Pass and roughly 12 kilometres (7 miles) from Ivdel. He said that he was on his own and it had been an uneventful shift. He was keen to get finished and had never experienced anything strange at the mine workings before. When the lights first switched on, he said it surprised him and the strength of them was so powerful, that it was like a searchlight. There were two lights fairly close together initially and they were in the forest about three hundred metres away from where he was standing in the open-cast mine. As he watched the lights, they started to move towards him very fast and they were moving around. When I asked him what he meant by "moving around" he said that, although they were still pointing in his direction, they were moving as if they were being held by someone and that they had previously been standing still and were now running towards him very fast, still holding the light and trying to keep it pointed towards him as they ran. He said that despite this seeming flurry of movement, there was absolute silence while all this was happening which unnerved him. He said that he felt compelled to look away from the lights because of their strength and, as they were coming towards him, they were dividing so there were more of them. It seemed, from his description, as if there were people running towards him and I asked him if he could make out any shapes or if there were people that he could see in the darkness but he said he could not and that the lights appeared to be on their own. He was dazzled by the lights, of course, so it may not have been that easy to see anything. The effect of the lights made him fearful and his instinct told him not to look at them. I then asked him about the

Forest Ranger named Valentin Rudkovsky who had experienced exactly the same phenomenon in the northern Urals. It turned out that when Rudkovsky had seen these lights he was in the forest about 100 kilometres (62 miles) to the west of where Yury Yakimov had seen them and roughly the same distance from the Dyatlov Pass. Interestingly, it was many months before Yury Yakimov learned of Rudkovsky's sighting of the lights, and when he investigated and spoke to Rudkovsky, it turned out that their individual sightings were less than two weeks apart – 29 August 2002 and 11 September 2002. Rudkovsky had seen the lights in the same manner as Yury and he too felt afraid and had to look away from them even though he was armed with a hunting rifle as part of his equipment for carrying out his duties as a forest ranger. I asked him what kind of a person Valentin Rudkovsky was and he said that he was a very grounded and stoic type of man, not easily flustered, which is why Yury felt his story carried some weight. Rudkovsky had spent years working in the forests, either on his own or in small teams and not a likely candidate to come up with a made up and outlandish story. He was retired now and kept himself to himself but had agreed to meet with Yury Yakimov to tell him what he had seen that night. Despite being a man who had lived and worked in the forests for many years amongst bears and wolves as well as being armed with a rifle, the overwhelming feeling that Rudkovsky had from the lights was one of fear. Yury also said that both he himself and Valentin Rudkovsky had felt very tired and sleepy for days after their encounters with the lights.

Yury Yakimov's opinion was that the members of the Dyatlov group had been killed by some form of energy directed weapon connected with the lights.

With regards to the source of the lights in both cases, I asked Yury what he thought could explain the strange lights? He felt that the phenomenon could only have been extra-terrestrial. Once, of course, this kind of explanation is mentioned, some people switch off. Whilst it is not a line I follow, I keep an open mind and really what is required is some kind of solid evidence to back that line of reasoning.

Yury Yakimov had tried to bring his story with regard to the lights and possible involvement with the Dyatlov deaths, to the attention of the

President's Office and it had been referred to the Chief Prosecutor's Office for the Sverdlovsk Oblast (administrative region). They had responded to him that the Dyatlov case had been concluded in 1959 and that there was no need for the case to be reopened. Irrespective of what anyone thinks of what happened to Yury Yakimov and the lights, the stock response of any official authority in Russia is that the case is closed and does not need to be investigated any further. It is worth noting that the prosecutor on the Dyatlov case, Lev Ivanov, followed the extra-terrestrial line of explanation. Most policemen tend to be hard-nosed types who have seen it all by the time they have reached the end of a long career in the police and Ivanov had probably seen his share of the worst of human nature in a large city like Sverdlovsk. He could have stuck with one of the more non-contentious theories such as an avalanche, with regards to the Dyatlov deaths, but he chose to keep to the line of them being killed by something out of this world. As will be seen, however, there may be other reasons why Lev Ivanov took the line he did.

After our meeting, we took some photographs outside the hotel, shook hands and said we would meet later at the Dyatlov Foundation when the group returned from the Pass. The group were due back the following day and I had time to kill. Whilst sitting in the nearest coffee shop I could get to, I looked at a brochure I had picked up in the hotel. The brochure was the same sort of thing you see in hotels everywhere. It was basically a tourist publication giving details of things to do and see in the Sverdlovsk Oblast. The Sverdlovsk Oblast is huge, about the size of England and Scotland and there was a long list of points of interest. The Dyatlov Pass was in there, although I couldn't imagine the average tourist passing through Russia going there as it required organisation and, as I well knew, a degree of physical fitness. It wasn't like hopping into a taxi in New York and asking to go to Times Square. However, looking down the list, one thing in particular caught my eye.

I had heard a story some years before which I took to be apocryphal, a kind of Soviet *Urban Legend,* and thought no more about it. I had assumed that if the story was true, then it would have taken place in the Ukraine where the famine, the *Holodomor,* had taken place and hit hard in the 1930s. However, here it was, in the tourist brochure in front of me, and it had actually taken place in 1932 in the Sverdlovsk Oblast, 355 kilometres (220 miles) from Sverdlovsk/Ekaterinburg in a village named Gerasimovka. The story may not have had the number of twists and turns of the Dyatlov story, but it was still a convoluted tale. The basic story is that a young boy named Pavlik Morozov, who was aged 13 years, found out that his father had been hoarding grain and hiding it from the authorities. The boy informed on him and the father was arrested, interrogated and finally executed. Pavlik Morozov was hailed as a hero and a shining example to Soviet youth by the authorities. Unfortunately, the tragic tale did not end there as he was found murdered shortly afterwards. Depending on which view of the story is taken, the village of Gerasimovka was viewed by the ruling Soviet authorities as a "Nest of Kulaks" and a massive crackdown was launched on the enemies of the state in the Urals area. Kulaks were rich peasants whom Stalin had launched a virtual war against, viewing them as obstacles to progress in collectivisation. With his murder, Pavlik Morozov became a martyr. Statues were built around the Soviet Union and poems were composed to him by Young Pioneers. The Young Pioneers was a Soviet mass youth movement for children aged between 10 to 15 years old, similar to Scout movements in the West. The hazy area of their relation to Pavlik Morozov is where the story gets murky. There is an attempt in official literature, such as the tourist brochure I was reading, to pass his murder off as the terrible murder of a young boy for reasons other than the fact he had shopped his father and his father was executed. This gives the impression of the boy being some kind of a *stool pigeon* in the vast prison camp that the whole Soviet Union was turning into. The tourist piece I was reading stated that when he was murdered, Pavlik "was not wearing his red neck scarf", implying that he had been murdered by someone who did not know who he was or could not identify him as a member of the Young Pioneers. However, Gerasimovka was a small village then and it is still a small village now and everybody would have known everyone else in the village, especially after the father's execution and the story that behind it. Later, I found that a Russian researcher had looked into the story and concluded that Pavlik Morozov had not been a Young Pioneer at all. Under the circumstances that seemed a bit peculiar because like all repressive societies, the Soviet Union was a place where it was wise to be seen to go along with whatever the rulers dictate. In the case of young

Pavlik it would not have been a good move not to have been a Young Pioneer when probably most of his friends and schoolmates were. The mere fact of him denouncing his father to the authorities suggests that he most likely was a Young Pioneer and if he wasn't, he had certainly taken on board what they stood for. What must have made this story difficult for the authorities to pass off as some kind of morality tale was the involvement of close family ties. It was not just a story of a young boy doing the right thing and telling the authorities of wrongdoing by a member of a class of greedy exploiters of food. It was also seen by many as the betrayal of a close knit community who were being attacked by outsiders and having the product of their labour being taken away from them. The worst part of the betrayal was that the boy's own father died as a result of his son's action.

What later research appeared to show was that the whole story was composed of half-truths involving friction between the family members, although the fact that a 13 year old boy named Pavlik Morozov was murdered in Gerasimovka is not disputed.

What I found was that few Russians I spoke to about it, did not seem to want to give an opinion or verdict on it when I mentioned it. All of them knew the story though. I later found that the case file had been transcribed and is available in English on the internet and in yet another odd twist, this download had been made available from the archives of the FSB. Basically, it was an ordinary police matter, if the later research is to be believed, and yet the record is held by the state security service.

If the blurb I was reading in the tourist literature was right, then perhaps the oddest part of the Pavlik Morozov story is that it now has almost a kind of a cult following, with ordinary people making visits to Gerasimovka to see his statue and leave notes there, using it almost as some kind of shrine. Gerasimovka is in the middle of nowhere, like a lot of places in Russia, so it is quite a trek which requires some motivation. I couldn't figure out what the draw would be to go and leave notes at the statue of a *stool pigeon* unless you were a die-hard communist. Had my knee not been in such bad condition, I would have hired a car to go and see what the fuss was all about, but I would have to leave it for my next trip.

Once the group I had travelled with up to the Dyatlov Pass arrived back in Ekaterinburg, about half of them had trains and planes to catch to other parts of Russia and had to travel on immediately. The other half of the group went back to the Dyatlov Foundation to discuss the trip. I took a taxi over to the Foundation with Marina, my translator. I was more than happy taking the trolley busses that crisscrossed Ekaterinburg but I could barely hobble more than a few feet with the help of a cane that Marina had loaned me which belonged to her grandfather. We were greeted at the door of the Foundation by Lisa, the Soul of the Forest and our ever jovial host Yury K. Among the others were Yury Yakimov, Alexey the Officer, Shamil, Sergey the guide, Nastya and Rashid. Shamil was going to head back to the railway station in a few hours to take a train back to Kazan but he had wanted to come back and discuss the trip. A nice spread of food including water melon and chocolates and drink had been laid on for us and we settled down in the study to first watch a taped interview that Yury K had made with a woman ATCO (Air Traffic Controller Officer) who was now retired. She had worked all her life at Uktus, the general aviation airfield which was only a few miles south of the main Koltsovo Airport for Ekaterinburg and when the city was known as Sverdlovsk. Although she was retired, she still lived near the airport and Yury K had interviewed her during the summer in her garden. She would pause during the interview to state what aircraft had passed overhead after taking off and say the type and where it was going. She said that her daughter had watched a programme on TV about the Dyatlov Incident and told her mother to contact the Dyatlov Foundation. After a few generalisations such as the behaviour of children nowadays, she proceeded to talk about her late husband. He had been a pilot and knew the area of the northern Urals very well as he often flew in the region in the old Soviet days when the city was known as Sverdlovsk. Her husband had flown Antonov An 2s, the old Soviet-era large biplane and she described an unusual incident around the time of the Dyatlov tragedy. He had flown north from Sverdlovsk towards Ivdel when he radioed in that he had seen what appeared to be a weather balloon and was going to investigate it. He turned towards it and as he approached the balloon or whatever it was, it rapidly ascended at a high speed out of his path and at a speed that he couldn't keep pace with and he lost sight of it. He said he had never seen anything like it before, and although he thought it was a weather balloon, it appeared to be under some kind of control which would have been impossible in the case of a normal balloon. Her husband also spoke of the lights in the skies of the northern Urals that he had seen along with other pilots, which appeared to have no rational explanation. It turned out that her husband had known Gennady Patrushev who had also flown in the northern Urals and was Sverdlovsk-based. Gennady Patrushev had seen a tent on Kholat Syakhl the day before the tent was discovered by Boris Slobtsov's search party. Myself, Marina and Yury were going to meet Patrushev's widow the following day.

We then watched a very interesting video presentation by Valentin Gerasimovich Yakimenko on his examination of the negatives taken from Zolotarev's and Krivoy's cameras. This presentation had been given at the last annual Dyatlov Conference held at UFU (Ural Federal University) earlier in the year. I have a copy of his paper and will go into it more fully later.

There was then a two hour discussion as to what exactly may have happened to the Dyatlov group on the night of 1/2 February on Kholat Syakhl. Much of the discussion related to the lights and Yury Yakimov's theory tied in with what had been found on the Zolotarev and Krivoy negatives, which looked like a burning plane or rocket. Yury Yakimov spent some time outlining his theory to everyone, as a number of them had not come across it before. While there was a general agreement that, going by Yakimenko's observations about the negatives, at least a few of the group had been outside looking at something and taking pictures, it didn't really explain the panic at the end. Alexey the Officer said to me;

*"You have heard all the evidence and what has been said Keith. What do you think?"*

It was a difficult question to respond to because what I have always looked for in this story is cold hard facts and there weren't a lot of them. Everything we had discussed about Yakimenko's observations on the negatives did not have an exact time frame. It seemed odd that if only a few of the group were outside at the end, I wondered why they would have sealed the tent entrance completely, although it can be understood in the freezing conditions to try and retain a little heat. Also, if there was something that had attracted their attention from outside the tent, so much so that they wanted to take pictures of the phenomenon, then why didn't they all go out to see the unusual sight? I said that the other thing that puzzled me about the slashing to the tent was the way it was slashed. I said that whether you were left handed or right handed, a slashing motion with a knife being done in a panic would have wide slashes at a 45 degree angle from the left to right downwards or right to left downwards depending on which hand you were using. I pointed out that many of the cuts in the picture of the slashed tent after it had been erected in the police station later showed that the cuts were very symmetrical and done in almost square shapes which didn't suggest a panic. Yury K said that some of the rescue party said they had made additional cuts to the side of the tent for easier access to get the items out from the inside. Mikhail Sharavin and Boris Slobtsov had used an axe to make the tear larger to get inside. Again that didn't make a great deal of sense as it would have been expected that extremely large cuts would have been made but some of the square symmetrical cuts at the top were quite small.

The consensus of opinion seemed to be that something had attracted the attention of some of the group in the sky and they had been taking pictures. Whatever had then happened had caused the members of the group in the tent to cut their way out and then as a whole group make their way to the tree line at the bottom of the mountain. It was all very plausible, but as with all the theories, it is still not enough of an explanation.

I really enjoyed the discussion as it was a chance to get together with people who all knew the story inside out and had developed their own theories as to what had happened. The problem with these discussions is you come out of it feeling no further forward because you follow a line of thought only to come up against a dead end and that is how I felt at the end of our get-together.

Vladimir Korotaev, the Ivdel Investigator who asked awkward questions at the
start of the case, but was told to get on with his job (Dyatlov Foundation)

The following day, I met Marina and Yury K at the Foundation and
took a taxi over to the other side of Ekaterinburg to meet Valeria
Gamatina who is Gennady Patrushev's widow. The area which Gamatina
lived in was full of old Soviet style blocks of flats. Nobody expected them
to be still standing well into the twenty first century, but they were. As
befitted my luck, Gamatina's flat was on the top floor of the block and lifts
were an unheard of luxury in these blocks. Any bending or pressure on my
knee was agony, so it took me some time to slowly pull myself up the
flights of stairs. Gamatina greeted us all warmly and she was a sprightly
looking and happy lady who looked much younger than her almost 80

years (her eightieth birthday was only a couple of months away). I considered myself lucky that she had agreed to meet me because she was no longer keen on meeting any writers or journalists. With Marina translating, Gamatina told me that just a couple of years previously she had been visited by a pair of TV journalists from a Russian station who were covering the Dyatlov story. When the interview was over, one of the journalists had asked for a copy of a picture that she kept on her wall unit in the living room. The picture was of her son who was also a pilot, in his uniform. She agreed but pointed out that the picture was of her son, not her husband who had died in the air crash. The journalists said it was OK as they wanted to use it in the programme they were making. When the show eventually aired she was watching it when the photo flashed up on the screen of her son who they said was dead. The implication was that it was her deceased husband who had died many years before. However, her son was still alive, but this ambiguity was not explained. It was a lazy and totally irresponsible piece of journalism but it gave her a terrible shock to see her son's picture on the television and to hear that he was dead. Such was the extent of the shock, she had to go to bed and stayed there for a couple of days to recover. I could well understand her reluctance to see anyone else after that.

She told us the story of her life, living with a strict father in Ulan Ude and Irkutsk in Siberia. She met Gennady Patrushev after he graduated from Pilot School in Sverdlovsk and they hit it off with each other immediately. He asked her to marry him not long after they had met as he was scheduled to go to Africa as part of his work as a pilot. Only single men could go and he was against going now that he had met his future wife. After her husband, Gennady, had died she had remarried at the insistence of her mother-in-law (Gennady Patrushev's mother). He second husband was now also dead and she was now long retired having spent her working life as a doctor.

Several years before, she had heard the full Dyatlov story from Yury K and asked if she could see all the paperwork relating to the story and the investigation. She was surprised to see no mention of her first husband, particularly as he had been involved in the search for the missing students and had seen the tent and radioed in the position on 25 February 1959 (the day before it was found by Boris Slobtsov and his team). Not only had he seen the tent that day but not mentioned in other accounts is the fact that he dropped a flag at the location to act as a marker. Furthermore, he (Gennady Patrushev), knew the approximate route the group had taken and was following it and on the day he saw the tent, he had seen also seen three people walking in the opposite direction much further away from the tent area. She believes this is why he later died in the plane crash 65 kilometres (40 miles) north of Ivdel. She told me that she and her mother-in-law met the coffin at Sverdlovsk airport when it arrived from Ivdel and she was told that his skull had been smashed in the crash of his Yak 12. She had been given a copy of his autopsy report which showed that death occurred at 4.30pm on the day he died. She asked for a copy of the crash report, which she was given, and she noticed that the time of the crash was given as the same time that he took off from Ivdel (4.30pm). She queried this apparent discrepancy as she pointed out it would have been impossible for the Yak 12 to take off from Ivdel and immediately crash as the crash site was 65 kilometres (40 miles) north of the airport. What she received back was silence and not long after this she was assaulted not once, but twice. The first assault happened at her husband's grave and the second assault took place in a quiet street. Being a young woman on her own, she was badly shaken up and decided not to pursue the matter.

After hearing her story she laid on a very nice spread for us and once again I was overwhelmed by the kindness and generosity I was to keep coming across on my visit.

After my meeting with Gamatina, I started to look at the Dyatlov story again in the light of some new evidence related to work carried out by Valentin Yakimenko in conjunction with Yury K.

# Chapter 7

Ome of the main problems with the Dyatlov story is finding a way to move it forward. To do that, what is needed is proper evidence, and that is the one thing that is lacking in every theory, or variation of theory that is put forward. Every year there are numerous visitors to the Dyatlov Pass, many of them with metal detectors. The area of the spur at the Pass, the tent location and the tree line must be one of the most heavily "metal detected" places in the world. Even when anything is found by the metal detectors, it doesn't necessarily prove there is a link with the Dyatlov group. For instance, some time ago, someone found a piece of metal that looked as though it was from a piece of Russian military equipment. Whilst that was entirely possible, it still does not prove a link to the group. There has long been military conscription in Russia and it is almost rare to find someone who has not been in the military or connected with it in some way. It is also common to see people dressed in military gear in the Urals as well as using second hand military equipment. So, for me, the idea that it might be possible to search around the area of the Pass and find something that will link back to the Dyatlov group is extremely remote. It doesn't stop people trying of course.

To add to the confusion, a number of Dyatlov forgeries have started appearing in recent years. For example, one document sent to the Dyatlov Foundation purported to be a copy of an original held in the KGB (now FSB) archives. The document stated an examination of the tent had been carried out by the KGB, and a dark stain found near the tent entrance was found to be blood. The document was proved to be a forgery but its appearance only shows how many twists and turns the whole Dyatlov story takes with all the different theories.

Another area of contention is the group's cameras and what they contained. Many people look at the haunting images to see if they might contain some clue as to what was going to happen. Tied in with this is the argument about the number of cameras that were in the group. Four were found in the tent and a fifth was believed to be with Zolotarev when his body was found. This is compounded by how many pictures were retrieved from those cameras and what was actually present on the negatives. There appeared to be many negatives in their film which had nothing on the frames. Matters were not helped because when the search parties located the bodies, some of the group's cameras were used by members of the search party to take pictures of the operation at the time. This was presumably due to the unavailability of cameras at the beginning, although a number of photos were taken later by members of the search parties who brought cameras with them.

At the annual Dyatlov Conference held at UFU Ural State University (formerly UPI) in 2013, a paper was presented by Valentin Yakimenko. The presentation by Yakimenko was one of the first pieces of real solid evidence put forward in the Dyatlov story for many years. The paper carried a lot of weight, not just because of the content, but also because the author himself, Valentin Gerasimovich Yakimenko, was Chairman of the UPI Tourist Club in 1959/1960 and knew the Dyatlov group members. He had graduated from the Faculty of Power Engineering in 1962 and went on to have a distinguished career heading up the design bureau of the Urals Hydroelectric organisation as well as being a prolific inventor with over 200 inventions to his name. Perhaps most importantly, he also took part in the search operations for the missing Dyatlov group in March 1959. It is worth mentioning here that "lights" play a crucial part in his presentation.

Initially, in January 2013, Yakimenko had written an article "A Dyatlov Group Message to us read 54 Years after", in a local Russian magazine named *Uralsky Sledopyt* (meaning *Ural's Pathfinder* – a monthly magazine printed in Ekaterinburg on tourism and history which covers ski sports and the outdoors). The translated meaning of the article's awkward sounding title was that it was meant as a message to us in the present time (2013) from the Dyatlov group. Yakimenko had based the article on the testimony of Captain Alexey Chernyshov of the Ivdel Gulag (Ivdellag) who had taken part in the search for the missing group in the month (February 1959) before Yakimenko was involved in the search. The original article was based on Zolotarev and Thibo being outside the tent on that last night and seeing the strange lights in the sky. The two of them called the others to come outside and see the light phenomenon.

The others came out and of the group, two of them, Krivoy and Rustem, took photos of the lights. After a while, either because they had seen enough or they were getting cold, or both, the others all went back into the tent and only Zolotarev and Thibo stayed outside. Yakimenko had based his assumptions, as stated above, on the testimony of Captain Alexey Chernyshov plus the autopsies and report on the condition of the tent. While going over his assumptions, Yakimenko decided to closely examine the negatives with a powerful microscope. He concentrated in particular on the main negative which shows a kind of light orb falling and which fills most of the negative. It was wrongly assumed by many people (myself included) that this was the last negative taken from Igor Dyatlov's camera. What Yakimenko found when he examined this negative under the microscope was the outline, at the base of the negative, of the tops of three heads of the others, which stood out against the brightness in front of them.

The tops of the heads of three of the group outside the tent watching the lights. They are identified as left to right: Thibo (he is the tallest), Zolotarev (in flapped fur hat), Zina (in skully hat) (Valentin Yakimenko)

A sharper view of the tops of the three heads (Valentin Yakimenko)

As Yakimenko concentrated on the research, he remembered remarks made by members of the search party on the day the final four bodies (Luda, Zolotarev, Thibo and Kolevatov) were removed from the ravine. This was 4 May 1959 and he remembered that the search party had said they had found a camera on Zolotarev's body. The camera is actually clearly seen on Zolotarev's body in the photo where he and another body are laid side by side. Zolotarev is lying on his back and the camera is clearly on his chest and had been hanging around his neck which suggests that he had made his way down the mountain immediately with the camera, without stopping to take it off. It occurred to Yakimenko that as Zolotarev still had the camera with him when he was found, then, he must have also taken photos of the lights in the sky that night. His (Yakimenko's) next task was to make some enquiries about Zolotarev's camera at the time of his body being found. Unfortunately, after over 50 years, two members of the original search party (Mokhov and Askinadzi) could no longer remember anything about the camera. There was no on-site inspection or report made of what was found at the time at the ravine where the last four bodies were found. Yakimenko also noted that the pathologist, Boris Vozrozdhenny, made no mention of a camera in the autopsy report, although he had made a note of clothes and the contents of Zolotarev's pockets. The camera obviously existed, but where was it and more importantly, where was the film inside it? Also, Yakimenko was concerned that as the bodies in the ravine had not been found for three months, the camera had lain under thick snow, so the next question was that assuming the film could be found, what would be the state of the film? The emulsion may have been affected by the long period in the camera surrounded by snow and also it may have been damaged when it was removed from the camera or at any point when it was looked at or developed in the film laboratory.

Yakimenko's next step was to consult with Yury K to examine the large number of negatives which had been donated to the Dyatlov Foundation by Lev Ivanov's daughter after he died. With Yury K's assistant, the three of them cut the film strips into lengths of six frames each and examined all the negatives including a number of seemingly "blank" negatives. They noticed that one of the strips had "Zolotarev" scratched on it. Who had scratched the name on it is unknown. More puzzling is that none of the cameras or the film recovered from the five group cameras were identified by the Investigators in 1959. It is reasonable to assume that all the film and the cameras were examined and some kind of attempt made to identify what film belonged to each camera and individual; but it would not have been easy as some group members would more than likely have given their camera to other members in the group and asked them to take a picture. Despite not knowing who had scratched the name "Zolotarev" on the particular strip, it seemed fairly certain that it had been taken from Zolotarev's camera.

Zolotarev's film appears to have been reasonably intact (*ie* not cut into strips) and it was cut into strips by Yakimenko. However, there were a number of other strips which had already been cut at the time of the investigation. The cutting of these other strips suggests that while the strips were in the hands of Lev Ivanov and/or the authorities, some kind of attempt had been made to examine them. Strictly speaking, if they (the larger strips) had not been cut, they should have been fairly easy to match to a camera and ought to have been handed back to the relatives when the investigation had ended. However, as they could not be identified easily, Lev Ivanov may have decided to just keep them.

The "Zolotarev strip" of film had ten frames in it and the cut edge matched the previous strip which had 17 frames. This previous strip of 17 frames covered pictures that Zolotarev had taken in earlier days. Both strips were free from emulsion damage but there was a small section of underdeveloped film on the ten-frame strip due to the layers of film getting stuck together in the developing tank. The most glaring item to begin with, in the examination of Zolotarev's film, was that nine frames were missing. There should have been a total of 36 frames but the two strips only had a total of 27 frames. So where were the missing nine frames? Whilst the dedicated conspiracy theorist can look for any evidence that points to a cover up of some kind, it could have been that the remaining strip or strips of nine frames had been lost. This is quite possible as there seemed to have been no formal cataloguing of all the items. Valentin Yakimenko felt that these missing frames contained important information and may have been "withheld" for that reason. The fact that these nine frames may have contained potentially important information will shortly be demonstrated because on the face of it,

Zolotarev was taking pictures outside the tent that night (1/2 February 1959) right up to the last moment before whatever event caused the tragedy started.

The strips were given a brief initial examination. The examination showed that all the shots from the ten frame strip with Zolotarev's name scratched on it were taken at night. At the time period the photos were taken, there was no visible moon. It did not appear until well after midnight and was waning (it was on its last quarter with 42% visibility and 23 days into its 29 day cycle before the new moon).

A brief first look showed nothing unusual. The light was so low that the edges of each frame could not be seen. What could be seen on the negatives were small black dots and some very small pale dots. To the human eye, these dots could not be identified. These dots were nothing like the much larger frame of the bright orb. The presence of the ten frames taken one after another showed that something in the night sky had attracted Zolotarev's attention and he took picture after picture of it.

Once this ten frame strip was scanned and examined under a powerful microscope, the edges of the frames could be clearly seen. Under magnification the frames showed fine bright and dull dots with lines which resembled the tracks of signal flares. The magnification also showed up very fine particles of dirt which had either been on the frame originally or had been picked up off the surface of the scanner. A comparison was made to the earlier frames in the 17 frame strip to see if there were any particles which matched the two frames exactly. That way, these objects or particles could be discarded, as they showed up in every frame.

The frames were examined using a microscope with x30 magnification. Once the superfluous items were put to one side, there were six frames of particular interest. The first one showed a small bright spot which was larger than the stars but several times smaller than the disc made by a full moon. This small object was rectangular in shape. In the second frame of interest Yakimenko found a larger object which appeared to be connected to a smaller object. The whole of this appeared to have a network-like structure, as Yakimenko described it. He named it *Lynx* to identify it because the front part resembled the outline of the head of a Lynx. This was purely an identification name, not a description of what he thought it actually was. In the next frame of interest, Yakimenko found another object which was quite bright and he gave it an identification name of *horn*, again because it resembled a horn.

The following frame yielded another bright spot. Yakimenko gave this the name *jaws* as it looked like a set of jaws opening. This identification name was not meant to imply anything other than what the shape looked like to Yakimenko, rather than an object that looked like it was going to attack the group in some way. The object in the next frame was named *Lynx 2* as it appeared to be the same shape as the *Lynx* object in the earlier frame. The last frame of interest was possibly the most interesting because it resembled the shape of an explosion. This was named *Mushroom* as it strongly resembled the shape of the cloud and smoke going upwards from an explosion at ground level. This frame was magnified and the mushroom shape appeared to have a bright centre nearer the top.

The *Mushroom* frame was the final frame of interest in the Zolotarev strip of nine frames. The whole sequence appeared to show something in the night sky approaching and getting larger as it approached, before what appeared to be an explosion in the final frame.

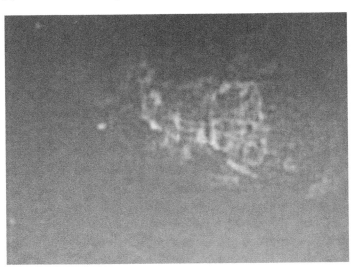

Lynx 2 (Valentin Yakimenko)

Mushroom (resembling an explosion) (Valentin Yakimenko)

Jaws (Valentin Yakimenko)

The important question is; over what time frame did this object or objects approach? It could have taken place very quickly or there could have been lengthy gaps of several minutes between the frames. Yakimenko, Yury K and Evgeny then conducted an experiment using an old Soviet FED camera. This particular camera belonged to the UPI tourist club at the same time as most of the Dyatlov group were students at UPI. It was presented to the Dyatlov Foundation by Yury Yakimeno along with a number of other cameras from that time. The FED is a rangefinder camera and was a crude copy of Leica cameras of the time. It was similar to the Zorky cameras used by the Dyatlov group. FED was the initials of Felix Edmundovich Dzerzhinsky whom the factory was named after.

In the experiment, they assumed that Zolotarev had made all 19 relevant shots on the one film, so using a stop-watch, they measured the time it took to cock the camera shutter, winding the film and take the picture. This was done 19 times. The average time worked out at five seconds per shot. Other factors had to be taken into consideration though. It was night time, Zolotarev would have been looking upwards and he would have needed to be sure of his footing in the snow. He would have needed to get the object in his camera viewfinder and then press the shutter release. This would take more than five seconds per shot. Yakimenko allowed for a period of eight seconds per shot which would take into account the extra factors. He (Yakimenko) describes the object or objects as a celestial phenomenon and that a total period of one minute and 36 seconds would have been needed for Zolotarev to take the pictures one after another. The time frame of this celestial phenomenon could have been longer than what had been covered in Zolotarev's photos as Yakimenko says he believes that Zolotarev may have run out of film before the end. This may account for the missing nine frames from Zolotarev's film mentioned earlier.

Perhaps the most important aspect of this sequence of shots is that Zolotarev appears to have captured the phenomenon as it appears in the night sky and descends towards the ground. It also seems that while he had caught mainly the beginning of it, Krivoy and Rustem had caught the end of it with their cameras which accounts for the very large white "orb" pictures that are so well known in this story.

Yakimenko's view of the investigation was that the investigators themselves remained unaware at the time that the cameras left behind in the tent might have contained any pictures of the light object in the night sky. There was, therefore, a failure to link all the film strips together to try and put any kind of a story to what they had seen. Yakimenko managed to link them, although this could not be done perfectly because there were a number of clippings rather than whole strips of continuous film which would have made the job considerably easier. There were seven separate lots of clippings apart from the large strips of film. He put them into seven groups and numbered them A1 (5 shots), A2 (1 shot), A4 (2 shots), C1 (5 shots), D1 (3 shots), D2 (3.5 shots), E1 (1 shot)[1]. The difficulty that he had was to match these clippings up with the larger strips of film to try and work out who had taken them. In the event he was only able to match up two of them – the three shots from D1 and the one shot from A2. He was able to match these up with two film strips. The three shots on clipping D1 was the first three shots of film strip No 13 (as he had designated it) and the 1 shot on A2 was the first frame of film strip No 16 (again as he had designated it). Yakimenko found that the line of cuts between the clippings and the main strips were a perfect match. The question remains as to why the investigators cut these frames away from the main film strips? It could have been for ease of examination. It also begs the question as to why frames from some of the strips (in addition to the missing nine frames from Zolotarev's film) are missing and where they are? The two possibilities for this are that the investigators found something of interest or incriminating (depending on your point of view) and withheld them or alternatively, they were simply lost, which is, of course, quite possible.

A further interesting observation that Yakimenko made when looking at the film strips was that in the sequence of photos taken of the tent being pitched at the spur of Kholat Syakhl on the late afternoon of 1 February 1959, some frames are missing from this sequence. Again, it seems odd that these should be missing as they would have just been straightforward

---

[1] Please see Appendix I for the table of descriptions in the sequences mentioned in this chapter. The table and actual photos are shown on my website www.dyatlov-pass-incident.com

photos of the Dyatlov group clearing the snow and pitching the tent, with Zina attending to Kolevatov's injured leg in the middle of it all. Why would the investigators want to examine this sequence more closely? The "event/s" happened some hours after this, although the interest may have been purely because these were the very last photos taken of the group alive. Also, although many in the group had removed their outer protective clothing, the investigators may have tried to match up the clothes being worn at the time of pitching the tent to the clothes on the bodies when they were found as it was only a matter of hours later when they left the tent and would have been unlikely to have changed. This would be confusing for anyone trying to match who was wearing what because some of the group were wearing clothes that belonged to others.

The next stage was for Yakimenko to examine the relevant clippings of the celestial phenomenon with the microscope at a much higher magnification of x1000. These clippings did not match any of the film strips, which meant that the sequence of film (frames) on each side of the clipping to the left and the right were missing.

Yakimenko made three significant observations. The first was that the bright object in the sky had been photographed by five different cameras in the group. The second observation was that there was a definite time element involved with members of the Dyatlov group having exactly the same shots as Zolotarev took but from later in the Zolotarev sequence. This infers that Zolotarev took the first shots and then called the others to come out of the tent to see for themselves. The shots they took exactly match Zolotarev's later shots and they would have all been standing there taking photos together. The relevant frames that match up are Zolotarev frames numbered 5, 7 & 10.

The third conclusion Yakimenko reached is that whatever the object in the sky was, it was moving over a period of time rather than being just one sudden flash of some kind of phenomenon in the night sky. It would have taken time for Zolotarev to take his first pictures, call the others and for the others to get their cameras and come out of the tent, get their bearings and start taking pictures.

The main issue facing Yakimenko was the dissimilarity of the objects in the different strips and clippings. Again (as with his previous exercise of examining the film under x30 magnification), he identified scanner faults, micro particles and miniature scratches. All these items differed in shape from the celestial phenomenon in the sky. It was more difficult to identify technical workmanship defects of the actual film itself. The best guideline for him was the repetition of the same objects in different strips and frames from different cameras. When he began examining the object/s under x1000 magnification, he divided the clippings into four groups and these groupings were by similarity of object/s.

## Group One Photos

- Photo 8 (clipping E1)
  Photo 8a (clipping E1 with background highlighted)

- Photo 9 (clipping A2)
  Photo 9 (clipping A2 with background highlighted)

The first group showed a luminous dot growing gradually larger in size from a size of 3 units to 16 units[2] in diameter. In the final shots, this dot was twice the size of the normal disc size of the moon (although the moon was not visible), so it was quite substantial in size. Both photos 8 and 9 are quite similar and were probably taken at the same time by different cameras. Yakimenko's view was that against the background of the bright luminous object was a structure which looked like spread wings and that this structure went out beyond the object itself. In the highlighted photo No 9 (clipping A2) he could clearly make out bright lines going down straight from the luminous object. The lengths of these bright lines were much larger than the luminous object size. He estimated their sizes at 100 to 180 units[3]. Clipping A2 had come from film strip No 16 and it was the first shot taken on this strip and the last shot taken of the luminous object. There were over thirty frames (or shots) left in this camera and this was

---

[2] The unit mentioned was devised by Valentin Yakimenko to give a scale to the objects in the frames. He based a unit on 1/1000th of the film frame width which is 36mm

[3] ibid

the camera which was used to take photographs by the search party at the end of February and beginning of March 1959.

## Group Two Photos

- Photo 3a (Zolotarev strip Shot No 5)

- Photo 6 (Zolotarev strip Shot No 9)

- Photo 10 (Clipping C1 Shot No 1)

The object in these three photos looked like some kind of a net which grew in size before eventually dispersing. There is no doubt that there appears to be some kind of netting effect in these photos which have come from two different cameras (two from Zolotarev's and one unknown).

## Group Three Photos

|  | Size con units | Strip/clipping | Photo No |
|---|---|---|---|
| Horn | 16x12 | Zlt shot 5 | Photo 4 |
| Piece of lopwood | 20x8 | D1, Shot 2 | Photo 11 |
| Figure-dummy | 26x7 | C1 shot 1 | Photo 12 |
| Wedge | 10x3 | C1 shot 4 | Photo 13 |
| Square with smoke | 216x216 | Krivonischenko's Strip | Photo 14 |

On the face of it, Yakimenko felt this grouping of photos was dissimilar to each other but that if they were viewed at different angles, they could be the same object spinning, but seen at different perspectives. Having said that, photo 11 and photo 14 were similar in shape. Overall, the object seen in Krivonischenko's film strip appears to be square shaped with smoke or steam coming out of it. Photo 14 is the last shot of some kind of object in Krivonischenko's film and there were two more frames in the strip which were both unused, so it can be deduced that the object was moving too fast over the group's heads for any more shots to be taken before it disappeared over the ridge. This last shot of Krivonischenko's and the shots in Group One (above) were the last shots of whatever this phenomenon was in the night sky.

## Group Four Photos

The fourth group of shots consisted of 3 frames of an object which resembled an aircraft. Yakimenko gave them the names *Plane* 1 to *Plane* 3

| Object | Size con units | Clipping | Photo No |
|--------|----------------|----------|----------|
| *Plane* 1 | 13 | A1, Shot 3 | Photo 15 |
| *Plane* 2 | 26 | A1, Shot 4 | Photo 17 |
| *Plane* 3 | 16 | D2, Shot 2 | Photo 16 |

Plane 2 (Valentin Yakimenko)

The *Plane* 1 frame from clipping A1 and *Plane* 3 frame from clipping D2 are almost exactly the same shape but *Plane* 3 is larger and therefore closer. *Plane* 3 was obviously photographed slightly later. The object in *Plane* 1 and *Plane* 2 are somewhat different in shape but again do have similarities. The difference in the size and shape (13 to 26 units respectively) can be explained by the fact that *Plane* 2 was photographed 8 seconds later with the object having come closer, and the shooting angle had changed. The most important thing about this grouping of frames is that clipping A1 and D2 came from different cameras. *Plane 2* is a very interesting photo because it closely resembles an aircraft or drone coming down to earth and breaking up as it does so.

In his findings Yakimenko entitled one section "The Mystery of Film Strip No 10". His research had showed that none of the clippings had coincided with the line of cut on Film Strip No 10. The lead end of the strip had 24 frames but 12 frames were missing. On this film strip (No 10), he found that in many of the shots taken in the earlier days leading up to the tragedy there were clear signs of emulsion loss on the strip. After scanning the earlier photos, there were clear defects on the photos of large and small oval-shaped spots with light borders. He put this down to the film layers in the camera's take-up spool, swelling and sticking together. Later, after the spool was taken out of the camera and the film was unreeled, the stuck emulsion was separated from its base.

Group in line shows original damage to photo (Valentin Yakimenko)

The negatives showed the emulsion damage in the form of what he described as "hillocks" and scars. The worst of this damage appeared to occur closer to the sprocket holes where the film was subjected to greater mechanical damage while it was being developed. Yakimenko concluded that the way the damage had been caused meant that Film Strip No 10 had been in a camera which had been in a damp environment for some time. In reality, this could only mean the ravine where the snow shelter had been located. This means it would have been in the snow for two months and for the last two to three weeks of that time the snow would have been very damp as it was starting to thaw with the onset of spring. The remaining question was: Who did the camera belong to? It was not Zolotarev as his film had already been identified (apart from the missing 9 frames). Yakimenko felt the camera could only have belonged to either Luda or Thibo. The investigation gave no clue as to who may have owned it either. Also, compounding the problem of ownership, was the fact that earlier shots on film strip No 10 included pictures of both Thibo and Luda. These were group shots and most likely the camera had been given to another member of the group to take the photos.

Yakimenko's attention was drawn to two photos in particular, which showed Luda moving on her skis at the end of the line behind Zina. From this he concluded that the camera, in all probability, belonged to Thibo. It was therefore Thibo who had taken the photos (along with Zolotarev) of the luminous objects in the night sky. The big question remaining then is: Was there something in the remaining and missing twelve frames that were withheld by the investigators because there was something in those frames that they did not want to be seen by anyone else outside the investigation? If so, what could possibly be on those frames that were to be withheld?

The other thing which puzzled Yakimenko was film strip No 2. This strip also had been given to the Dyatlov Foundation by Lev Ivanov's daughter. There were 12 frames on this strip and the first one was the well-known photo of the large orb.

The following 10 frames were photos of the Dyatlov group bodies in the morgue in Ivdel. The last frame is completely blank. However, the lead end (*ie* the start of this film strip) is missing and there are 24 missing frames. These 24 frames come before the large orb picture, so it seems peculiar that the large orb picture is present but what presumably happened just before it, is missing.

In his article in the magazine *Uralsky Sledopyt* (*Ural's Pathfinder*) Yakimenko had stated that he believed that the large orb photo had been taken by Rustem when he left the tent. He (Yakimenko) had originally believed that after looking at the tent inspection report, he believed that the last person out of the tent was Rustem, who had turned around to take a picture just before the object disappeared behind the ridge. However, since he had written the article and after considering his findings by examining the film strips closely, he now believes that Rustem had probably taken several shots of the luminous object. So the absence of Rustem's 24 frames, 9 frames of Zolotarev's and 12 frames of Thibo's imply that the three of them had photographed the majority of the progress and final stages of the celestial phenomenon. Whatever anyone believes may have happened to these three missing pieces of film, Yakimenko's view is that all three of them are held in the same place.

It is known that the cameras of the group were used by the search party and investigators after they were found, which is why Rustems's Photo No 2 of the large light orb on Film strip No 2 is followed by the morgue photos. This camera would have been in the hands of the Investigator, probably Lev Ivanov. The other two cameras which contained film strips Nos 13 and 15, which contained the shots of the phenomenon in the night sky were later used by the search parties as they contained pictures of the search operations. The film in Rustem's camera was most likely developed in the middle of March 1959, from which Yakimenko deduced that Lev Ivanov would have seen the light orbs on the film and wondered about their presence. At that point (mid-March 1959), the bodies of Thibo and Zolotarev had yet to be discovered and the Zolotarev's camera had yet to be discovered. Yakimenko also mentions the fact that the recollections of the search party members Sergey Sogrin and Piotr Bartolomey, was that Ivanov had questioned them very closely about earlier hikes undertaken by members of the Dyatlov group. Both Sogrin and Bartolomey knew the group members and had been on other hikes with them. With a policeman's instinct, Ivanov appeared to be interested in the dynamics within the group as if the answer might lie there; but despite his extensive questioning of Sogrin and Bartlomey, he was not making much progress. It is stated that Ivanov was then (in March 1959) suddenly summoned to Moscow. Sogrin and Bartolomey said later that they both noticed a quite abrupt change of behaviour in Ivanov, who had made it clear he wanted no further contact with them. Whether or not Ivanov had indeed been summoned to Moscow and his change in behaviour was down to that is unknown, because as will be shown later, Moscow was to come to Sverdlovsk in the shape of Deputy Prosecutor General Urakov.

The film in Rustem's camera was most likely developed in the middle of March 1959, from which Yakimenko deduced that Lev Ivanov would have become aware of the event in the night sky as that camera had contained the most prominent picture of the orb/s. However, the question has to be asked as to how much Ivanov knew before he set off from Sverdlovsk for the northern Urals. Ivanov was no fool and once he had been up to the Pass and returned and had seen the orbs on the developed film, his concerns about what had caused the deaths must have taken a troubling turn for him.

Yakimenko wound up his examination of the film strips and clippings with a number of observations. He felt that the film strips of the group's cameras had captured the whole of the celestial phenomenon and that the celestial phenomenon was technology-based (in other words human-made). The group had pitched their tent on the southern slope of Kholat Syakhl, so the area of the sky that could be seen by them was the southern part, as the northern and north-western parts of the sky were hidden by the eastern spur of Kholat Syakhl. The duration of the celestial phenomenon he estimated to be between 1.5 to 2 minutes and the size of the luminous dot growing from shot to shot to the size of two moon discs shows that the movement was in the direction of the group and the Pass. In the 8 strips of film examined, there were 25 luminous objects found and the fact that the same object/s were spread across all the films is conclusive evidence that the orb/s existed. The first two shots of the celestial phenomenon found on Krivoy's and Rustem's film strips showed the luminous objects were large and there was a trail of steam or smoke over one of them.

Yakimenko then stated that although they had found something, he was not sure what it represented. This is the crux of the problem – what exactly had the group seen and photographed?

In his original article Yakimenko had put forward the notion that there had been a launch from Baikonur of an R-7 missile to the moon. However he was informed by AB Zheleznyakov, a member of the Russian Academy of Sciences, that a moon launch of an R-7 from Baikonur on 1 February 1959 would not have been possible due to the fact there was no R-7 and Lunar Probe available for an attempted launch at that time. Yakimenko accepted this, but pointed out in his original article that what had appeared was possibly either a spacecraft or another type of missile, including possible anti-aircraft missile systems. He explained that the problem with the object being a rocket or missile was the time frame of the photographs. He had estimated the time frame of the unusual celestial phenomenon would exclude the possibility of a rocket or missile because if they had observed the flight of a rocket or missile, it would have had to be many kilometres away as a missile travels at speeds of around 3 to 6 kilometres a second. Therefore, the rocket or missile would have been too far away to present a danger to the group. If the rocket or missile had been much closer to the group, it would have passed over them or close to them; it would have appeared and gone in literally a matter of seconds and there would not have been enough time to take 30 plus photos with the different cameras of the group. The time frame of 1.5 to 2 minutes from the first frame of Zolotarev's film suggests the bright spots was a missile, possibly 250 – 300 kilometres (155 - 186 Miles) away from them. The scene was that the group were watching the Southern part of the sky, saw the luminous object/s for a period of 1.5 to 2 minutes and took their photos before the missile or rocket or unknown object disappeared behind the stone belt ridge (the ridge where the Dyatlov memorial rock is now located).

Yakimenko made the point that what appears to be light coming from the objects in the sky could well be reflected sunlight as the pictures were taken not long after sundown and it would be dark in the area of the Pass hidden from the sun by the ridge and the mountain. I can vouch for this effect because the night I spent up on the Pass itself (as opposed to being down in the Auspia Valley where we were camped), I noticed the Pass became very dark once the sun went behind Kholat Syakhl and the ridge, but the sun still had not set properly.

In his research piece about the examination of the film strips and clippings, Yakimenko finished with what he termed "The Final Minutes". He stated his view that once the members of the group had finished watching the celestial phenomenon they all got back inside the tent. He believed that Zolotarev and Thibo stayed outside the tent and walked about 20 metres away (65ft), probably to relieve themselves. The rest of the group were inside the tent and starting to undress and discussing the celestial phenomenon they had just seen. He believed that Rustem was the last member of that part of the group to crawl inside the tent and he put his camera on the ground near the entrance. He had closed the flaps at the tent entrance, taken off one boot and was about to take off another when whatever it was that caused them to flee the tent, happened at this point.

Yakimenko stated that the research he had done was on actual documentation ie hard evidence from something that had belonged to the Dyatlov group. What was needed now was an interpretation of that evidence.

The fact that something was in the night sky does not prove that it was the cause of what happened to the Dyatlov group. There is no direct cause and effect but a number of scenarios can be put forward. The fact that these are the last photos in the various cameras suggests it was very close to the time when the group fled the tent. Had they survived the night it would have been expected that in the daylight they would have taken some pictures of Kholat Syakhl and the surrounding mountainside as a memento of the journey. The mountainside topography was quite unlike anything they had seen on their journey to that point, as it was the first time they had come out of the forested area.

It may be possible that after the pictures had been taken, most of the members were inside the tent while some went outside to answer the call of nature, *etc* and then the event occurred, with the group members slashing their way out after the calls from those outside. In other words, that whatever was happening in the night sky was over. Whilst that is a possibility, it is a remote one and it really lends support to the view that the event in the night sky took place very close to the time they all left the tent and that whatever it was, it was the reason for their flight. It seems too much of a coincidence that the events in the night sky were so close to their evacuation of the tent that they would be unconnected.

Could it be that whatever happened at the tent, started to happen so fast that Zolotarev and Thibo started screaming at the others to get out of the tent fast and get away, which would account for the slashing of the side of the tent?

# Chapter 8

The revelations brought about by Yakimenko's research introduce an element of certainty to the events of the last night of the group. Before examining a possible scenario in respect of this, it is worth looking at the various discrepancies at each of the different stages of the journey and later events. These stages can be broken down into rough, but distinct, "areas"; the deviation of the group to pitch their tent on the slope of Kholat Syakhl; their evacuation of the tent and descent to the tree line; the final positions of the bodies at the tree line; the findings of the autopsies. Intermingled with each of these "areas" is the behaviour of the authorities before, during and after the investigation.

When Yury Yudin left the group at the abandoned geologists' settlement (second severny) to return to Sverdlovsk, the group's journey could be summarised as: "so far, so normal". Their trip was going along more or less as planned and there was nothing which happened to mark the journey out as any different to others undertaken by members of the group or countless other ski tourists in the Soviet Union. Using the group's diaries, and with knowledge of the route that they had planned to take to Mount Otorten, the first discrepancy is the deviation of their route taking them up out of the Auspia Valley up onto the ridge at Kholat Syakhl and the pitching of their tent there. Lev Ivanov had concluded in his final report that Igor Dyatlov had taken a route which was 500 metres (1,640ft) towards Kholat Syakhl which took them up onto the mountain whereas if he had stayed 500 metres (1,640ft) to the right they would have come out into the middle of the Pass between Kholat Syakhl and elevation 880 (the location of the stone belt ridge), which would have been an easier journey. Before departing, Igor Dyatlov had agreed his route with Evgeny Maslennikov who was a highly experienced ski tourist and knew the area so well that he acted as an advisor/consultant to ski tourist groups and clubs in the region. This was secondary to his job as a mechanical engineer, but nevertheless, his opinion was highly respected. The question is; why would Igor Dyatlov have deviated from this route?

It is quite possible that, on his own initiative, Igor Dyatlov wanted to add in an extra layer of difficulty or test for the group by altering the route to make it tougher. I covered the route they took in the summer and it was hard work even without the winter conditions, although I am not in the best of shape. They were young and in peak fitness and even though they had left behind any unnecessary equipment at the cache (store) they had prepared, it would have been a good test of their fitness and abilities. The level of difficulty, or rating, for their trip was set at grade 3, the then highest level, and they would all be qualified to grade 3 on completion of the trip. Some observers have also pointed to the fact that Igor Dyatlov did not start their journey from the Auspia Valley up to the ridge until around midday. Some say just before and some say after midday. 'Guesstimates' can be made from the angle of the sun in the final photos as they made their way up to the ridge. Quite why he (Dyatlov) left it so late before setting out is unknown. It could be that seeing the mountain from the floor of the Auspia Valley, Dyatlov had not anticipated travelling much further as he wanted to pitch the tent on the slope of the mountain. Either way, he had not left much margin of time as it was close to sunset when they eventually pitched their tent.

What Yakimenko's conclusions do show is that the Dyatlov group were there on the slopes of Kholat Syakhl on the night they died. There is one strong line of thinking which subscribes to the theory that they died elsewhere and that the tent and their bodies were brought to the scene and the scene was staged. The first person to suggest this was journalist Gennady Kizilov and it was a theory which many agreed with. It seemed to explain the weird scene on the slopes of the mountain and the tree line. The reason for the removal of the bodies and tent would have been to take them away from where they died so that there would be no evidence nearby as to what may have caused their deaths such as a large blast, which would leave evidence in the form of damage to trees and vegetation as well as fragments and shrapnel.

Moving the bodies and tent seems a great deal of trouble to go to in order to stage the scene of an accident but is understandable in order to hide the actual place where the deaths occurred. This could only be done by someone with the facilities to do it *ie* manpower and access to vehicles and/or helicopters able to deal with the extreme conditions. However, there are contradictions to this theory as well because the diaries were kept almost right up to date with the last entry in the group diary made the day before they left for Kholat Syakhl; although it has been suggested that the diaries had been tampered with (some entries removed and different handwriting).

One issue with the suggestion of the group dying elsewhere and the tent and location of the bodies being "staged", is the testimony of pilot Gennady Patrushev and navigator Karpushin who claimed to have flown over the mountain and seen the tent and two bodies beside it on 25 February 1959, the day before the tent was discovered. The criticism of this is that it was felt that they could not have seen such a small object as the tent from the air at a distance of 25-30 kilometres (15-18 miles) as they stated. It is possible that Patrushev and Karpushin may have seen the staging of the scene whilst it was in progress; it is unlikely to have happened while the whole area of the route was being combed by search parties. Nor would it account for the fact that the bodies of Luda, Zolotarev, Kolevatov and Thibo were already lying under several metres of snow or they would have been found in the following days. Some commentators have played down the observations of Patrushev and Karpushin, but, as will be seen, there is an interesting aspect as to what happened to their radio communications that day (25 February 1959). Furthermore, the criticism that they could not have seen the tent at the distance they claimed is not necessarily valid because one of them would have been flying the aircraft and the other acting as observer and would most likely have been using binoculars as they were searching the ground.

The photos of the objects in the sky on Zolotarev's camera shows that if there was some kind of an event or explosion, it happened either at or close to the tent or down closer to the tree line. The analysis of the negatives shows that the group were actually up on the ridge by Kholat Syakhl on that last night. In particular, one of the frames appears to show the line of the stone belt ridge about half a kilometre from the tent location. The proof of the photos means that the deaths occurring at another location and the bodies brought to Kholat Syakhl can be discounted.

The next stage to examine is the actual evacuation of the tent itself. Damaging the tent to get out of it as quickly as possible as well as moving away from it to the tree line does not make any sense unless they were in extreme and imminent danger, and that danger was in the vicinity of the tent. On the face of it, this is quite plausible but the flaw with this is that the footprints as described by the search parties appear to show an orderly descent at a walking pace to the tree line a kilometre and a half away (0.9 mile). That the footprints show a reasonable, almost measured walk, is attested to by several witnesses. It seems peculiar that the side of the tent would be torn apart in a frenzy to get out, only for the group to calmly walk down the mountain to the tree line. Furthermore, the relatively calm descent is odder still because not only did they leave behind many items that they needed to help stay alive but most of them had no footwear for the extreme conditions. It seems too much of a coincidence that at least Zolotarev and possibly others were outside taking pictures in the night sky and within a very short time-scale, they are all moving away from the tent to try and get away from it.

Zolotarev's body was found with the camera and strap still around his neck which implies that he was outside the tent at the end still taking pictures, and moved away without removing his camera, or possibly had just gone back into the tent and had not removed the camera yet. If he had received the severe injuries to his ribs up at the tent, he would probably have needed help to move down to the tree line (despite testimony from the searchers saying the footprints seemed to be of people moving without help) and it would be expected he would have taken his camera off. When I was at the tent's location in 2015, the rest of the group I was with, had moved off to the tree line while I was taking more pictures and I was some distance behind them. I had my camera around my neck and was moving fast to catch up with them. The camera was a nuisance as I didn't want to stop to pack it away in its case, but equally I found it a distraction as it kept swinging and bouncing around. I stopped and took it off and swung it over my right shoulder so it was then bouncing on my right hip as I moved down to catch up with everyone. If Zolotarev had been moving fast in fear for his life, injured or not, I would have expected him to take it off and throw it on to the snow with a view to maybe collecting it later, depending on what danger they were facing.

Leaving aside the matter of the lights in the night sky, the strongest contenders as to what could have made them move away from the tent quickly are in order of possibility: an avalanche, an external threat such as the Mansi or military forcing them to move away to the tree line or some kind of disorientation caused either internally or externally (*ie* something they had eaten or breathed in or some kind of external force acting on them). These three factors are the first issues which come to mind. There are numerous other possibilities but these three are the most plausible in my opinion. The avalanche theory has been put forward by many people and dismissed for the usual reasons of the low angle on the slope (varying between 15 to 30 degrees, but with a general agreement by most that it was nearer to 15 degrees); the lack of any history of avalanches in the northern Urals and the lack of any sign of an avalanche when the search parties reached the abandoned tent. On my visit to the tent location, I was with a large group of Dyatlov "enthusiasts" for want of a better word and each and every one of us dismissed the idea of an avalanche just by looking at the scene. The slope was far too shallow and the location was too close to the top of the ridge. It was a non-starter as an explanation. The possibility that the group were forced to the tree line from the tent by either Mansi or military are equally possible. The Mansi argument is that the group were trespassing on a holy site on Kholat Syakhl, although there are conflicting arguments about this, with some saying it was a holy site and others saying the site had little or no relevance to the Mansi at all. The possibility of any military involvement mainly rests on the premise that the group had observed secret tests and had to be silenced. What argues against both these possibilities is that there were no other footprints visible. The search parties spoke of "eight or nine pairs of footprints" going down to the tree line with no mention of any other footprints.

The footprints themselves can also be somewhat contentious because, dependent on the exact climatic conditions, fresh snowfall falls in such a way as to "raise" footprints above the level of the snow around them giving the 'column' effect seen in the photos. However, separate groups of skiers have tried to recreate the conditions of the Dyatlov group at the same time of year. They found that the footprints and ski tracks they made from the area of the tent down to the tree line had completely disappeared within a matter of days and in some cases hours. Whilst there may have been heavier snowfall in the later experiments, it also raises doubts about another discovery close to the Dyatlov tent. The first person in charge of the case, Ivdel Prosecutor Vasily Tempalov, observed old traces of urine close to the entrance to the tent. As part of his summing up of the scene, he made the statement that "nobody approached the tent without me". However, the search party led by Boris Slobtsov and Mikhail Sharavin were actually first on the scene and Tempalov did not arrive on the scene until two days later. With the amount of snowfall evident on the tent, it is unlikely that urine traces from three weeks previous would still be visible. This suggests that someone else either in Sharavin's search party or someone else in another party had relieved themselves and that this was nothing to do with anyone from the Dyatlov group. What or who this other party may be can only be guessed at, but it would suggest the presence of someone at the site very close to when it was discovered. The area around the tent was so trampled down that it would have been difficult to try and make any sense of comings or goings and numbers. If others had been present at the scene before the arrival of the search parties, it also suggests the use of a helicopter or helicopters due to the lack of any footprints approaching or leaving the tent, apart from those of the group. A related minor issue is how witnesses estimated distances of which there were considerable variations. Of the more than half a dozen witness statements taken, the number of footprints varied between seven and nine pairs of footprints and the distance they started from the tent varied from eight metres (26ft), estimated by searchers Yury Koptelov and Mikhail Sharavin to Ivdel Prosecutor Vasily Tempalov estimating it at 50 to 60 metres (164ft to 197ft). Tempalov estimated that the footprints continued for only 50 metres (164ft) whereas searchers George Atmanaki and Vladimir Lebedev estimated that footprints continued for 800 metres (2,625ft). The Sverdlovsk prosecutor Lev Ivanov estimated the distance as 500 metres (1,640ft); so there were considerable variations. What was odd about the descent of the group to the tree line was that to some of the searchers the footprints appeared to them as if the group had been combing the slope, as if they were searching for something or possibly looking for something in order to avoid it. Two sets of footprints had diverged from the main group of prints and came back again at one point. Some wore felt boots but some were in bare feet in the snow and some wore socks.

Whilst the searchers said that the footsteps did not show anyone being assisted or injured, these interviews were conducted later and were with the benefit of hindsight. Originally the footsteps would have been noticed and assumed that the group were still alive and had gone to the trees for safety. Once the first bodies were found, it was just a case of finding the remaining bodies. There is nothing in the protocols which state that once the bodies were found, they had then gone back to examine the footprints more closely. By this time the other search parties had converged on the mountain and any proper examination of the area would have been impossible.

There is also the lack of any tracks from the Dyatlov group leading up to the site of the tent from the Auspia Valley. These tracks could have been obliterated by climatic conditions. It is odd that the tracks down to the tree line survived but the tracks leading up to the tent didn't, despite being made within twelve hours of each other.

There were a number of items found at the tent which raised doubts as to what they were doing there. These included a Chinese-made lamp, a damaged ski pole and a flask containing what was believed to contain Vodka. The issue with the lamp is that it was found lying on the collapsed part of the tent and barely had a sprinkling of snow on it, whereas everything else had been covered in snowfall to at least a depth of 10cm (4 inches). Nobody recognised the damaged ski pole as belonging to anyone in the group. The empty flask of Vodka was strange, because according to the sole survivor of the group, Yury Yudin, none of them had any alcohol and he mentioned the problem they had trying to get medicinal alcohol to take with them on the trip for first aid purposes. They had been unable to procure any. Nevertheless, these are all relatively minor items and can probably be explained one way or another. For instance, it was thought that Alexander Kolevatov had some alcohol and had kept it to himself. And it is possible that when the searchers arrived at the tent, possibly one of them may have picked the lamp up off the tent and placed it down again without anyone else noticing and then assuming it had lain there all the time.

It must be remembered that, at the arrival of the search party at the site, nobody had any idea they were looking for people who were already dead and that the evidence at the site needed to be preserved in any way. Ivdel Prosecutor Vasily Tempalov gave the impression in his statement that he took control of the scene but this was probably with the benefit of hindsight following the discovery of the first bodies, and in an effort to give the impression that the investigation was being conducted in a proper manner at the site of a potential crime scene, with him in charge. The probable truth is that initially, it was a virtual free-for-all. In fairness to Tempalov, he would not have known the group were all dead. It is also likely that the appointment of Lev Ivanov to replace Tempalov on the case would not just have been the appointment of a "Big City Cop" with more experience, but also a possible rebuke to Tempalov in his initial handling of the case.

Finally, on the issue of the escape from the tent and the journey of the group down to the tree line, comparisons have been made with another incident which took place in Yakutia, fourteen years later.

The River Alakit lies deep in Siberia in the Republic of Sakha (Yakutia), roughly 2,575 kilometres (1,600 miles) to the east of the Dyatlov Pass and can be considered to be as remote as it gets in Russia. In 1973 four geologists ran away from their tent and died from hypothermia. Their bodies were found two to three kilometres away from their tent after they had failed to make contact with their centre. There seemed to be no explanation for their behaviour as nothing could be found which pointed to an external threat. What is interesting though, in this comparison with the Dyatlov group, is that the geologists ran in different directions away from each other, which would suggest panic. Their tent had also been cut and they too were only partially clothed, which again suggests that whatever happened, happened very suddenly and must have been life threatening. Some observers of this incident have stated that the geologists were running away from an avalanche. However, although they were in an area of gentle mountains, they were actually camped on a relatively flat area of land close to the River Alakit. So again, the possibility of an avalanche can be ruled out. Like the Dyatlov Incident, there was no clear explanation for the deaths of the geologists or more correctly, what caused them to flee their tent which, in turn, led to their deaths.

The finding of the bodies of the Dyatlov group down by the tree line raised a question by survival experts which was; why did they not go deeper into the forest for better protection from the elements, especially the wind, which was blowing fairly strongly that night. The raised area by the cedar tree where Doroshenko and Krivoy were found, gave a view of the tent but they would have known that they were struggling to stay alive and it would be expected that shelter was more important, which should override picking a position to watch the tent. Similarly, the final positions of where the bodies were found broke another survival rule which was for the group to stay close together. Although there is some dispute of the location of the snow shelter, the fire was some distance from it and it would have made more sense to build the fire closer to the shelter. One of the suggested locations of the shelter was some considerable distance from the cedar tree and the fire, although there was no rock there which matched the one that Luda's body was found on.

Another issue is the way the bodies were laying when they were found. When Rustem's body was found on 5 March 1959, Moses Axelrod in the search party had commented that the heat from his (Rustem's) body had melted snow beneath his body and formed a kind of ice layer. In contrast, none of the others had heated the snow beneath their bodies in the same way, which suggested there was virtually no heat in their bodies by the time they lay down and died. It seems as if they died literally standing up, and fell over. Igor Dyatlov's body was on its back with his arms raised up in front of him which is very odd as it would have been expected most of the bodies close to death would have assumed a foetal position in an attempt to keep warm. Only Zina's body exhibited anything like this. The other exceptions were the bodies of Doroshenko and Krivoy, who appear to have been laid side by side after the others had removed clothes from their bodies once they had died.

Threaded through the timeline of the Dyatlov group's journey north to when the search parties found the first bodies and the aftermath, is the rather contradictory and peculiar attitude of the authorities. To a casual observer, the attitude of the authorities went from being what appeared, at the beginning, to be an almost total lack of interest to a tight control of all aspects of the case by the end.

The first suggestion of any involvement by the authorities was the start of a rumour at some point in February 1959 which circulated through the students at the UPI (Urals Polytechnic Institute) which was that the Dyatlov group were using their trip north as a cover to try and defect from the Soviet Union. It was an outrageous and preposterous suggestion and offended many of the students including Yury Yudin when he later heard of it. Why would anyone start such a baseless and offensive rumour, without any foundation, which blackened the characters of all in the group? Could it have been someone who bore a grudge against one or more members of the group? Possibly someone was jealous of Igor Dyatlov himself as a skilled and respected ski tourist, who had also won the affections of Zina, one of the most attractive girls at UPI. However, there remains the strong possibility that such a dreadful rumour had the backing of the authorities who already knew that the group were dead and such a rumour could have been started by one of the numerous KGB informers embedded throughout Soviet society. It could only have been started by a deliberate instruction. This rumour on its own would not have explained away much once the bodies were found, but it appears to be the beginning of a major disinformation exercise.

The sudden closure of the case on 28 May 1959 following the autopsies of the final four bodies, and the closure of the area of the Pass for four years brought down the curtain on the deaths as far as the authorities were concerned. The results of the autopsies on the final bodies ought to have been the beginning of a deeper investigation because of the strange and unexplained car-crash type injuries, particularly on Zolotarev and Luda. However, the opposite happened.

The closure of the area around the Pass seemed totally unnecessary, even allowing for the unfortunate deaths. The area was not so much closed as permits were not given to anyone who had no reason to go there. This obviously did not affect the forestry workers or the Mansi who lived in the region. The area was no less safe than any other similar area used by hikers and ski tourists in the Soviet Union. If anything, what happened to the Dyatlov group should have called for instructions to go out to clubs and institutions for greater awareness and better training for ski tourists attempting hikes in the most extreme conditions. By refusing to permit ski tourists or anyone who had no reason to go to the area of Kholat Syakhl where the Dyatlov group died, it appears as if the only fault lay with the landscape rather than anything else.

# Chapter 9

After looking at the separate areas involving the physical evidence of the deviation to Kholat Syakhl; the scene at the tent and the locations of the bodies, the enquirer is left with no real answers. There are so many conflicting pieces of evidence that it is almost impossible to arrive at a conclusion that can answer all the queries raised by each aspect of the scene on the mountain. That then leaves the autopsy report itself to try and piece together all the evidence to reach a conclusion.

If all the deaths were attributed to hypothermia, then the obvious question would be why did they leave the tent in such a hurry, where they were all safe, and what on earth could have caused them to do it? If all of them had received the same terrible car-crash type injuries as suffered by Luda and Zolotarev, then the answer begins to look a little clearer. There can be a number of reasons for mechanical injuries (broken bones), the most obvious under the circumstances is a blast of some kind. Although explosives can be used by civilian organisations such as mining, the military are the main users of explosives. So, if the autopsies showed they had all died from the effect of a blast, it raises awkward questions, not least because it appears that the physical scene had been doctored to make it look as if something or someone else was responsible for the deaths. It is possible that only a few of the group were affected by an initial blast and the rest had to get away from the tent in case of a further blast, but they succumbed to the effects of hypothermia. Whilst the tent would not have afforded any protection from a blast, it is possible that Zolotarev and Luda may have been outside, further away and up behind the tent in the area where they had dug the snow out to allow them to help flatten the ground to pitch the tent. Being at a lower level, those inside the tent would have escaped the worst of the blast and the snow which covered the tent when it was found by the rescuers may have been as a result of a blast. One of the most telling comments is in the statement dated 28 May 1959 made to Lev Ivanov by the forensic pathologist Boris Vozrozdhenny. The deposition is in the form of questions and answers. Ivanov asks Vozrozdhenny for an explanation as to what could have caused the severe injuries to Luda and Zolotarev and whether it had one cause? Vozrozdhenny replies that the injuries were similar to Thibo and that in his view, the kind of force that would create such damage without leaving an external mark on the body were very similar to the trauma created by the shock wave of a bomb. The mention of blast injuries was an avenue Ivanov obviously did not wish to pursue. Ivanov asked one more question after this answer which was: How long did he (Vozrozdhenny) think that Luda and Zolotarev would have lived after this? The response was that Luda and Zolotarev would have lived for ten to twenty minutes. The questioning was then ended and the deposition was signed and dated by both of them. It can also be noted that some people who have looked at the face of Doroshenko in the Ivdel morgue say that it looks as if he has suffered blast injuries.

When faced with an unsolved mystery, people tend to focus on what facts are available and then tirelessly scrutinise those facts as though the answer lies in them but have not yet become clear. Only by constant study of them will the enquirer hopefully find the missing answer that is constantly eluding them. The problem with the autopsies of the Dyatlov group is that there are so many apparent discrepancies that no single answer seems to cover it. On the face of it there is such a range of discrepancies that it almost seems intentional. It is a set of autopsies with what appears to be several possible explanations.

The major discrepancy is that there are two causes of death within the group, roughly half dying of the extreme cold and the other half dying of what appears to be blast type injuries. They, of course, are not referred to as blast-type injuries as that may start to lead the enquirer down a particular path the authorities don't want them to go.

Scattered throughout the autopsies are a number of what can only be described as "red herrings". These include supposed fight type injuries to the fists of Rustem and the group leader Igor Dyatlov. Rustem was found roughly 180 metres (590ft) away from Dyatlov on the slope going up towards the tent. The implication of the autopsy for the fist injuries on both is that they had either been fighting each other or someone else. There was a superficial knife wound across the palm of Dyatlov's left hand which may have been accidental, but also gives credence to the possibility of a fight. It would have been expected that they would both have had similar types of injuries, and they both had facial and leg abrasions. Another red herring is that Rustem is believed to have died from brain trauma. He (Rustem) had haemorrhaging in his right and left temporal muscles as well as a crack in the left temporal bone of his skull which was 6cm (2.36in) long. He also had gaps in some skull sutures on both sides of his head. With these types of injuries, it would have been expected for Rustem to have been with the other group near the snow shelter who had suffered mechanical injuries of this nature. Why would someone suffering brain trauma, try to return to the tent, when it would have been expected that he would have been at the snow shelter with the other seriously injured members of the group? Rustem was behind Zina and in front of Igor Dyatlov, as though the three of them were trying to get back to the tent in a line, with Zina leading.

The autopsy report for Zina gave her death as due to hypothermia, which is fairly straightforward although she had abrasions on her palms and hands; but these could be explained by her making her way through the undergrowth at the tree line, as well as helping to prepare the shelter.

Among the first group who died of hypothermia, and the first bodies to be found, were Krivoy and Doroshenko. They were much closer to the second group of seriously injured near the snow shelter and had been tending the fire. Another anomaly is that, although the fire was not too far from the snow shelter, it was still some distance away. It would have made more sense for the fire to have been built as close as possible to the shelter, even if it necessitated carrying branches and twigs a little distance. Both Doroshenko and Krivoy had similar injuries to each other, including severe frostbite on their fingers and toes and both had a profusion of abrasions, cuts, scratches and bruises on their upper body and legs. Given that they were tending the fire, it is understandable they would receive several cuts and abrasions. Both of them also had burn marks to their hands and feet. Additionally, Doroshenko had foamy grey liquid coming from his mouth and this same liquid was discovered in his lungs. This could be attributed to his chest being squeezed or a seizure. Doroshenko and Krivoy were found lying side by side, and it was believed they had been left in that position by the others after they had died and their clothes had been removed so the others could keep warm.

The four bodies (Luda, Thibo, Kolevatov and Zolotarev) which were found several weeks later on 5 May 1959, were a relatively short distance away from the cedar tree and had received terrible injuries (with the exception of Kolevatov) with another set of anomalies. Thibo died from a severe head injury as his skull had been fractured. Luda had multiple rib fractures on both sides plus there was haemorrhaging in the right ventricle of her heart. She would not have lasted long and died from bleeding in the right ventricle of her heart along with the rib fractures and internal bleeding in her chest cavity. She too displayed the same grey foam found on Doroshenko which was found in her larynx and bronchial passages. Luda was missing her lower teeth, upper lip, eyes and, possibly the biggest red herring in the whole story, she was missing her tongue.

Like Luda, Zolotarev had received massive chest injuries with rib fractures and haemorrhages in the adjacent intercostal muscles. There was almost one litre of blood in his pleural cavity. There was also a wound to his head exposing the parietal bone (these two bones form the posterior roof of the skull) and his eyeballs were missing. Besides the camera around his neck, Zolotarev was discovered clutching a notebook and a pencil in each hand. Considering the mess his body was in, would a notebook and pencil to write out what was happening have been uppermost in his mind, considering also that his hands and forearms were frostbitten up to the elbows? It is quite probable that Zolotarev knew he was dying. Alternatively, it may have been another red herring left for people to ponder over on top of all the other rapidly mounting anomalies at the scene. Although the notebook and pencil were witnessed, the question could be asked: Were they placed there by someone else?

There is also a great deal of speculation about Zolotarev (his role in the group, his tattoos, his burial etc) which is beyond the scope of this book.

The oddity or red herring in this group found near the snow shelter is Kolevatov. Although he had suffered a broken nose and a deep wound was found behind his right ear, he was reported to have died of hypothermia. He still had bruising on his left knee which was wrapped in a bandage, and had happened prior to their arrival on the mountain.

Another area which confuses the whole issue is that of the radiation tests conducted on the clothes and bodies. These tests were only carried out on the bodies and clothes of Zolotarev, Luda, Thibo and Kolevatov. After these final four bodies were found in early May 1959, the radiation tests are generally assumed to have been carried out under the instructions of Lev Ivanov. Despite Ivanov asking for the tests to be carried out, the instruction came from an authority outside the Sverdlovsk Prosecutor's Office and it can only be assumed that it was from Moscow. It is highly unlikely Ivanov would have asked for tests to be done without instruction from a higher authority and that higher authority would have had to come from outside the Prosecutor's Office. Anything to do with radiation would be a sensitive subject and by its nature would involve the military. It also seems peculiar that Lev Ivanov only asked for the tests to be carried out on these four and not all nine bodies. If he had suspected that radiation had in some way been responsible for their deaths, then why did he not arrange for the exhumation of the first five bodies (who had been buried by this point) to corroborate the theory (assuming there was a theory)? Radiation is hardly likely to have confined itself to the small area the four were found in and they were not a huge distance from the other five. Both Doroshenko and Krivoy were within speaking or shouting distance from the four found at the snow shelter, and although they had been buried by the time of the tests, they were not exhumed to be tested.

When the last four bodies were found, they had mummified to a considerable extent and they were all clothed at that point. Their "supposed" injuries would have become apparent at the autopsy. At this stage Ivanov must have received instructions for radiation testing to take place. Otherwise, why did he take a sample of soil from underneath where Kolevatov was found? He would not have known of the serious injuries when the bodies were found, so unless he suspected radiation in some form when the bodies were discovered he would have had to return to the location to take the soil sample. Also, why only take a sample of soil from where Kolevatov was found? Kolevatov was found close to Zolotarev but he was out of the stream on the bank, despite the initial report of Vasily Tempalov, who stated all four bodies were in the water. Considering the other three were being tested for the presence of radiation and they had all been in the stream, it would seem obvious to take a separate sample of the stream water itself for testing. However, this wasn't done. Although Kolevatov was then currently a student at UPI, he had previously worked at a nuclear facility in Moscow and this may have had some bearing on Ivanov's actions.

The outcome of the radiation tests was that three items of clothes showed significant levels of radioactive contamination. This contamination could have come from either dust in the atmosphere, which was regarded as unlikely as it would have been more evenly spread over not just the group but the whole area or Kolevatov may had had his clothes contaminated through his work, but other clothes besides his were also affected. What is then left is a highly-localised event and this comes back to the military. Soviet artillery in the form of large calibre mortars and field artillery were capable of firing rounds with small tactical nuclear warheads. Tactical battlefield rockets could also be fitted with small nuclear warheads. In the air, whilst Tu 95 *Bear* bombers were strategic weapons and carrying nuclear bombs of much greater power, if they were conducting a training mission they may have carried training weapons with a much lower yield. In addition to this, there were a number of other missiles being developed at the time (*see Chapter 14*) that could have leaked radiation.

There was also the presence of the nuclear warhead storage and warhead assembly/disassembly area to the south of Kholat Syakhl at Nizhnayaya Tura / Lesnoy. Could there possibly have been some kind of leak from there? It has to be said that a much greater area would have been affected by this if that was the case.

So, to conclude the autopsy results: Igor Dyatlov and Rustem may have been fighting either each other or someone else, but Igor died of the cold and Rustem died from brain trauma exacerbated by the cold. Kolevatov, Krivoy and Doroshenko died from the cold but someone may have been compressing Doroshenko's chest. Zolotarev and Luda died from massive internal chest injuries and it is reckoned that neither Zolotarev nor Luda would have had the time to make it down from the tent to where they were found, so bad were their injuries, which would then suggest they received their injuries at the tree line or where they were found. Thibo died from a severe head injury within two to three hours of receiving it. Zina appears to have died the most "normal" death, if anything can be called normal about this story. She died of the cold and when found, her body appeared as if it was moving into a foetal position.

Three of them (Thibo, Luda and Zolotarev) would have been unable to walk without help, and as stated previously, it is unlikely that neither Luda nor Zolotarev would have made it down to the area of the snow shelter before they died from their injuries had they received them at the tent. From the position of the tent, it took me at least fifteen minutes to reach the first position (the area where Zina's body was found) at a reasonably fast pace, and this was in the summer. Zolotarev and Luda would have been close to death in that time. Some of the group of Zolotarev, Luda, Kolevatov and Thibo had traces of radiation on their clothes. However, where this radiation came from is not fully explained nor accounted for in the test results. Chief Radiologist Vladimir Levashov stated the facts as he found them and his report was issued on 27 May 1959, the day before the case was officially closed.

Ivanov would have been very much aware he was going into areas that did not concern him. Nuclear matters were treated with the utmost secrecy and it would have been a foolhardy policeman to have conducted his own investigation into a case which had a possibility of radiation somehow being at least partially responsible for the deaths, with the attendant blame being laid at the door of the military and the authorities.

If the purpose of the autopsies was to mislead and confuse (by placing red herrings), which they have certainly done, then is it possible to try and pick out what may be genuine in the autopsies and deduce what may have happened?

The autopsies should have given some kind of definitive answers of what happened to the group, but much of what they contained doesn't make a lot of sense and raises many questions. It also raises the serious question of whether the autopsies are actually genuine in what they state. For instance, the master stroke of all the red herrings is Luda's missing tongue – was it ever really missing? No matter what theory anyone comes up with, there seems to be no real explanation for her tongue to be missing and why her and nobody else? It is such a bizarre item and one which really throws everything into confusion on top of all the other anomalies in the case.

It can be said that these are official documents raised by a legal authority; but in the case of the Soviet Union, that does not mean much. With regards to the leak of the Anthrax spores from the military bio-warfare laboratory in Sverdlovsk (Ekaterinburg) in 1979, the KGB had confiscated all the medical records of those who had died and arranged that the records and death certificates be reissued to show that the deaths from Anthrax had occurred because of eating contaminated meat, not inhalation. It is telling that neither the KGB nor the military officially said anything to the Sverdlovsk civil city administration for a full week after the accident. The eventual verification of the truth was only possible because a laboratory worker had kept some of the affected tissue and this was examined by an investigating team from the USA in 1992. It is worth noting that from a complete denial of the facts up to the time of the break-up of the Soviet Union, to a partial admission of the truth during the Yeltsin era, the official line at the time of writing is now back to a complete denial of the facts.

Why would the government wish to hide the truth or facts which may help to arrive at the truth? The answer in the case of the Anthrax deaths was because the Soviet Union was in contravention of the Biological Warfare Convention signed in 1972. In the Dyatlov case, it suggests there is some kind of government/military complicity. Nobody in authority seems particularly interested in opening the Dyatlov case up for a review, despite the level of public interest and speculation on the case. One person who had written to President Putin's office recently about the case had the letter passed to the Sverdlovsk Oblast administration to be dealt with and the response was that no new facts had emerged since the closure of the case to justify reopening it.

This obfuscation of the facts by the autopsies is very useful to anyone wishing to close down any further investigation into the case, because none of it can be verified by an outsider. Unfortunately, this total focus and reliance on the autopsies leads any enquiries up all sorts of paths and dead ends. An example of this over-reliance on one set of evidence can be shown by what happened in a case of several murders in England.

From 1975 to 1980 a series of terrible murders of prostitutes in the north of England gripped the country. The man who carried out the murders, Peter Sutcliffe, had been dubbed the *Yorkshire Ripper* by the media (a reference to the original *Jack the Ripper*). The police poured a lot of resources into trying to catch him, without any success to begin with. During the course of the investigation, a number of anonymous letters and an anonymous tape recording were sent to Assistant Chief Constable George Oldfield, the policeman in charge of the case. The tape and letters were purportedly from the *Yorkshire Ripper*. The strangled vowels of the voice on the tape taunted the detective:

*"I'm Jack, I see you are still having no luck catching me......." and ending with ".....I reckon your boys are letting you down George. They can't be much good. Can they?"*

Oldfield was seen listening to the tape for hours on end and it sent the investigation off in entirely the wrong direction, allowing the Ripper to murder more victims because the police were completely focused on the voice taunting them on the tape. This used up valuable time and resources which were completely wasted. When the Yorkshire Ripper, Peter Sutcliffe, was eventually caught he said that the tape had been nothing to do with him and it had been a hoax.

The Dyatlov autopsy reports are, of course, not a hoax. However, because of all the seeming inconsistencies and oddities in the reports of each death, the question has to be asked if they are a true and honest version of what happened to each member of the group. In the same way that George Oldfield focused on the *Ripper* tape, everybody who examines the Dyatlov story focuses on the autopsy reports; but, of course, there is no real answer and that is what is most likely intended. The autopsies give two different sets of conclusions.

Even the final conclusions of the autopsies are awkward for the authorities because there is no real answer without implicating the military. In the Cold War, certain events could be explained away by the machinations of imperialist and capitalist aggressors. However, in this case it would raise the embarrassing question of how imperialist aggressors and saboteurs had managed to penetrate into the heart of the Urals without being stopped or identified. When Mathias Rust flew his Cessna 172 from Helsinki through some of the most heavily defended airspace in the world and landed in Red Square in May 1987, the Chief of Air Defence, Marshal Alexander Koldunov lost his job.

Are we really to believe that a case which had attracted a great deal of attention in the Soviet Union at the time was to be given a final postscript by the pathologist and endorsed by the investigators as "We don't really know what happened?" and that this would be accepted without question by the authorities? Given the nature of the hierarchy and how things were done then, the autopsy reports and conclusions would have gone straight back to the Sverdlovsk Prosecutor's office, with the instruction – if you don't know what happened, then find out. However, as it turned out, it was quite apparent that the authorities were not particularly interested in what the Sverdlovsk Prosecutor's office had covered or uncovered in their investigation.

# Chapter 10

By 1990 Lev Ivanov was long retired from the Sverdlovsk Prosecutors Office and was living in Kustanay in Kazakhstan and working as a barrister. That year he published an article in the newspaper, *Leninsky Put'.* The article appeared in two parts on 22 and 24 November 1990. The translated article follows:

*We are gradually getting used to the fact that, in pursuit of sensation, some papers tend towards publishing unverified or plainly unreliable information. My attention was drawn to a reprint in the Leninsky Put' of articles from American sources about UFOs (LP No. 210, 30 Oct 1990). I was attracted by trustworthiness of the material, since more often than not official authorities try to suppress obvious facts of UFO sightings.*

*This is really so. But I would like to look into the ways such things are done in this country.*

*Thirty years ago I, in my official capacity, had to deal with a similar problem myself, with the only difference that in my case it was related to a tragic occurrence.*

*All I am going to tell you about is documented officially and filed in the criminal case kept today in the Sverdlovsk Oblast State Archives. In consideration of the above I give the real names of* the persons involved and the real dates. The information I present is free from any "artist's supposition", on the initiative of the editorial board of the Sverdlovsk newspaper Uralsky Rabochyi the documented facts have been made known to the public – after almost thirty years, in 1990.

On some day in April this year the telephone rang in my room. The talker on the other end introduced himself as the Uralsky Rabochyi newspaper correspondent Bogomolov, he asked me for a personal interview for which he was ready to fly from Sverdlovsk. He was interested in details of some sensitive issue. So I agreed. And there we sit far into midnight in my flat, and I answer his questions about events of long ago.

What was it that had excited the public in Sverdlovsk so?

The Urals Polytechnic Institute has a tourist club named after Igor Dyatlov, a student who long ago had perished on a hike with a group of UPI fellow students. There is a memorial at the St. Michael cemetery dedicated to nine UPI students who all died on a hike in the Near-Polar Urals in 1959. But no one knew what had caused the death of such a big group of tourists, they were buried in closed coffins, no explanations had been given to the incident. Thirty years had passed since then. But students are of the persevering kind: they continued their own search. It happened so that perestroika had its effect on special archives as well, in other words: the ultra-confidential files stored in archives were declassified, and among them the criminal case which had been under investigation back in 1959.

Students, members of the tourist club, after getting familiarized with the materials and secret files kept in the case felt confused: the then official version of tourists' death had nothing to do with the information they found in the declassified criminal case. They started looking for people who might have known at least something about the incident but not one such person had been located. Finally, they came to a decision to find a prosecutor or an investigator who might have been involved in the investigation into that case.

*Boris Yeltsyn in his book "A Testimony On A Bespoken Subject" remembers how, already as 1956 graduate of the same Institute, he liked going on hikes with his friends. At the time described by Yeltsyn, complex tourist hikes in the Near-Polar Urals of the highest (third) category of difficulty, according to the existing classification, were very popular among young people, because they developed courage, stoutness, attachment to friends, and selflessness. The case I am talking about belonged to exactly such category.*

*At the end of January 1959 a group of skiers, students and graduates of the UPI (two girls and seven men) went on a hike registered as one of the 3rd category of complexity, with a goal to traverse (cross) the mountains in the Near-Polar Urals, with an ascent to Mount Otorten located north of Ivdel, in the upper reaches of the river Auspia, a tributary of the Lozva.*

*Under conditions of adverse weather (snow storm, sharp frost), the skiers were approaching the mountain behind schedule. Despite the bad weather and thickening twilight, they decided to complete their ascent, make camp and spend the night on the mountain top, with a view to traverse to the other mountain top in the morning.*

*When they had already pitched up the tent and were preparing for sleep, some force threw them all, undressed, out of the tent and scattered over the valley. All the tourists died.*

*The search for the dead was conducted by army specialists and student volunteers with the support of aircraft of the Urals military command. It continued from February to May. The bodies were found at different time within a 1.5-km radius of the tent, were brought to Sverdlovsk and buried. And that was about all the relatives and the public in Sverdlovsk could find out. It was explained to all that the tourists met with an emergency situation and froze to death.*

*However, that was not quite true. The real cause of death of those people remained hidden from the public, the actual facts were known to but a few: former First secretary of the Oblast Party Committee (Obkom) A.P. Kirilenko, Second secretary of Obkom A.F.Yeshtokin, Oblast Prosecutor N.I.Klimov, and the writer of these words the case investigator. None of them are alive today.*

*This is how things were moving. On 31 January 1959, the group of tourists led by experienced hiker Igor Dyatlov set up a store to leave part of supplies in the valley of the Auspia, and started the ascent to the Otorten. According to the route schedule, Dyatlov with the group were expected to appear at the check point, v. Vizhay, by 12 February and inform the sports committee in Sverdlovsk with a telegram about their completion of the route. But by the appointed date the group did not appear in Vizhay. One tourist (the tenth member of the group) who had been left to stay in Vizhay due to illness and could not continue on further hike with the group was the first one to raise alarm.*

*The Obkom executive committee immediately organized a rescue team which included army engineers, aircraft and student volunteers. General supervision of rescue operations was entrusted to Master of Sports (Tourism) Ye.P.Maslennikov, I was put in charge of conducting the investigation. We went to Ivdel by plane, and further, by military helicopters, to the taiga. Also attached to our group were experienced trackers from the corrective labour camp and several Mansi hunters.*

*It was my official duty to get in the investigation, or lead the investigation process on the most complex issues. Evidently, the above circumstance, and also my former experience of service at the front had played the decisive role. So, I found myself in the middle of the impassable Urals taiga, in a tent, in the most severe winter time between February and May.*

*My purpose is not to go into details of the search and the investigation process. All that might be very interesting and educative, but the paper column sets its limitations. This, definitely, with a good share of imagination, has been described by one of the participants of our expedition Boris Yarovoi in his book "Of the Higher Category of Complexity" which came out 20*

129

*years ago in Sverdlovsk. I only want, as I have promised above, to talk about the mysterious phenomena, which from time to time get manifest on the planet Earth but which no one has managed to give adequate explanation so far.*

*When we landed in the taiga and moved on skis up the Otorten, there, on the very top of the mountain, we found the tourists' tent buried in snow.*

*As we examined the tent we found tourists' outwear: jackets, pants, backpacks with all their contents and untouched. As is known, even in winter, tourists preparing for sleep in a tent usually take off their outerwear. That was what we did in our tent, despite that the temperature inside never rose above minus four [°C – transl.].*

*It was clear from the view of the clothes and practically all personal items, including diaries, photo cameras, foodstuffs left in the tent, that people were leaving it in a great hurry. Later, I established that the two long cuts in the wall of the tent, through which people were getting out, were made with a knife from inside.*

*Not even a single drop of blood inside or around the tent showed that all tourists had left the tent without bodily harm. The latter circumstance will be regarded very important in the future.*

*At times eight, at times nine, tracks of footprints led from the tent down the slope and into the valley. In mountain conditions, with overcooled snow, tracks do not get covered up but, on the contrary, look like columns, because of the snow getting compacted under foot, while loose snow around gets blown off. The presence of nine tracks of footprints confirmed that all tourists were walking by themselves, no one was carried by others. And there we come to a mystery. At a distance of one and a half kilometres from the tent, in the river valley near the old cedar tree, tourists made fine after escape from the tent – and started dying one after the other.*

*Using the developed films with shots made by the tourists before they started preparing for sleep, with account for the negatives density and film sensitivity (the boxes for films were found in place), diaphragm and exposure settings of the cameras, I had a chance to time the shots and obtain a wealth of information, but all this failed to answer the main question: what had made the tourists run away from the tent.*

*There are no secondary details in an investigation, the investigator's motto is "take heed of details!" Near the tent we found a natural evidence of the fact of a man leaving the tent "for number one". The person came out bootless, wearing woollen socks only ("out for a minute"). And further the track of the same bootless feet is traced on slope leading into the valley.*

*I had every reason to develop a theory that it was that man who had raised alarm and had no time to get shod himself. It means that there must have been some frightful force which threatened him and the rest, making them leave the tent in a hurry and run down the slope, seeking shelter in the taiga. The task of the investigation was to identify that force, or, at least, try to take a step closer to solving the puzzle.*

*On 26 February 1959, we found remains of a small fire at the foot of the hill near the forest edge, also there were found the bodies of two tourists: Doroshenko and Krivonishchenko, without clothes, in their underwear only. Later, almost in line in the direction of the tent, were found the bodies of Igor Dyatlov, and, at a short distance from him, of two more people: Slobodin and Kolmogorova. Without going into more detail, I will only add that the last three had been most fit physically and most strong, they were crawling from the fire to the tent for clothes – that was absolutely clear from the positions of their bodies. Further autopsy showed that those three courageous people had died of overcooling. They froze despite being clothed better than others.*

*Later, already in May, under five-metre thick snow not far from the fireplace, the bodies of Dubinina, Zolotarev, Thibeaux-Brignolle and Kolevatov were found. On external examination no injuries on the bodies were noted. A sensational discovery was made later when, in conditions of the Sverdlovsk morgue, an autopsy of the bodies were carried out. Dubinina, Thibeaux-Brignolle and Zolotarev were found to have received extensive internal fatal injuries. For example, Luda Dubinina had broken ribs: 2, 3, 4, 5 on the right side and 2, 3, 4, 5, 6, 7 on the left. One fragment of a rib had even penetrated into the heart. Zolotarev had 2, 3, 4, 5, 6 ribs broken. Note, the heavy injuries had no visible external signs. The injuries of the kind may result from action of an immense force on human body, for example, if hit by a car moving at a high speed. Such injuries could not have been obtained from an accidental fall from a standing height. In the vicinity of the Otorten and the surrounding area we saw boulders and rocks of different shapes hiding under snow, but these were not in the way of tourists' retreat (remember tracks of footprints!), and naturally no such rocks could have been hurtled on the tourists. Hence there must have been some selective directional force which acted on individual people and excepted others. There were certain other circumstances which I would like to discuss.*

*When later in May Ye.P.Maslennikov and I examined the scene of the incident, we noted that some young spruces at the edge of the forest had traces of burning, but their location was neither concentric nor otherwise systematic. There was no epicentre either. That was one more proof of directional nature of, say, a thermal ray or some unknown, at least to us, energy of selective action: no traces of melt in snow, no damaged trees were noted either. We got an impression that after tourists had walked on foot over five hundred metres down the slope, someone had dealt with a few of them in a directional way.*

*There is much talking nowadays around the period of the fifties, in order to put the onus of the past on some people. That time was the period of strict or, I should say, point-blank discipline, particularly in the work of the law-enforcement organs. Beria (Lavrentiy Beria, 1899-1953, Soviet politician, chief of secret police, NKVD – transl.) had been dismissed and gone, but Beria's ways and methods still lived, and even today we are not always ready to part with them.*

*When, together with the Oblast Prosecutor, we presented the initial information to First secretary of Obkom L. P. Kirilenko, he gave us a clear-cut instruction: all work must be made secret, not a word of information to be leaked. Kirilenko ordered to bury the tourists in closed coffins and explain their relatives that the tourists had died of hypothermia.*

*Khrushchev was informed about the incident from the very beginning and, as is known from the publication of one of the rescue party members, a newspaper correspondent, spoke against any publications on the matter until the investigation is completed and all tourists are found. But at the end, when the rest of the group had been found and the above details revealed, it was Kirilenko who held back the information. So finally the case came to naught at the highest level. All requests from relatives were shelved. Such was the then order in the country and we had no say in that matter.*

*The fact is that at the time of our investigation the Tagilsky Rabochiy newspaper published a small article about sighting during the students' ascent of the Otorten of a Fire Orb, or, as we call it today, an Unidentified Flying Object (UFO) in the sky above Nizhny Tagil. In absolute silence the strange light crossed the sky in the direction of the northern tops of the Ural mountains. The author of the article questioned: what could that be? The newspaper editor was severely reprimanded for this publication, and I, in my turn, received orders from the Obkom to abstain from research into this topic. Supervision of my investigation into the case was taken over by Second secretary of the Party Obkom A.F.Yeshtokin.*

*We knew very little about UFOs in that period, and almost nothing about radiation. The ban on the said topics was caused by danger of even unintentional disclosure of rocket or nuclear engineering information, the really intensive development of such technologies was only at an early stage, and the world was living through the period which later received the name of the Cold War.*

*But the investigation must go on, am I not a professional crime investigator, I must solve the puzzle! So, despite the ban, I continued my investigation into this particular topic in conditions of top secrecy, since other theories, such as human or animal attack, a fall under a storm, etc., were excluded based on the gathered data.*

*I had a clear understanding in what sequence and who were dying, this information was the result of thorough examination of the bodies, their clothes, and other data. Only the sky was left, with all its contents and an unfathomable energy that had turned out to be beyond human strength.*

*With the assistance of scientists from the Urals Branch of the Academy of Sciences of the USSR I undertook extensive tests of clothes and some organs of the deceased for presence of "radiation". Notably, we compared the obtained results with clothes and internal organs of people killed in car accidents or who had died a natural death. The results were amazing. Non-specialists would see nothing special in the results of analyses, but let me name just a few: the radioactive decay readings of the brown sweater that belonged to one of the tourists with bodily injuries showed 9900 counts per minute (cpm), and after washing of the sample in water, the reading was 5200 cpm; this testified to the fact of washing off of the radioactive contamination. It should be noted that, before the bodies were found, they had been subjected to intensive washing with snow melt water: there were real streams of water flowing under snow. Hence, the radiation contamination at the moment of death of the tourists must have been many times higher.*

*As a prosecutor who, at that time, had already had some experience in dealing with certain secret matters of defence, I discarded the version of nuclear weapon tests in that area. It was then that I came to deal directly with Fire Orbs.*

*I questioned many witnesses of UFOs flying over or hovering, in other words, visiting the Near-Polar Urals. As a matter of fact, I disagree with those linking the appearance of UFOs with aliens. A UFO is an Unidentified Flying Object, and that's that. Many data show that those may be "bundles of energy" acting on their way on objects of organic and inorganic nature, which modern people fail to understand, and modern science and technology to explain. Apparently, ours was one of such phenomena.*

*Given below are abstracts from the materials of my interviews and some documents. As I have noted earlier, all of them are now kept in the archives.*

*This is what weather observer Tokareva told me:*

*"On 17 February, at 6:50 am, an unusual phenomenon was viewed in the sky, in the form of a star with a tail. The tail resembled thick cirrus clouds. After some time the star separated from the tail, became brighter and moved across the sky, gradually swelling like a big balloon wrapped in a haze. Then a star lit up inside the orb, first it looked like a small sphere and was not so bright. The bigger orb started gradually going down and turned into a blurred spot. At 7:05 it disappeared altogether. The direction of movement was from south to north-east."*

*Should I add here that sky observation was part Tokareva's professional duty. And that no comets had been visiting this Cisuralian area at that time.*

*The same fire orb was sighted in the vicinity of Ivdel by military officer A. Savkin, whom I interviewed as well:*

*"On 17 February 1959, at 6:40 am, in the time of duty, I observed a brilliant white orb appearing from the south, at times getting wrapped in a shroud of mist, with a bright spot of a star in the middle. The orb moved north and was visible for 8-10 minutes".*

*Further it was a matter of technique: to find other people who would have stayed awake outdoors, in their duty execution, at night time in the period of January-February 1959. It's no secret today that the Ivdel area in those times was one big "archipelago" of prison camps – the 24-hour guarded Ivdel-lag.*

*I had similar records of interviews with witnesses Novikov, Avenburg, Malik. The same orb was sighted on 31 March. An identical orb was viewed on the night of the tourists death, that is, on the night of 1 to 2 February, by tourists – students of the Geography faculty of the Pedagogical Institute. Witness G.Atamanaki saw an orb over the Otorten on the night of 1 February.*

*I believe the case study to be totally convincing today, and back then I held to an opinion that tourists' death had been caused by some action of an Unidentified Flying Object. On the basis of the evidence before me the role of a UFO appears quite obvious. Correspondent Bogomolov who interviewed me wrote in his publication that "criminal prosecutor Ivanov had a clear understanding of students' death being caused by an unidentified object, although in his final document he chose to resort to a 'casual result' formula". My response to a question by the correspondent whether my view of the cause of tourists' death had changed in the past thirty years was that yes it had, but only in respect to technicality of the action. Where earlier I believed that the orb had exploded emitting some unknown but radioactive energy, in my opinion today the action of energy from the orb might have been of selective nature and directed to three persons of the group only.*

*When I reported about my discoveries, the fire orbs and radioactivity, to A.F. Yeshtokin, he was very categorical in his orders: absolutely everything related to the must be made secret, classified, sealed, sent to special archives and forgotten. Am I to explain that orders had to be and were executed right off?*

*Today's reader may wonder at so much secrecy about this all. But, if you remember, shortly before the described events the so-called radioactive "exhaust" had occurred in Kyshtym. Many publications about the Kyshtym accident may be found in the press today, but one could hardly imagine anyone trying to tell about such things back then! A great amount of decontamination work had been carried out in the vicinity of Kyshtym, but despite that only a limited group of people knew, and those who knew preferred to kept mum. The older generation remember those times: the recent launch of the first man-made earth satellite, news about tests of atomic and hydrogen weapons. Many people were apt to associate the above enigmatic events, UFOs including, with military tests, but our investigative results convinced us that the Dyatlov case incident had little to do with military tests. And today, when we come to learn more about testing sites and nuclear tests, our early version of students' death that had appeared in that period is getting even stronger confirmation today.*

*The current generation should not judge us too harshly for our work, I must remind that still today, while witnesses of old-time events are still living, all truth is still hard to be revealed.*

*Recently I read in the national press that in the operation of shooting down the spy plane of Gary Powers near Sverdlovsk one more plane led by pilot Safronov was also crashed. The story was told by Major Voronov, former battery commanding officer, it was his battery that had shot down both planes. And look: the fact of two planes, one of them ours, being destroyed had been known to thousands of people. Thousands of people watched our fighter plane hit the ground near Degtyarsk, a small town near Pervouralsk – and not a line in the press on the length of thirty years! I, like many others, had watched first one, then another rocket cross the sky, and the planes falling, one in the direction of the town of Syssert (Powers), and the other, in the southern direction, towards Revda (our plane). The publication about the event appeared many years later.*

*With my over forty years' experience of work in prosecution, where most of the time I had top secret clearance, I cannot stop wondering what the lies the authorities kept telling people were needed for?*

*It is not my purpose to find excuses for my actions on classifying information about the Fire Orbs phenomena and death of a big group of people. I asked the correspondent to publish my apologies to relatives of the deceased for perversion and concealment of the truth, and, because no room was found for these in four newspaper issues, I apologize in the present article to relatives of the deceased, particularly the families of Dubinina, Thibeaux-Brignolle, Zolotarev, for distortion of the truth. At the time I tried to do my best, but the situation in the country, as lawyers would define it, was one of an "overwhelming force", and only on our days an opportunity has appeared to overcome this force. And, again, getting back to the Fire Orbs. They did and do exist. We only want to keep information of their sightings open, and try to understand and study their nature. The majority of onlookers note their peaceful behaviour, but, as you see, fatalities also occur. Something or someone had wanted to either frighten, or punish the people, or demonstrate their strength – and they did it, killing three people. I know the circumstances of the event in detail and can definitely assert that only those who piloted those orbs know all. But had there been "human beings" inside, and are they always present there, no one knows yet.*

*And one last thing. What was it that caused the young people to go on such dangerous hikes? What force was driving them? Reading Boris Yeltsyn's story about his participation in tourist hikes in the North Urals and comparing it with his today's character, I see a direct relationship there: in such extreme situations real men are shaped. Courage, valour, daring, will power, honour – all these result from long, since young years, development of character and true grit. Far back in February 1959, when we came near the cedar tree under which the tourists had tried to make fire, after we examined the site and tried to put things together, we were amazed at the courage and spirit of the young people as they struggled for lives of their own and of their companions. Imagine a tree trunk 50-60 cm thick. They climbed up this tree in turn to break branches for their fire (they had managed to light a fire). We found frozen (so horrible to just pronounce such a thing!) muscle fragments from thigh interfaces, and scraps of cloth from their underwear stuck in the tree bark. Later, in May, we dug out the bodies of Luda Dubinina and the rest. They had been the first to die from extensive internal injuries, but had not been left alone. They were taken away from the fire and carefully laid on the ground. Those men took care of the dead, through perishing themselves. Only real men will behave so. A message from the past, a lesson we must learn. And so mean seems to us today the behaviour of some people unable to overcome even minor everyday difficulties.*

*And what about pilots of the Fire Orbs? If they exist, they will sooner or later manifest themselves, and circumstances will bring them in contact with our civilization. I don't doubt that.*

*L.I.Ivanov, Barrister.*
*Kustanay"*
Published in the Leninsky Put' newspaper 22 and 24 November 1990

At the beginning of the article Lev Ivanov refers to the publication of the Dyatlov case in the Sverdlovsk newspaper *Uralsky Rabochyi* bringing the case to the public's attention for the first time since 1959. Ivanov probably felt ready to speak on the subject given that the Soviet Union was in the process of breaking up and a journalist (Bogomolov) was ready to help him get his supposed view of events out to a wider audience. He (Ivanov) refers to reprints of some U.S. UFO articles in the *Leninsky Put'* newspaper as the catalyst for speaking out on the Dyatlov case. However, it can be seen that he chooses his words carefully;

*All I am going to tell you about is documented officially and filed in the criminal case kept today in the Sverdlovsk Oblast State Archives.*

He goes on to describe the make-up of the group, their route up to Mount Otorten and the difficulty of the hike they were undertaking. These are all well-known facts now but were still relatively new at the time of his interview with Bogolomov.

With regard to the event that caused them to flee their tent, Ivanov states;

*When they had already pitched up the tent and were preparing for sleep, some force threw them all, undressed, out of the tent and scattered over the valley....It was explained to all that the tourists met with an emergency situation and froze to death. However, that was not quite true. The real cause of death of those people remained hidden from the public...*

With this second statement Ivanov tells us that there was a cover up of some kind but he later proceeds to give a less than satisfactory explanation. Before his explanation he makes a couple of incorrect points;

*One tourist (the tenth member of the group) who had been left to stay in Vizhay due to illness and could not continue on further hike with the group was the first one to raise the alarm.*

*The Obkom executive committee immediately organized a rescue team which included army engineers, aircraft and student volunteers. General supervision of rescue operations was entrusted to Master of Sports (Tourism) Ye.P.Maslennikov*

He says it was Yury Yudin (the tenth member of the Dyatlov group who had turned back) who raised the alarm, This was not the case, it was the relatives of the missing ski tourists who were deeply worried at the group's non-appearance who were strongly pushing for something to be done and he gives the impression that the Obkom *immediately* leapt into action, when nothing could be further from the truth. They appeared to drag their heels as much as they could. Furthermore, although Maslennikov may have had general charge of the mechanics of the search due to his undoubted skills and knowledge, Ivanov fails to mention Colonel Ortukyov who had the authority to call in whatever was needed from the military by way of logistical support. Neither does Ivanov make any mention of his replacing the Ivdel Prosecutor, Vasily Tempalov. It could be said that after thirty years, Ivanov's knowledge of the exact details may not have been perfect and perhaps he can be forgiven for this. He does say;

*My purpose is not to go into details of the search and the investigation process.*

Ivanov explains that his purpose in this article is;

*I have promised above, to talk about the mysterious phenomena, which from time to time get manifest on the planet Earth but which no one has managed to give adequate explanation so far.*

With this statement, we begin to see where he is coming from on the whole subject. He goes on to describe the terrible injuries found in some of the last group of four in the group and says that they (the Prosecutor's Office) were instructed by the head of the local Communist Party that no mention was to be made of any of this,

*... together with the Oblast Prosecutor, we presented the initial information to First secretary of Obkom L. P. Kirilenko, he gave us a clear-cut instruction: all work must be made secret, not a word of information to be leaked. Kirilenko ordered to bury the tourists in closed coffins and explain their relatives that the tourists had died of hypothermia...*

*....at the end, when the rest of the group had been found and the above details revealed, it was Kirilenko who held back the information. So finally the case came to naught at the highest level. All requests from relatives were shelved. Such was the then order in the country and we had no say in that matter.*

Whilst Kirilenko may well have instructed him to say nothing, Ivanov makes no mention of the fact that Kirilenko would not have instructed him to do this without himself being instructed by a higher authority. The unasked question which would surely be asked by Ivanov himself would be; why would a local party boss try to cover up the facts of the deaths?

Ivanov then starts to expand on his UFO theory beginning with the radiation aspect;

*Only the sky was left, with all its contents and an unfathomable energy that had turned out to be beyond human strength.*

*With the assistance of scientists from the Urals Branch of the Academy of Sciences of the USSR I undertook extensive tests of*

*clothes and some organs of the deceased for presence of*
*"radiation".*

With red lights and warning signals all around this case, Ivanov would not have undertaken radiation tests on his own initiative as he implies here. The truth is that he was instructed to do so, as we will see.

After the discussion of the tests for radioactivity, Ivanov makes the following statement which firmly takes the subject away from the military and into the realm of UFOs;

*I discarded the version of nuclear weapon tests in that area. It was then that I came to deal directly with Fire Orbs.*

He describes various witness sightings of orbs/lights in the skies in the northern Urals, along with his interviews of the witnesses. Significantly he mentions the sighting of one of the orbs on the night the Dyatlov group died (1/2 February 1959) by the students of the Geography faculty of the Pedagogical Institute in Sverdlovsk and mentions witness Georgy Atamanaki seeing the orb. Atamanaki was to take part in the search.

Ivanov is quite categorical in his views and conclusions and takes care not to link the military with them. He also takes care to refer to objects that are unidentified in the sky but not extra-terrestrial;

*I believe the case study to be totally convincing today, and back then I held to an opinion that tourists' death had been caused by some action of an Unidentified Flying Object. On the basis of the evidence before me the role of a UFO appears quite obvious....My response to a question by the correspondent whether my view of the cause of tourists' death had changed in the past thirty years was that yes it had, but only in respect to technicality of the action. Where earlier I believed that the orb had exploded emitting some unknown but radioactive energy, in my opinion today the action of energy from the orb might have been of selective nature and directed to three persons of the group only.*

It is not an entirely satisfactory statement as he has refined his thinking to say the orbs only killed Luda, Thibo and Zolotarev using some kind of energy beams but offers no explanations as to why they fled the tent and why the others should have all perished as well. He says that on reporting his conclusions regarding orbs and radioactivity to AF Yeshtokin, Second Secretary of Obkom, Yeshtokin instructs him to file everything away as secret and not to say anything. As if to spell it out and distance the military from what happened, Ivanov says;

> ....*our investigative results convinced us that the Dyatlov case incident had little to do with military tests.*

And yet he says some kind of energy type weaponry is involved but it is nothing to do with the military. He says that regarding any accountability for what happened;

> *It is not my purpose to find excuses for my actions on classifying information about the Fire Orbs phenomena and death of a big group of people.*

Ivanov does offer an apology to the relatives of Luda, Thibo and Zolotarev in particular, for what he says was "distortion of the truth". One gets the sense that Ivanov deeply regrets something and feels that after 30 years he is making some kind of amends, particularly as he was nearing the end of his life.

Going back to the earlier part of his account, Ivanov states the following;

> *...the actual facts were known to but a few: former First secretary of the Oblast Party Committee (Obkom) A.P. Kirilenko, Second secretary of Obkom A.F.Yeshtokin, Oblast Prosecutor N.I.Klimov and the writer of these words the case investigator. None of them are alive today.*

At various points in the overall statement, Ivanov tends to give the impression that he was only accountable to the local Communist Party hierarchy. Whilst it is true that they had taken control of the case and he would have been required to keep them abreast of what was going on, Ivanov actually worked for the Sverdlovsk Prosecutor's Office and Ivanov mentions his overall boss, Nikolai Klinov in the Prosecutor's Office. However he leaves out one name which is all the more surprising, as this was his direct superior. His direct superior was still alive at the time of

Ivanov's article and, as will be seen, he had a very different take on the Dyatlov deaths to that of Lev Ivanov

# Chapter 11

There is one person who rarely crops up in accounts of the Dyatlov tragedy. He held a very senior position in the investigation and remarkably at the time of writing (2016), he is still alive and lives in Moldova. In effect, he was also Lev Ivanov's boss during the investigation. In 2013 he was 94 years old and gave an interview to two journalists from the *Komsomolskaya Pravda* regarding the Dyatlov tragedy.

He remembered the case very well and he found it quite mysterious. In 1959, Evgeny Fyodorovich Okishev was Deputy Head of the Investigative Department of the Sverdlovsk Oblast Prosecution Office and was directly responsible for the supervision of the case including Lev Ivanov's handling of it (Ivanov was subordinate to Evgeny Okishev and had replaced Vasily Tempalov, the Ivdel Prosecutor, very early in the investigation). His interview was as follows (*Interviewers questions and comments are in bold italics, Okishev's responses are in ordinary type*):

"EO – When it became clear that the tourists had died, we organised an investigation team under the direction of criminal prosecutor Lev Ivanov, and I was appointed to supervise their work. The impression of the examination of the tent, with its cuts and remains of food inside, was that the tourists had just sat down to supper and suddenly felt panic that made them all rush out. We tried to collect more facts about the Pass. We learned that the location was a sacred site of the Mansi, and that women were not allowed to go there. Since the tourists' group included two girls, the Mansi were the first we suspected. However this version was soon discarded.

– How did you check it out? What made you discard it?

EO – I called the Ivdel district prosecutor and asked him to find a literate Mansi, an activist with whom I could talk. So, when I came to Ivdel, there were already three Mansi men coming there at the prosecutor's request, one of them a quite literate person, People's Deputy to the Regional Council. I had booked a room for the three of them at an Ivdel hotel. But they refused to stay in it. They preferred to sleep outside, in the snow, with their dogs. This is how the Deputy (*Mansi*) explained it to me: "I ride my sledge dogs even when I go to attend a session of the Regional Council, and I always sleep with them because I feel it hard to stay indoors". We talked with him about the Mansi and their traditions. He asserted that the place where the tourists died was in no way sacred. On the contrary, any Russian appearing among them would be looked upon as something divine. People would try to touch such a person, make him their guest, as this holds good promise to all. It was absolutely clear from his behaviour that the man was telling the truth. After this talk the Mansi assassination theory became irrelevant. But the question of panic remained. It is worth noting that, for some reason or other, the two men that were found in the forest under the cedar tree had been trying to make a fire for quite a long time: the proof to that was a great number of dead matches were found scattered around.

– Do you remember this for sure, had there really been dead matches?

EO – Absolutely, matches were also mentioned in the on-site inspection report.

– But in a month's time matches must have become covered up with snow?

EO – I believe the inspection report. (It is worthy of note that the copy of criminal case kept in the Sverdlovsk Oblast archives bears no notice of matches. So, this is one more mystery of the Dyatlov Pass. – *Interviewing Journalist written comment to Okishev's comment "I believe the Inspection Report")*

- Why had the military become involved in the search?

EO - To say the truth, this was done on our request. And there were reasons for that. Shortly before that we met with a worker of one of the prison camps in the North Urals. He described strange flashes of light which he and his wife saw late that evening on their way home from the cinema. The light came from the direction of the supposed accident with the tourists. We also received evidence from other local residents, and all of them spoke about a similar phenomenon, all testimonies were entered on our records of interrogation. We got a suspicion of existence of a military test field somewhere around, could that be true? Could flashes be caused by a failed rocket launch that had killed the tourists?

- But, again, there is no such record in the criminal case! So, what happened then?

EO - A group of the military under the command, if I am not mistaken, of Colonel Artyukov, arrived. I talked to him, and he convinced me that no such facilities were nearby and no possibility of missile launches. But, there was one instance that put us on the alert. When the last bodies were found later in May, an order came to collect all items found at the pass and send them for radiological examination. Also, all people who had been in contact with the things found in the tent and nearby were ordered to undergo body counting. So it was done, but neither a reassuring, nor any other results were made known to us. And again, the fact of some secret military tests being held was coming to mind. We applied with a letter signed by the Oblast Prosecutor to either the Prosecutor General of the USSR or the Federal – I don't remember exactly now – asking to explain what really we were investigating into? And how it was related to radiation? Could it be so that even the top commandant of the Urals Military District knew nothing of any tests of armaments held there? In response to our letter, Deputy Prosecutor General, comrade Urakov came to meet with us and gave orders that we were to all tell anyone who asked that the tourists' death was an accident. Urakov evaded all our direct questions about tests of armaments. I mean, he did not deny this version, but simply avoided direct answers. What's more, Urakov took absolutely no interest in the course of our investigation, as if the picture of the scene was absolutely clear to him already. He, however, took the case away with him. With that, our investigation came to an end. Just imagine: at the very height of the investigation, when dead bodies with strange injuries have just been found, the case is being taken away! And I clearly remember when we were signing our letter in the office of Oblast Prosecutor Klinov, he himself asked in doubt whether we had omitted something and had not fully checked one or the other evidence? We told him that if the top officials discard the military incident version, then all is left to us is to consider other possible versions. He found our considerations convincing, and signed the letter. But, again, the reaction from Moscow was such that our suppositions of a military involvement had been neither confirmed nor disproved...

- What's your idea, why Urakov ordered everybody to say that was an accident?

EO - Evidently, such was an order from the CPSU Central Committee.

- Do you admit that other structures could have been involved in investigations into this case:, the KGB, for example, or some other agency?

EO - I think they had been involved, really, only I was not let in on that. The KGB investigators must have been attracted. Such was the usual practice then. I can even suppose that while we sweated over fact-finding they had already known more – with their powers.

- We have recently got through to the then head of the KGB Investigative department for Sverdlovsk Oblast. The officer's answer was "we were not engaged in that case, definitely". He, however, refused to meet with us in person.

EO - So much for their involvement: why did he refuse to meet with you if the KGB had reportedly not been involved? Why then should he fear to repeat that to you openly? It may well be that his department had really had a hand in the investigation. This is the function of investigators of the Committee (KGB – *Transl.*). Such was their top secret activity. And your interlocutor had simply no right to discuss their work with you.

.- We may suppose that the tragedy was caused by some tests. From the very beginning the KGB performed their own investigation into the case. They quickly find out that, say, the plane had dropped the bomb in a wrong place. A disgrace at government level that must be concealed by all means. It may well be that it was decided to bury the worst injured bodies in four-meters deep snow in hope to find some better solution before they are found. Meanwhile the case was assigned to a civilian investigating office, which, on Urakov's instruction, would file the case away in storage as an accident ... .

EO - We can suppose many things here, but I prefer not to, in the absence of facts.

- According to eyewitnesses, when the last bodies were found, prosecutor Ivanov's behaviour changed abruptly. He looked depressed and in despair. Could this change be related to Urakov's order to write it all off to an accident?

EO - I don't know what to relate it to. We, Ivanov and I, were in a very difficult situation then. Parents of the young people came to my office, some of them cried and called us fascists trying to hide the truth from them. I lost sleep after such charges. But could tell them nothing beside what I was instructed to tell by my superiors. Just imagine the situation; mother or father of a student in my office. They come crying, saying they had lost their only son, or daughter. Like you want to ignore it altogether, don't do any real investigation, allude to an accident. We told them it might be an earthquake, a storm or anything like that ... But look, what else could we tell them? We knew absolutely nothing ourselves. Parents wrote letters to the authorities at all levels, I think, to Khrushchev too, asking for investigation to be continued. The investigation was nevertheless closed – not on our initiative.

- Many people mentioned the unusual red colour of skin of the deceased.

EO - Yes, the skin colour was really unusual. Ivanov mentioned this in his report to me. Who else would have known such things if not him, a war veteran and a criminal investigator, he had seen many people frozen to death before. But nothing like this, ever.

- So what could have happened to them?

EO - I have a strong suspicion, after all those expert examinations (particularly after the radiation analysis made by some order from the top authorities), that there had been tests of some secret weapon or a launch failure. By that time the USSR and the USA had signed the test-ban and nuclear weapons production cut-back treaty. New extra-power devices needed to be created. It may well be that due to special secrecy, tests were conducted at locations unknown to the enemy. The students might have walked into a test area and got injured by fragments of a missile or something of the kind.

- Right, and forensic expert Vozrozhdenny, too, described heavy injuries as if bodies had been hit by an automobile. So, talking of rocket fragments, where could they have disappeared?

EO - The military might have collected them.

- And where could the notebooks of some of the tourists have gone? Also the film strips from the tourists' cameras?

EO - You are putting me in an awkward position. I would then have to disclose our work methods. There could be anything; withdrawal of documents, other material evidence. Anything that might expose, unfavourably, the involvement of the top authorities had to be destroyed.

- But, at the same time, a few undeveloped films were found left in the tent, and you took them. The military, or whoever else, could not have left a film so you could find it; it could carry shots of armament tests.

EO - It may well be that no orders to withdraw films were given. The thought is important to take away fragments as the most evidential items. I also admit those people had been in a big hurry and overlooked some details.


- And could it be this way; the KGB officers develop a film and understand there is nothing special on it. Then they superimpose the developed film on the undeveloped one and after exposure obtain a "negative-positive", develop the second film and again superimpose it on the third one. After exposure the third film presents an exact copy of the original film. This last copy may be loaded back into the camera, and now let the investigator develop it...

EO - I don't know how much technically feasible this could be, but it is a fact that the KGB could work miracles in those years. Let me tell you one story. In summer of the same year 1959 Richard Nixon comes to the USSR and visits Sverdlovsk. And there, in Sverdlovsk he asks: May I visit the Beloyarskaya nuclear station construction site. The people who escort him are at a loss; not just myself, but even much higher authorities did not know anything about construction of a nuclear power station in Beloyarka. How could Nixon know about that? And what to do? At last, after consultations with Moscow, the permit is given. So he goes there with a crowd of his journalists. The KGB people somehow manage to arrange it so that not one of them photographs anything. God knows how they did it, closed the lens with their bodies, or what. Nixon photographed too, and who would dare to obstruct the lens for him? He took quite a few shots of different secret facilities. However on the same night his escort persuades Nixon to visit the Russian steam baths, where, needless to say, all steam room attendants happen to undercover KGB officers. So while some attended to him in the steam bath, others spoiled all his films. I heard that later he felt much upset.

- In some sources we read that in the fifties, after Beria's old guard people were dissolved, the KGB men were no good at all: mostly green and cowed.

EO - Right, different people could be met in this service then: Baboons after hardly six classes at school, and true professionals as well.

- It is said that had there been any cover-up of the events at the Pass it must have involved many people, and later someone would inevitably have spoken up. But no such testimonies have been made so far ...

EO - But who knows the destinies of, for example, the military men who participated in the search? You don't? I don't know either. What has happened to colonel Artyukov, do you know?

- As far as we know, he soon died of cancer.

EO - There now, make your own conclusions ..."

END OF INTERVIEW

Towards the end of 2013, Evgeny Okishev had a meeting with Leonid Proshkin. Leonid Proshkin was a recognized defence lawyer with a long career and the meeting with Evgeny Okishev was arranged through the auspices of the *Komsomolskaya Pravda* journalists Nikolai Varsegov and Natalia Varsegova. The following is a record of their conversation:

Proshkin: - I have thoroughly studied the Dyatlov case. I have one question to ask: Why there is no case number on the file?

Okishev: - I really don't know how this could happen. Maybe because the case was altered later?

Proshkin: - From the available documents we learn that criminal proceedings on the case were initially carried out by Ivdel prosecutor Tempalov. Then all of a sudden we learn that it is taken over by

152

criminal prosecutor Ivanov. However the file contains not a single order on institution of proceedings on the case!

Okishev: - Look here, all the documents had been in place. I remember that well.

Proshkin: - And had there been any orders on expert examinations? They are missing in the case too.

Okishev: - All these orders had been in place. Otherwise no experts would have started working. I don't know what had become of them. Maybe someone had had a relation to that case, and the documents of importance had been taken away by someone later?

Proshkin: - I worked a long time in investigating murders as a criminal investigator for the Kemerovo Oblast. We kind of competed with your Sverdlovsk Oblast in the number of murders.

Okishev: - Right so.

Proshkin: - Anyway, I can't say I ever heard of the Oblast Prosecutor being present at autopsies. But, in the Dyatlov case, Sverdlovsk Oblast Prosecutor Klinov must have had some reason to come to Ivdel and spend three days in the morgue observing autopsy of the five bodies.

Okishev: - This is the only case in my practice, too.

Proshkin: - Does this mean that investigation was regarded as one of special significance?

Okishev: - This means that the Party organs took control over the case. Note, control not just at the Oblast, but at the Central Party organs level. Before Klinov took this position, he worked at the Oblast Party Committee and maintained good contacts afterwards. I remember well that he had connections among his former colleagues. He had probably been prompted to take the case up himself, this being too serious a matter. Who could advise him? Yeshtokin (*Second Secretary of Oblast Committee in 1959 – Komsomolskaya Pravda journalists identifying his position*) could well be such a person, or that might be anyone else, even Kirilenko himself (*First Secretary of Oblast Committee – Komsomolskaya Pravda journalists identifying his position*). By the way, Kirilenko was later transferred to Moscow. In what concerned the autopsy, I remember it was mentioned that one of us had to be present in the morgue. I also remember well that Klinov said we would do everything ourselves.

Proshkin: - It was a pleasant surprise to see the name of Yeshtokin in the case. After Sverdlovsk, Yeshtokin worked in Kemerovo as the First Secretary of the Oblast Committee. I reported to him on several concrete cases. But now, tell me why, after the snow melted away, there was no repeated examination of the incident scene carried out? As you know, repeated examination can bring even more important results.

Okishev: - When the version of military tests arose, we considered visiting the site one more time, with soldiers, for detailed examination as the snow would be melting away. We even included the trip in our investigation work plan. We wanted to make a thorough study of rags (clothes, tent), and all kinds of expert examination. But nothing came out of it.

Proshkin: - Why?

Okishev: - Taboo! No permit. For that reason no repeated examination was conducted.

Proshkin: - Was it for the same reason that there were no radiation tests on the site, when the last four bodies were found?

Okishev: - Our investigation team did not conduct site radiation tests. But such tests had definitely been carried out because after the last four bodies were found, all who had been in contact with the items at the Pass were sent for radiation examination. But for us, other events were unfolding at that time. Deputy Federal Prosecutor for Investigations Urakov arrived and immediately asked us to bring him the case. He told us to write the closing statement. He went to the Oblast committee and took Klinov and Ivanov with him. When Ivanov cane back he told me that an order was to close the case. We argued: how can we close it, on which grounds? There are nine dead bodies in it!

Proshkin: - Yes, the proceedings were instituted on finding of dead bodies!

Okishev: - Right. But at that moment we knew nothing about radioactive contamination. We, Ivanov and I, then decided to close the case with regard to organizing a trip, but only suspend proceedings on the case of the dead bodies. Hoping to continue after a respective permit is obtained. A bit later I received an express order from Urakov to tell parents it was an accident. We all then felt something strange about this case. We suspected this to be something connected either with rockets or some tests. It was the most we could do and what we really did. Anyway, the case was already taken away from us. No doubt, Urakov could have told us, but preferred not to. Because he himself must have received orders from the Procurator General who, in his turn, executed orders from his superiors. And it looks like so: all of a sudden, in the midst of investigation, there comes Urakov and closes down all work.

Proshkin: - How long had Ivanov worked as a criminal prosecutor?

Okishev: - Since early 1954, from the moment this position was created.

Proshkin: - Was he a good investigator?

Okishev: - I should say, excellent. Meticulous and very thorough.

Proshkin: - This explains his appointment. I understand this as a former criminal prosecutor myself. But tell me, with your transfer, was there any pressure on you at that time?

Okishev: - No. They only asked what I thought about a transfer. And I had no arguments to say no. Klinov was against my departure, but he had to carry out the Procurator General's orders. And so I was transferred to the position of deputy head of an investigation department.

Proshkin: - But getting back to the Dyatlov incident expedition. Who photographed the bodies at the scene?

Okishev: - The scene investigator. I don't know details how this work was organised, this was done either by himself or someone under his guidance.

Proshkin: - And what about weather conditions as of the time of the incident, were they studied?

Okishev: - Surely! I remember low temperature and piercing wind were mentioned. There was such a document in the file.

Proshkin: - But it is missing now. And this is an important point.

Okishev: - I remember the detailed description of snow, and foot tracks on the slope. As far as I know, there was a snowfall after the tragedy. When Ivanov came back from the Pass he gave me a detailed account. We discussed possible versions together. It was clear that the Tourists left the tent in a panic and were undressed. The tent was ripped. Later Dyatlov, the group leader, was found lying closest to the tent. And then those dead matches scattered under the cedar tree in attempts to make a fire ...

Proshkin: - The closing statement on the case says that the Tourists' death was caused by forces they were unable to overcome. What hides behind this phrase?

Okishev - (*sighs heavily*) Whet else would you hear from an investigator when no version has been fully verified? With any development of the main radioactivity version being simply banned. Just look: where could radiation come from in the open?! Only tests, I am sure of that.

Proshkin: - May I ask a personal question? When you get an order to stay away, when it is explained to you that it's taboo, such words, as a rule, will only arouse interest to what really happened there? It's true, the official investigation was closed, but interest in the matter must have remained all the same? Such is human nature.

Okishev: - It is exactly for this reason that I got interested in the matter. Could there be some tests conducted? I got a clue from some nuclear specialists who mentioned the existence of a nuclear test field in one of the republics in the Caucasus. But in the late 50s a moratorium was called on nuclear tests*. Western intelligence agencies knew about that test field and kept an eye on it. Ivanov and I then suggested that tests might have been moved to the North Urals. The same mountainous terrain, with neither people, nor inhabited areas for 100-150 kilometres around. I asked the above nuclear specialist (I don't remember his name now), do you admit tests could be conducted at the time of the moratorium. He smiles and says: "look, let's not discuss that, I have no right to talk about such things".

> *\* In 1958, the USSR, USA and Great Britain entered into a nuclear weapons testing moratorium which was observed during 1959, 1960 and the first six months of 1961 until in the middle of 1961 it was violated by Khrushchev.*

Proshkin: - Maybe he refused to talk because he himself participated in violating the moratorium? There was a situation when, at one stage, I stood at the head of a group investigating events in 1993. In particular, we investigated the Ostankino incident in which many people were killed. Reportedly, first there was a shot made from a grenade gun, and then the "Knights" group (trl; special forces) started shooting at people. When we examined the scene we understood that there was no shooting from a grenade gun. If it were so, this would have caused much greater destruction. A "Knights" man was killed then, he was posthumously awarded the Title of Hero of Russia. Then we drew specialists into our investigation. Once when we relaxed and had a drink together, a specialist from the Ministry of the Interior suddenly says, "you know I was in Ostankino at that time, and I know of the death of a soldier from an explosion of some special weapon. The said "Knights" had just come back from the North Caucasus bringing their special weapons with them. I know what had exploded there but cannot tell you what". When I tried to press on him to tell more, he refused point-blank. Just can't talk, and that's that!

But let's get back to the Dyatlov theme. At a glance the case suggests a complex set of questions; there is no case number, it lacks expert examination reports and other procedural instruments. It is unclear who investigated the matter. Tempalov initiates the investigation and then we see him being interrogated himself. How can that be? I have a feeling that case papers had been thoroughly "tidied up".

Okishev: - Sure! It can't be called a criminal case in the full sense of the word, it is only scraps left over and raising no suspicion. No conclusion can be based on such fragments. Hackwork, nothing else. An awful example of an investigation case. It's worlds different from what we had done then, like night and day.

Proshkin: - But there is an inventory list for the case compiled by Ivanov! Does it mean that Ivanov was making a list of an already sanitized case?

Okishev: - He did what his superiors told him to do, and the case had to look exactly so. What else could he do?

Proshkin: - But there's also the Oblast Prosecutor's signature under the statement. Was he aware of its content? It might well be that he just signed without looking.

Okishev: - Oh no. We finalised the text of the statement together. We were both bound hand and foot. All we had to do is close the case, having nine dead bodies left and without knowledge of what had caused their deaths. We go to prosecutor Klinov and ask him, do you agree to close the case the way we are doing it, putting the blame on the administration for negligence? He only lifts hands in dismay: there's no alternative. I can only add this; should I meet such an investigator in another situation, I would kick him out for a statement like this. Dead bodies in the case, and the blame for them being put on the people having absolutely no relation to them. Can you imagine how painful it was for Ivanov and me to carry out Urakov's order? At the height of the work we get a slap on the wrist.

Klinov calls us and says; round it off, orders must be executed, without discussion. It was at that moment that we put in this phrase about a "compelling elemental force".

Proshkin: - I read in reminiscences that on 25 February one of the fliers saw a tent at the pass, and that practically near it, two bodies lay in the snow. One of them had long black hair, presumably it was a woman.

Okishev: - I am a former flier myself and I know well how one may be visually mistaken. Once, when I was getting near the airfield, looking down from the altitude of 300 m (the first approach circle) I had a feeling that we were at 10 metres, not 300. Low enough to jump down! Such was the illusion. I therefore suggest that the flier might be mistaken in his eye estimation of the distance between bodies and tent.

Proshkin: - I wonder about one thing. From the first moments of the search there are 5 to 6 radio-telegrams every day filed in the case. But exactly on the 25th when the flier had reportedly seen the dead bodies, there are none. While the same are present for the 24th and 26th. How can that be?

Okishev: - I don't remember such details.

Proshkin: - Back to radioactivity. I am sure the terrain was then checked for radiological contamination. But that was done outside the framework of this particular criminal case.

Okishev: - No doubt!

Proshkin: - Because at that time the word "radiation" itself was pronounced ... with awe!

Okishev: - And not just this. Suppose there had been some tests, then every piece of evidence had to be cleared out. Prompt measures had to be taken. I wouldn't exclude some special orders coming from the top. And the same top people might have introduced their amendments. Ivanov

159

and I came to understand this when the question of secrecy arose. So, our theory concerning presence of a test field may appear to be true.

Proshkin: - Tell me, in your days as an Investigator, can you name any other criminal cases taken for investigation from the Sverdlovsk Oblast to the Federal Public Prosecutor's office, or even that of the USSR?

Okishev: - No, nothing of the kind. In my long practice the Dyatlov case was the only one ever taken to Moscow. We can only guess how much importance was attached to it."

END OF DISCUSSION BETWEEN THE TWO MEN

After his meeting with Evgeny Okishev, Leonid Proshkin met up with the two journalists from the *Komsomolskaya Pravda* later on to give his impressions:

> *"Proshkin: - I am sure Evgeny Fyodorovich has told us almost all he remembered. But still there was something he kept back. As a former criminal prosecutor myself I asked him many procedural questions. He gave clear-cut answers, adding details, but when I asked him why the case had no number, he looked slightly at a loss and could not give a definite answer. There is not a single document in the case that could point to who was carrying out the investigation. That is, we have Ivdel prosecutor Tempalov instituting the criminal proceedings. And that is clear. Some investigative actions are carried out by Ivdel investigator Korotaev. And that is clear, too. Although he must have been included in the investigation team, and the case should have carried some notice of that. But there is none. Furthermore, the investigation on the case is being carried out by Oblast criminal prosecutor Ivanov. That makes sense, but is such be the case that he takes over further processing, there must be notice of him being included in the investigation team, while the latter, judging*

160

*from the documents in the file, had not been formed at all (!). Note, the case was under control of the Federal or even the USSR Prosecutor's office. There was attention to it at the regional party committee level, too. It is worth noting that at that time the party committee was the top administrative organ in the Oblast. Therefore such procedural omissions are absolutely unexplainable. Or rather, they may be explained by one fact: the whole case is a fake. And one more interesting aspect. The Ivdel prosecutor opens up and then investigates the case. Then he gets interrogated as a witness, and after that continues the investigative actions. This is not permissible, absolutely. A person can never appear as a prosecutor, an investigator and a witness at one and the same time. I got an impression that as the investigation was going on everything had been clear well beforehand. People continued working but someone else had already decided that all necessary materials would be extracted to another case, leaving the remaining part as a dummy. The more so, there is one curious procedural moment to which Evgeny Fyodorovich has given a good answer. Here we have an order on institution of criminal proceedings into the fact of the deaths of the Dyatlov group. But the order on closing down the investigation refers not to the death of people but to neglectful bureaucratic actions of the UPI workers. It also mentions that the Tourists had become victims of an unnamed force. Okishev wrote those lines together with Ivanov, the closing statement was approved by the Oblast Public Prosecutor Klinov. In answer to my question about such formulation he said, "We realized that it was wrong to close the case this way. The death of the Tourists had remained under-investigated but we had no alternative." I understand and am absolutely sure that prosecutors of that time would not have written SUCH a statement for no particular reason. They deserve credit because they did not fear to write such a statement and did not write lies. While they had been under pressure, there is no doubt about it."*

### END OF LEONID PROSHKIN'S COMMENTS

There are several interesting points to come out of both interviews. The journalist mentions a bomb being dropped in the wrong place and how that would be a disgrace for the government that would have to be covered up. Okishev, however, refuses to be drawn and he doesn't mention the exact nature of the deaths. He does agree to the suggestion that radiation may be involved due to the colour of the skin of the deceased. Although Okishev mentions the last four bodies and nature of the injuries, he does not dwell on them too long. In particular one would have expected Okishev to say something in detail about the injuries to Luda and Zolotarev. Is it possible he already knew exact details or had guessed they had died in a blast and he didn't want to draw too much attention to that aspect of the mystery? He does say that the students may have walked into a test field and may have been injured by missile fragments or something similar.

Among the oddities mentioned by both Okishev and Proshkin is the presence of Sverdlovsk Oblast Prosecutor Klinov at the autopsy in Ivdel. Klinov was in overall charge and therefore the boss of both Okishev and Ivanov. Klinov approved the final statement made by Okishev and Ivanov. The fact that both Ivanov and Okishev were senior men with long experience in their jobs makes it all the more strange as to why Klinov should have thought it necessary to officially approve of their final conclusions and statement. Klinov would have been mindful of the instruction from Urakov to close the case and wanted to be sure there was nothing contentious in the closing statement.

Okishev also assures the interviewers that Artukyov (Ortukyov) told him that he knew nothing about any military exercises or missile launches in the area of the Pass. Artukyov (Ortukyov) was a Colonel attached to UPI for military liaison, but he would not have been privy to any secret exercises going on in the northern Urals, especially if it was a branch of the Air Force or anything nuclear-related which was involved, such was the nature of the compartmentalisation of information in the Soviet military. Even if he had managed to find out what was going on unofficially through his contacts, he would have been very wise to keep

162

this information to himself. Further on in his interview Okishev says that possibly even the head of the Urals Military District (UMD) may not have known about secret tests in the northern Urals. So if the head of the UMD would possibly not have known about such tests then it can be taken as fairly certain that a mere Colonel attached to a University in that district would not have known. It is unlikely that the head of the UMD would not have known what was going on. The UMD has since merged with the Volga MD and has now become the Central MD, but the position as head of the UMD was always held by a senior army figure and at one point after the War the position was held for six years by Soviet war hero, Marshal Georgy Zhukov. Stalin had wanted Zhukov out of the limelight in Moscow and the position was beneath his capabilities. However, being head of the Urals MD was by no means an insignificant position. The commander of the UMD at the time of the Dyatlov expedition was General Dmitry Danilovich Lelyushenko. His headquarters was less than half a mile from the Urals Polytechnic that the Dyatlov group set out from. Lelyushenko was a highly regarded and much respected former Soviet tank commander. It was largely due to Lelyushenko's aggressive moves that Hitler's Operation *Typhoon* was blunted before Moscow. After further action at Stalingrad, Lelyushenko also led the last major action by the allies in Europe during the Second World War when his forces crushed Nazi resistance in Prague on 5 May 1945. So Lelyushenko was a tough, no nonsense veteran with plenty of authority. In 1959, the year of the Dyatlov deaths, he was promoted to the rank of General of the Army and was twice awarded the title of Hero of the Soviet Union. The possibility that any secret military exercises or tests would have been going on in his area of command without his knowledge is highly unlikely.

Proshkin also points out the anomaly of Ivdel prosecutor Tempalov acting as a prosecutor, investigator and a witness at the same time, which was highly irregular. Proshkin was probably very close to the truth when he said that his impression was that, although the investigation had started, behind the scenes the outcome had already been decided. He also refers to the fact that many of the relevant materials had been withdrawn from the "public" investigation and that the "real" investigation was going on behind the scenes. This would certainly account for the lack of a case number on the front of the file of the materials that are available for public consumption.

One query raised by Proshkin for which no adequate explanation was forthcoming is the fact that there is no record of the radio message about the sighting of the tent and two bodies sent by Gennady Patrushev on 25 February 1959, whereas the messages sent on the 24 and 26 February are available in the records. He pointed out that on each day, there appeared to be on average five to six messages a day but on the 25 February 1959, there were none.

It can be mentioned here that at the annual Dyatlov Conference held at the Ural Federal University (UFU - formerly UPI) in February 2014, some women were present who had been running the communications centre (as students) at UPI for the Dyatlov search operation in 1959. They described the closing down of their section when one day some "stern" looking men in uniform appeared and confiscated all paperwork and told them their job was over.

The interview with Evgeny Okishev shows that when the last four bodies were finally found, it was apparent that something very unusual had happened. However, the question must be asked – did they know anything before the arrival of Deputy Prosecutor General Urakov from Moscow? He (Okishev) mentions the fact that Klinov was present at the autopsies of the first five bodies in Ivdel and points out that this was highly unusual, particularly as Ivdel is 400 miles away from Sverdlovsk (644km). Why would Klinov have felt the need to go up there while the autopsies were being carried out, unless he had previous knowledge of some kind? Whilst Okishev was being fairly open in his interview with the *Komsomolskaya Pravda* journalists and his discussion with Leonid Proshkin, Proshkin himself points out that he felt Okishev was holding something back. In particular he mentioned the lack of a case number which supports the view that the real case file is elsewhere and that the one for public consumption is just a dummy as has long been suspected by many observers of the Dyatlov story.

The arrival in Sverdlovsk of the Deputy General Prosecutor of the USSR - Deputy Prosecutor General Urakov is of great significance. The fact that one of the most powerful men in the Soviet legal system arrives from Moscow to deal with an accident to nine skiers and takes away the case files with him seems highly unusual. He appears to have no interest in what they had to tell him about the course of the investigation and before he leaves, he instructs them (Klinov, Okishev and Ivanov) to say that the deaths were due to an accident. It is worth repeating here what Okishev said about Urakov's visit;

> *Urakov came to meet with us and gave orders that we were to all tell anyone who asked that the tourists' death was an accident. Urakov evaded all our direct questions about tests of armaments. I mean, he did not deny this version, but simply avoided direct answers. What's more, Urakov took absolutely no interest in the course of our investigation, as if the picture of the scene was absolutely clear to him already. He, however, took the case away with him. With that, our investigation came to an end. Just imagine: at the very height of the investigation, when dead bodies with strange injuries have just been found, the case is being taken away!*

Okishev also says that in all his years as a prosecutor, this was the only one which involved a high ranking official arriving from Moscow and taking the case away with him. Would the second most powerful man in the Soviet legal system have bothered to travel from Moscow to Sverdlovsk if the Dyatlov group had died in an avalanche? A simple murder case involving locals? A wind vortex of some kind causing them to wander down the mountain to their deaths? Murder by escaped prisoners or locals (Mansi) etc, etc? It would have been more or less an open and shut case of murder or death by misadventure.

Urakov reported directly to the chief prosecutor of the USSR, Procurator General, Roman Rudenko. Rudenko was from the Ukraine and not a man known for tender mercies. He had been the chief Soviet prosecutor at the Nuremburg trials and was the chief prosecutor in the trial of pilot Gary Powers. He had also been commandant of NKVD (The forerunners of the KGB) Special Camp No 7 at Weesow (later moved to Sachenhausen) where approximately 12,500 German prisoners and people sentenced by Soviet military tribunals, died of malnutrition and disease. Rudenko was also the judge who handed down the death sentence to former secret police chief, Lavrenti Beria at his trial. With people like this in the background, it can be understood that Ivanov, Okishev and Klinov and the local Sverdlovsk Communist Party hierarchy would be keen to be seen to follow orders.

# Chapter 12

Whilst the progress of the book has been to look at a military accident involving somehow the lights in the night sky, there are other theories that are worth looking at. Among the other main theories is that of the Mansi. People who look at this, seem to fall into two groups; that the Mansi were directly connected to the deaths of the group or the complete opposite view, that there is no way they could have been responsible, directly or indirectly. It is one theory that is endlessly chewed over and discussed.

Perhaps the main view put forward by many is that the Mansi could not have been responsible for the Dyatlov group deaths because they (the Mansi) appeared friendly and were well disposed towards the search for the missing members of the Dyatlov Group. In other words, the Mansi were "too nice" to have been involved in the deaths. Despite all the talk of the Mansi being well disposed towards Russians, even if they were, any group will contain one or more individuals who don't follow the norms of that group. To say that "all Mansi were nice people" would be about as factually correct as saying "all Welsh people are good singers" or "all Frenchmen are great lovers" etc. It is true that the Mansi knew the area better than anyone and were able to offer guidance and support as well as using their dogs in the search and that help seemed to be willingly given. At the time of the searches for the missing group members, the impression given by the relations between the Mansi and the authorities, represented by the search parties and investigators, was one of friendly cooperation between near equals. However, it is worth going back to around 15 years or so before the Great Patriotic War (World War II) against the Nazis to see how relations developed between the Mansi and the state.

This was a period of repression and is probably most remembered for the crackdown on the *Kulaks*, the better off peasants who became among the first victims of the government's attempts to collectivise agriculture which started in earnest in 1929. At around the same time the authorities identified various groups they viewed as threats to the state. These included Germans, Finns, Swedes, Turks and a number of similar ethnic groups who were all mercilessly repressed with thousands arrested and either imprisoned for lengthy periods or shot. This was followed in the late 1930s by what historian, Robert Conquest called 'The Great Terror' when virtually nobody was safe from Stalin's paranoia.

During this period of repression, ethnic tribes, such as the Mansi, who lived in remote areas, came under scrutiny. The attitude towards the Mansi was not the same as the targeted groups, who were alleged to be a threat to the Soviet system. Nevertheless, although officially they were known as 'Indigenous Peoples', they (the Mansi) were viewed by some as 'Natives' or 'Aborigines' to be educated and brought more into the Soviet system. Others viewed them, less charitably, as simply 'Savages'. The main political power in the northern native lands was the state-run *Committee of the North* and the native regional executive committees (known as *Tuzrik*) which were responsible for carrying out reforms in these areas. It is true however, that up until this period, the Mansi generally led their lives as they had always done with little interference. With the arrival of Communism, the aim was to integrate the natives of the northern areas into the new economic and political structures that the state foresaw for the future. The way they intended to do this was through education and accordingly by 1934, a total of 15 'Culture Centres' were set up right across the remote northern areas of Russia within the native areas. For the Mansi, the Culture Centre was set up at Sosva, approximately 80kms (50 miles) to the South East of Serov, where the Dyatlov group had changed trains and spent the most of the day on 24 January, before they departed for Ivdel.

There was another Culture Centre set up at Kazym to serve the neighbouring Khanty and Forest Nenets tribal areas to the east of the Mansi. Each Culture Centre had a boarding school for the tribal children and each Centre was expected to contain up to 250 workers who could travel out into the surrounding areas. These workers included vets, teachers, doctors, party workers and it could be said that it was organised in the same way Christian missionaries took the Gospel to African or Pacific native peoples. The Communists, of course, had deep hostility to any kind of religion but the methods they were using here were the same as the Christian missionaries. Many of the Centres had ethnographers to study the languages and ways of the locals, but even here, the identification of 'class enemies' needed to be taken into account and *Kulaks* identified. A Mansi tribesman who possessed a herd of between 200 to 300 reindeer was considered rich by the authorities and therefore a *Kulak*. Along with the outreach into the native lands, the natives were forced into *Kolkhozes* (cooperatives/collectives) in keeping with what was going on in the rest of Russia.

Part of the problem was that many of the 'enforcers' of the collectivisation were rough, brutal men. Most were Red Army veterans and several were Siberians but from a Cossack background and many had developed a taste for pushing people around. This was apparent in the way that confiscations were made. Whilst the process of Collectivisation was going on, if they decided that a tribesman had a gun, dogs or geese he shouldn't have, it was confiscated whether or not the tribesman was supposedly a rich *Kulak* or not.

So, all in all, the Culture Centre in Sosva became Moscow's 'face' to the Mansi. There were two things that were most definitely not welcome at the Culture Centre and the outreach workers and that was the Mansi way of worship of the natural world and the Mansi Shamans. There were two types of Shamans; the first could carry out the functions of a Shaman (usually under the influence of Fly Algarics) and connect to the spirit world and the second type were basically fortune tellers. Oddly enough, despite the lower status of women, a woman could be a Shaman.

The Mansi incorporated all natural elements into their worship of the world around them (Mikhail Petrov)

Despite the deeply embedded way the Mansi worshipped the land and the associated spirits of water, land and the sky, these were viewed by the authorities as superstitious rubbish to be eradicated as quickly as possible. The Shamans were viewed as much an enemy of the people as the *Kulaks* were, and they had their political rights taken away and were repressed. There was also a concerted campaign to ridicule the Shamans with, for example, children's skittles games with Shaman figures for skittles to be knocked over. There is plenty of evidence of the official disdain the Shamans were held in, although there were some stories which were probably exaggerations. Some studies on the repression of Shamans in the Soviet Far East mention Shamans being taken up in helicopters and thrown out and told to fly. Another story concerned a KGB officer who lured Shamans to a remote area under the pretence he was ill and he needed the services of a Shaman to help cure him. Once they turned up, he shot them dead, disposed of the body and kept the Shaman's drum they were carrying as a souvenir. The KGB was formed in 1954 so this would have taken place after this date and helicopters were not in general Soviet use until the 1950s. While these stories may or may not be true, it gives a good idea of the contempt the authorities had for Shamans and by extension, the tribes they came from.

Once the authorities began to impose more and more on the way of life of the Mansi, it was only a matter of time before there was friction. The schools for children was one source and another was the seeming interference in the habits of the Mansi, such as encouraging them to be more hygienic and to use *Banyas* (Saunas). Improvements to health issues were also introduced including better medical care and facilities for childbirth. Veterinary care in the form of reindeer husbandry and research into reindeer diseases was also introduced.

One of the main problems which arose from all these changes is that they were presented as Russian 'improvements' to the Mansi way of life. Despite all the positives about the way the Culture Centres and the veterinary workers appeared in the Mansi lands, the 'help' was offered in a way that didn't brook a refusal. The 'help' came along the lines of the saying used for new conscripts to the Red Army - "If you can't, we'll show you. If you won't, we'll make you."

The effect of this intrusion into the way of life of the various tribes led to deep resentment by many of them. There is an account of a female geologist being tied up and thrown into a lake in the 1930s by Mansi tribesmen. Other than a brief mention of it in some Dyatlov Incident accounts, details of this murder seem to be non-existent, which is not to say that it didn't happen and the details have not come to light yet. It is more than likely that this incident is based on an event in the Kazym uprising (*see below*) in nearby tribal lands close to the Mansi.

Conflict between the peoples of remote areas and the central authority was not new. The idea of a great white chief rising up and leading an uprising to conquer Moscow was popular throughout all the indigenous tribes in Siberia since an uprising in the mid-19th Century. Some tribes reacted more violently than others. In the neighbouring Khanty tribal areas to the east of the Mansi, there was serious trouble. It started with a raid by Khanty and the Forest Nenets tribesmen who went to the school at the Kazym Culture Centre to take back 43 of their 48 children who had been taken there by the authorities in the autumn of 1931. In the two years that followed, a number of tribal elders and leaders were eliminated from

Soviet elections, followed by the arrest of four Shamans in March 1933. With the discontent growing, what really set the violence off, was a visit by to Lake Num-To by representatives from the Culture Centre at Kazym. Lake Num-To (known as *Heavenly Lake* literally translated as *Sky - the Lake*) was close to the upper course of several tributaries of the River Ob and was held to be sacred by the local Khanty and Forest Nenets people. It was only used by them for sacrifices. When the representatives from the Culture Centre arrived there on 26 November 1933, they started fishing despite being told by the local tribesmen that the lake was sacred and nobody was allowed to fish there. There was a female Communist activist in the group named Polina Shnaider. She wanted to travel to an island (known as *Saint Island* to the locals) on Lake Num-To. She was told it was taboo for women to go onto the island as it was a sacred area. She went anyway. It is believed by some Mansi scholars that what happened to Polina Shnaider has morphed into the story of the female geologist being tied up by the Mansi and thrown into a lake and drowned.

The action by Polina Shnaider in ignoring the sensitivities of the local people by still travelling out to the island on the lake after she had been told it was forbidden, would appear to be crass insensitivity. The Khanty and Forest Nenets tribespeople would have seen it this way but it must be remembered that she was a Communist Party activist representing the central authorities. The central authorities had stipulated that these superstitions were to be completely stamped out and that as far as they were concerned, this was an island in the middle of a lake that anyone, including women, could travel to if they so wished. It was the setting for a physical clash of ideologies which would cost Polina Shnaider her life, along with the propaganda team she was with. After her trip to the island, the propaganda team moved from the Lake into the Taiga and just over a week later, on 4 December 1933, they were taken prisoner by the locals. The conditions set for their release was an impossible list of demands which the authorities would in no way agree to. Part of the problem was that the locals had no real idea of the power they were up against and so it proved. The demands for the release of the prisoners included; a ban on fishing in Lake Num-To, the release of the arrested Shamans, the restoration of voting rights to both Shamans and *Kulaks*, abolition of taxes on richer natives, termination of reindeer confiscation and forced labour for the Kazym Culture Centre, free fish and fur trade, the closing of all trading posts in the Tundra, a demand that their children no longer attend the boarding school at the Culture Centre in Kazym, that natives should not have to appear in court outside the tribal area and finally a demand that all Russians leave Kazym. There was only ever going to be one answer to such a list of demands, but before that, an extraordinary event took place. A gathering of local Shamans held a ritual in which they said that the Gods had demanded an offering of the captured propaganda team that was being held prisoner. In other words, they were to be sacrificed. The whole group was tied up and taken to a hill on sleds. When they arrived on the hill, they were all strangled with a long rope in the same way that reindeer were sacrificed. After the murders, seven reindeer were also sacrificed and a traditional ceremony was held. Retribution was not long in coming and a few weeks later, state security troops arrived in the area. There was a small skirmish in which several of the tribesmen were killed and many arrested. A number were released, but trials were still held with most sentenced to long terms of imprisonment and eleven of the tribesmen were sentenced to death. The death sentences were commuted to 20 years imprisonment on appeal. Most of them died due to the harsh conditions in the prisons. It was a salutary lesson and an unfortunate by-product of this episode was that all the men imprisoned were unable to provide for their families, which resulted in several women and children suffering from starvation.

The odd thing about the repression of the Shamans is that in 1936, they had their civic rights restored, followed by further easing of the restrictions at the end of the war and the post-war period with the Constitution allowing religious freedom. Despite this, the official view of the Communist Party was that religion was based on superstition and was to be eventually eradicated. Stalin had called a halt to the persecution during the War because he needed national unity and in 1944 a council was set up to handle the affairs of 'Religious Cults' which in reality, meant keeping a close eye on what the natives were up to. The Russian Orthodox Church had its own council. In practice, what this meant was that if state officials wanted to treat the Mansi or any of the other tribes any way they liked, they were free to do so.

From 1936 onwards, the attention of the state seemed to turn more to the economic exploitation of the northern areas.

Coming back to the Dyatlov group in 1959, despite the Mansi showing goodwill by assisting in the search, the local Mansi did not have to look too far to see what they would be dealing with for any displays of hostility towards the state. Sitting on their virtual doorstep was the Ivdel Gulag with its sub camps and groups of guarded prisoners working in the forest areas through which the Mansi lived and hunted. Whether or not the Mansi turned a blind eye to what was going on, they could not help but notice the harsh treatment doled out to the prisoners over the preceding years despite the supposed running down of these camps by 1959.

Another aspect of the openness and willingness of the Mansi to help was shown by the arrival in Ivdel of the three Mansi representatives from the area to meet Prosecutor Yevgeny Okishev, albeit at his summons. After the meeting, Okishev ruled the tribespeople out as possibly being complicit in the deaths (*see chapter 11*).

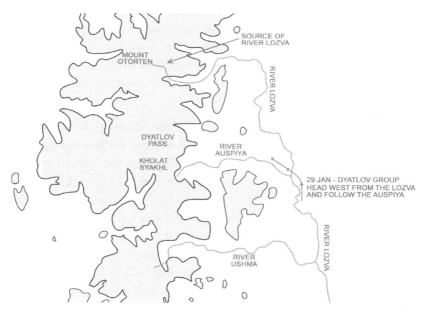

Map showing the region of the upper Lozva and the point at which the Dyatlov group turned west from the Lozva along the Auspiya
(BHARDWAZ – Fiverr)

Once the search for the missing Dyatlov group had started, the local Mansi were visited and questioned. There were three Mansi clans, the Bahtiyarov clan, the Anyamov Clan and the Kurikov Clan living in the approximate area of the latter part of the Dyatlov group's journey. They were questioned as to what they had seen and heard rather than being accused of anything that may have been done to the members of the group. What came out in the statements of the members of these clans was a curious mix of statements. Among these was a statement by one of the Bahtiyarov Clan who said that the prayer mountain was located in the upper Vizhai River area and anyone could go there including Mansi. He also said that there were not that many religious Mansi and his interesting statement that (surprisingly) there were no other sacred Mansi places in the area, was not correct. There was a prayer pit in the area of the upper Lozva River and the upper Lozva also contained water spirits which were sacred to the Mansi. Even if Petr Bahtiyarov, who had made this statement, put himself in the group of non-religious Mansi, he must surely have known about the prayer pit and the water spirits. Despite the groups of Clans living apart from each other, they were still relatively close knit. Petr Bahtiyarov had even less reason to claim a lack of knowledge about sacred places in the area because there had been a Shaman within his Clan who had been arrested and imprisoned in 1938 for Shamanic activities as well as for falling into the class of being a *Kulak*. Rather than appearing to have something to hide, it is more likely that he was being vague as he wished to distance himself from any problems, knowing what the official view was of anything to do with Shamans and places of worship. It is curious, though, that there was no mention by anyone of the water spirits that resided in the upper Lozva and that women were forbidden to go on the banks on that part of the river, notwithstanding the fact it was frozen over at the time of the Dyatlov group's journey.

In the search for the missing Dyatlov group, Mansi Stepan Kurikov was reputedly a Shaman and it should be stressed here that his status as a Shaman would have meant little to the Russians in the search parties. Whilst they found his help of use in the search, there would have been a few who looked upon him with some derision in line with Communist Party ideals, which still saw Shamanism as superstitious and anti-scientific.

So, what could have driven a group of Mansi to the extent that they were prepared to kill and invite possible severe punishment on the Mansi tribe by doing so? In addition to the suppression of the ways of their immediate descendants, many of whom would still be alive to remember what happened in the 1930s, there was also the increasing search for oil and minerals by the state. The search for minerals and oil took no account of Mansi sensibilities.

The Mansi and their ancestors had lived in the region for Centuries. With the coming of the Communists and the push for industrialisation with its demand for resources, the Mansi had seen their tribal lands walked over, driven over, dug up and exploited in every way possible with the attendant pollution and despoiling of the land, rivers and lakes. It is inconceivable that some of the Mansi were not outraged at what they saw happening to their ancestral lands. Tied in with the despoiling of the land was the desecration of revered holy sites by outsiders entering them and ignoring any formalities associated with those sites. For instance, a sacred mountain would have strict boundaries which could not be crossed for any reason. If a Mansi was hunting an animal and the animal passed over the boundary onto a sacred mountain, the hunt had to stop immediately and the animal could not be pursued. Despite the fact that these ways were passing into history by 1959, there were still many Mansi who respected the ways of their ancestors even if they didn't strictly observe the formalities. There were also still a number of older Mansi who did follow the practices and traditions of worship and respect for the natural world around them.

The theory about the Mansi being responsible for the deaths, centres on the women in the Dyatlov group, Luda and Zina, transgressing onto the Mansi sacred mountain of Kholat Syakhl. It has to be said that women occupied a particular place in Mansi society which was of lesser status to men. For example, females could not be in a physical position that was higher to men. This is one of the reasons that led to the Kazym uprising (*See above*) as the female children who were boarding at the Culture Centre slept on a higher floor to the males. Another example is that it was considered shameful for a female to step over a male Mansi who might be lying or sleeping on the ground. Also some Mansi dwellings had attics where sacred items for worship were kept and females were not allowed to go, not just because of any sacred items but also by being in the attic, would place a female in a higher position than a male who might be below.

In relation to sacred areas, there were some where no male or female Mansi could go, but there were other places where men could go but women could not. Additionally, there were some sacral places where both sexes could go but each had to approach in different ways. While the argument continues about whether Kholat Syakhl was sacred not, there was something in the area that was considered sacred by the Mansi and that was the upper reaches of the River Lozva. The Lozva was frozen at the time the Dyatlov group were making their way towards their destination, but they followed its course for part of their journey. On the route that the Dyatlov group took, they were close to two rivers which contained water spirits. The head of the Vizhai River contained a water spirit and water spirits were said to reside in sections of the upper Lozva, close to Mount Otorten. In Mansi tradition, the upper Lozva, in particular, needed to be treated with great respect and approached in different ways and separately by men and women.

The Mansi would have been aware of who was in or travelling through their territory at any one time. It is quite possible that the Dyatlov group were observed making their way up the Lozva with the assumption that they were heading towards the upper reaches of the Lozva near Mount Otorten. The scenario that a small group of armed Mansi may have been aware that the Dyatlov group have been not far from the upper reaches of the Lozva and feeling that enough was enough of constant transgressions on their land, could have pushed them over the edge into doing something about it. It is a possibility as the theory suggests, that a group of Mansi may have watched the Dyatlov party pitch their tent near the ridge on Kholat Syakhl and then later forced them out of the tent and down the mountain at gunpoint. The group may have been left with the threat they would be shot if they tried to make their way back to the tent would have forced the group to try and make shelter as best they could in the conditions. The finding of the bodies of Zina, Rustem and Igor Dyatlov in a line as if heading back to the tent, could well be construed that they felt it safe to return, but didn't make it.

After the Dyatlov deaths, it could be argued that the restriction of permits (ie the closing down of the area for four years) to go into this area was done by the authorities as a gesture towards the Mansi to stop travellers and others tramping through their areas and disrespecting their way of life. It may well be, although the evidence doesn't really back it up, considering what had happened in the Polina Shnaider case in 1934 and the view the authorities had towards religion in 1934 and in 1959. It certainly didn't stop the central authorities from continuing to exploit Mansi lands for minerals and oil. A process which accelerated from the 1960s onwards, in one case in 1973 using an underground nuclear device in the area for exploration purposes.

The above scenario that the Mansi could have been responsible for the Dyatlov group deaths has its flaws like every other theory out there. It does not explain the only nine sets of footprints leading down the mountain to the tree line and more importantly, it does not explain the serious injuries suffered by Zolotarev and Luda. There are attempts to 'shoehorn' these injuries to fit the theory by saying that could have been caused by blows or by falling onto a rock, but to me they have been caused by a tremendous localised force like that from a blast. The footprints anomaly could be explained by the Mansi approaching the tent from another direction, possibly from the Auspiya valley or from over the ridge behind the tent, forcing the group at gunpoint down to the treeline and then after a time making their (the Mansi) way back from where they had come. Had they approached from over the ridge behind the tent, the prevailing winds would have removed footprints from both sides of the top of the ridge in the time period before the tent was discovered.

It does not necessarily answer all the questions but what this theory does do, is to give some of the Mansi who felt strongly enough about it, a motive for their actions.

# Chapter 13

*I*ntuitive Communication / Remote Viewing /Mediums is another area that people either agree or disagree with. There is no doubt that some people have these skills and the Police in the USA and Europe have used them, sometimes successfully and other times not so successfully.

I was contacted by a remote viewer from the USA who had earlier (in 2014) carried out an *Intuitive Communication* with Luda. This is what he has concluded and what follows is entirely the words and work of *Intuitive Communicator* Bill Ohm:-

## KHOLAT SYAKHL

$$\bigcap_{i=1}^{9} S_i = \, ?$$

Keith and others wanted the case reopened. It was originally denied. Keith informed us on 1 February 2019, the 60th anniversary of the Dyatlov Pass Incident, that the case would be reopened.

Below is part of the foreword in *Mountain of the Dead (The Dyatlov Pass Incident)* which was written by Keith McCloskey.

Foreword

...

...

The core of the mystery is not so much how the various members of the party died, but what caused them to flee from the safety of their tent in what appears to have been blind panic, for their lives.

...

...

The real problem is that there is very little evidence to go on, everything is conjecture.

...

...

The only thing certain is that nine young people in the prime of their lives died dreadful deaths and, like the Marie Celeste, it is probably that the truth of what actually happened will never be known for sure.

Consider the statements below:

There are no mysteries in the universe. What is a mystery to one life form might not be a mystery to another life form. We need only to consider the Golden State Killer, Jimmy Hoffa, JFK, or the reason that a male teen who ran along the perimeter of a soccer field collapsed and died.

Suppose that you were eight years old when the hikers passed on Kholat Syakhl. You might be alive today, which is 1 February 2019. Suppose on 1 February 1959 you are 20 years old. You know what happened on Kholat Syakhl. You might be alive today. Also older people can tell younger people about this case.

...

...

My point of view is as follows:

*Some people at the present time do not understand the events that occurred on Kholat Syakhl on 1 February 1959. But, these events were known by someone.*

*We did an Intuitive Communication (IC) on 28 July 2014. At this time, Lyudmila Dubinina provided information, which provided insight, at least for us, about the events that occurred on 1 February 1959. Since the above IC we often thought about the same type of communication with the other eight hikers. Finally, we decided to do this. We needed a name and a photograph of each hiker.*

*Keith sent these to us.*

*We hope that the results provide at least the following:*

- *They provide additional insight about the events that occurred on 1 February 1959.*

- *They provide the family members of the hikers with some closure.*

*On 1 February 1959, 9 hikers camped on Kholat Syakhl. Each passed that night or early 2 February 1959. Before the hikers passed, each experienced a set of events.*

*Consider any of the 9 hikers. This hiker experienced an infinite number of events prior to their death. We are interested in a subset of these events. What is this subset?*

*Each hiker experienced a finite number of main events. The key is main event. A main event is an event that is used to explain what happened on Kholat Syakhl on 1 February 1959 at the tent. In particular, what are the main events that will answer the first statements in the Foreword above.*

*Let $S_1, S_{2...}, S_9$ be sets. Each Set contains the main events of a hiker. What main events are common to these sets? We establish a one-to-one correspondence between the hikers and the Sets above as follows:*

- *$S_1$; Yury Doroshenko*
- *$S_2$; Lyudmila Dubinina*
- *$S_3$; Igor Dyatlov*
- *$S_4$; Semyon Zolotarev*
- *$S_5$; Zinaida Kolmogorova*
- *$S_6$; Alexander Kolevatov*
- *$S_7$; George Krivonischenko*
- *$S_8$; Rustem Slobodin*
- *$S_9$; Nicolai Thibeaux-Brignolle*

*We proceed as follows:*

*We use the photographs that Keith sent (See the page after page 96 in Keith's book, which was mentioned above for photographs). We write only what is received. We edit scribbles. This makes them easy to understand, but the idea remains the same.*

*An IC was done for each hiker. Each IC reflects the personality of a particular hiker. An excellent example is the IC with Lyudmila.*

*We start IC with $S_1$. The IC with the others follows in the order above.*

*$S_1$: Yury Doroshenko (=Y)*

*Ug: Y, can we please communicate with you?*

*Y: Yes.*

*Ug: What happened on Kholat Syakhl on 1 February 1959, at the tent? Will you help?*

*Y: I'll gladly help. I can tell you quite a bit.*

*Ug: That would be nice. We will ask you questions. But, please feel free to add information.*

*Y: No problem.*

*Ug: Was everyone in the tent?*

*Y: Yes.*

*Ug: Was everyone asleep?*

*Y: Yes.*

*Ug: Did everyone sleep until morning?*

*Y: No, we were woken up.*

*Ug: What woke you?*

*Y: It was another hiker. He was frantic.*

*Ug: Can you tell us the events?*

*Y: Sure.*

> *He woke me. He Pointed. We heard sounds. They sounded like natives. They were talking to each other. I don't know what they said. Then the tent started moving..*

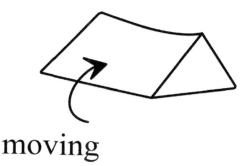

moving

*Soon there was a hole in the tent.*

*Everyone was frantic.*

*Without hesitation we slashed the opposite side of the tent.*

*Some hikers ran fast through the snow (down a slope).*

*Two males confronted outsiders. (Yury and another male hiker)*

*The outsiders were dressed with light brown (tan) coats.*

*Their heads were covered (hood).*

*They had spears. Spears were pointed at us.*

*We stood and we fought. But, two on one does not work.*

*I felt the pain as I landed. I didn't know if I could get up.*

*As far as I know, I lay flat on the ground as they stooped over me.*

*I was grabbed and I was pulled.*

*I eventually crawled with back against tree. My head slightly turned left.*

*I could feel the pain.*

*I died there.*

*Ug: Y, they were what type of people?*

*Y: Natives because of speech, strong men.*

*I could not smell anything.*

*Ug: What did their faces look like?*

*Y: Not young, eyes deep set, eye brows (small & dark).*

*Nose (sharp & pointed slowly at end).*

*Face (reddish brown).*

*Chin (might be slightly rounded).*

*One man about 5'6"*

*Other man slightly taller.*

*Weight is hard to tell (clothes).*

*Fur around edges of hood.*

*Pants (tan).*

*Boots (tan, laced, about 10"height)*

      He fought Y.

*S2: Lyudmila Dubinina (=L)*

*Ug: L, Can we please communicate with you?*

*L: Yes.*

*Ug: We IC with you before. But, we try again.*

*L: It is Okay.*

*Ug: Will you help with Kholat Syakhl on 1 February 1959?*

*L: I most certainly will.*

> It was a disastrous night. Not just for me, but for everyone.
>
> And, it need not happen. We did not offend anyone.
>
> And, some interfered with us.
>
> Why? They are totally ridiculous and stupid.
>
> Sorry. But why should I be calm?

*Ug: It is Okay.*

*L: Thanks. How do you expect me to act?*

*Ug: You're fine.*

> Are you willing to talk about why 9H left tent?

*L: Of course, it does anger me.*

*Ug: Was everyone in the tent?*

*L: As far as I know, yes.*

> *I was tired. And, I was not interested in goofing around.*
>
> *I just spent a lot of time hiking on whatever you call it.*
>
> *And, I looked forward to the end.*

*Ug: I assume that you slept?*

*L: I was "knocked out".*

*Ug: Did everyone sleep until morning?*

*L: Of course not. We were woken up by some idiots.*

*Ug: What woke you?*

*L: Yury yelled "Get the hell out of here. Hurry!"*

> *At first we did not know what to do. He yelled "Cut the damn tent!"*
>
> *I ran right through as fast as I could, away from the tent.*

*Ug: Were you with other hikers?*

*L: image*

another hiker was
not far from her

*Ug: Did anyone chase you?*

*L: Yes. And I beat the idiot as much as I could.*

> *Both arms were swinging. It was useless.*
>
> *I was pushed back. I landed in the snow.*
>
> *A man came over me. I saw a knife.*

*I blanked out.*

*Ug: Do you know what the man looked like?*

*L: I really don't know.*

*Ug: How far did you run from the tent?*

*L: It is hard to say. I ran.*

*Ug: Did "they" speak?*

*L: The man breathed hard over me. He had to catch me.*

   *When he grabbed me I fought.*

*Ug: What else can you say?*

*L: I looked down from above.*

   *I saw:*

I could see the men.
Everything was quiet.

*Ug: Is there anything else you can tell us?*

*L: I've said enough. It brings anger to me.*

   *Not only about myself, but about the others too.*

*Ug: Sorry.*

*L: Sorry about what? They were plain idiots.*

*Ug: Thank you.*

*L: You're welcome. It's not UG's fault.*

   *But, tell others who are still alive to move on.*

   *You can't change what happened.*

   *You can fantasize.*

   *But, how does one bring 9H back from the dead?*

*What can people really do?*

*Let's quit. But, common sense tells you that search, cry, anger and so on will not bring us back.*

*I always say "you dig your own hole."*

*And that is what these men did.*

*When they get in the hole, it will be covered up.*

*Bye!*

*END*

*S3: Igor Dyatlov (=I)*

*Ug: I, can we please communicate with you?*

*I: It will be fine.*

*Ug: Are you willing to discuss 1 February 1959 events on Kholat Syakhl?*

*I: It will be fine. It was a terrible event.*

*Ug: Sorry.*

*I: It is Okay.*

*Ug: Are you ready?*

*I: Sure.*

*Ug: Was everyone in the tent?*

*I: It is not like we all poured in the tent all at once. We slowly came in. It was a few minutes apart. We were glad to stop. It was a long day. Maybe not by hours, but, by use of body.*

*Ug: Did you sleep?*

*I: I definitely fell asleep. I was extremely tired. I toted a lot of stuff.*

*Ug: Did everyone sleep till morning?*

*I: The answer is definitely no. We were woken up by people outside our tent. When they attempted to get or come through tent, we were on our way out.*

*Ug: Can you explain this?*

*I: I can tell you some. Others woke me.*

> *I only know that Yury yelled, "Get the hell out of here."*

> *He rushed others out. I went too.*

*Ug: How did you get out?*

*I: The tent was already slashed. I went out the slash.*

> *Some others had already left. I'm not sure where they went.*

*Ug: When you exited the tent, what did you observe?*

*I: Yury was fighting. I went to help. It wasn't long before I landed.*

> *I turned to my right side with my hand against my face.*

> *That was the end of me.*

*Ug: Were they men?*

*I: They appeared "Eskimo" to me. They were not excessively tall. Of these I saw, they were less than average height. But, they are definitely strong.*

> *And after I landed, one acted as if to say, "I took care of him."*

> *I was not approached again.*

*Ug: Can you describe the men?*

*I: When they are bundled up, it is hard to describe. But, as I said, the men I saw were, as appeared to me, medium built and their complexions were on the dark-reddish side.*

*Ug: Did you hear a voice?*

*I: From the time that I confronted it was a fight. I heard nothing after I landed.*

*Ug: Thank you.*

*I: You're more than welcome.*

*Tell others "it just happened".*

*Ug: Will do.*

*I: Thanks.*

*Ug: Thank you.*

*Ug: Do you know the type of men?*

*I: I would be only guessing.*

*Ug: What is your instinct?*

*I: I do not think military. The same applies for other non-Earth beings.*

*From their appearance and my knowledge, I would say local people.*

*Other hikers do not do this.*

*Ug: Thanks*

*END*

*S4: Semyon Zolotarev (=S)*

*Ug: S, can we please communicate with you?*

*S: You are most welcome. I have been waiting.*

*Ug: Are you willing to discuss 1 February 1959 on Kholat Syakhl?*

*S: Sure.*

*It was a terrible event to say the least. But, it happened. We must move on.*

*This includes others. You can learn from the past. But, don't dwell on it.*

*This is my opinion. And not all people are nice.*

*Ug: Was everyone in the tent?*

*S: Definitely. 8 were in. Then the last male entered.*

*Ug: Were you asleep?*

*S: I definitely was. Tiredness was not the word. I slept like a baby.*

*Ug: What woke you?*

*S: I woke when I heard the commotion. It was in disarray. People started leaving the tent. I thought that it was crazy. But Yury yelled "Get out of here."*

*I sailed out of the tent only to see unknown men. They had "Eskimo" type clothes.*

*They were not extremely big.*

*Ug: Can you tell me about these men?*

*S: They definitely were not friendly. They had spears.*

*There was also a knife belted around the waist of a man.*

*They said nothing. Then I heard "jo mif". This was said to a man that he knew.*

*I sensed that they were talking about me.*

*Ug: What did you do?*

*S: I took off. I knew that I could not win against them.*

*Ug: What nationality were they?*

*S: From my observation (face, dress etc) I would say that they were locals.*

*Ug: Do you think that the military was involved?*

*S: If they were, it was indirectly.*

*Ug: Is there anything else?*

*S: You know. We were tired. We worked hard to get this far.*

   *It is a shame that others interfered.*

*Ug: How many men did you see?*

*S: I saw 3. Then I saw a 4th. A 5th crawled out of the tent.*

*Ug: Was tent slashed by others before you left?*

*S: I don't know. I left quickly.*

*Ug: Thanks.*

*END*

*S$_5$: Zinaida Kolmogorova (=Z)*

*Ug: Z, Will you please communicate with us?*

*Z: I first thought no. But I will.*

*Ug: Thanks. What happened on Kholat Syakhl on 1 February 1959 at the tent?*

*Z: I would like to know why it happened.*

   *I've yet to justify the events. It makes no sense to me.*

   *What were we doing that caused it?*

*Ug: We do not have an answer. Was everyone in the tent?*

*Z: Yes there were 8. The last male was slow.*

*Ug: Did everyone sleep until morning?*

*Z: No way. We only got a few hours of sleep.*

   *Then we heard noise outside the tent.*

*Ug: What did you hear?*

*Z: Men were talking. They seem to ask questions.*

*What is this? Why is this here? But, I cannot be sure.*

*Ug: Did you hear cars, airplane and so on?*

*Z: I heard only voices.*

*Ug: Did you know the language?*

*Z: It was more or less broken language. It was not strange or unusual language.*

*Ug: What is the closest language?*

*Z: It could be Indian. But it is not American Indian.*

*It was clear that they spoke it often.*

*Ug: After you heard the voices, what happened next?*

*Z: It was clear that the others were startled.*

*What should we do?*

*But, when slit occurred I saw a spear.*

*It was time to exit. No one hesitated.*

*Ug: Did you see people outside?*

*Z: I took a quick look. Then I ran through the snow.*

*I thought that the further I was, the better off I was.*

*This was not the case.*

*I always wondered: Suppose we stayed. What would happen? There are 9 of us.*

*When you spread out you are less of a threat to others.*

*Ug: What else do you think caused you and others to exit?*

*Z: It is simple. There were men outside the tent.*

*If they were friendly or had some sense they would yell (say) loudly,*

*"Who is there? Please come. We wish to talk (or something equivalent)."*

*You don't start cutting the tent.*

*Ug: Okay. Do you have anything else to say?*

*Z: Yes. I froze. It was not pleasant.*

*Why? These events were unnecessary.*

*Ug: Did you see what the other hikers did?*

*Z: I didn't stay long. The "order" was: Get the hell out of here fast.*

*Ug: Thanks.*

*Z: You're welcome. I'm glad that we talked.*

*END*

*SUMMARY: Ug, $S_1$, $S_2$, $S_3$, $S_4$, $S_5$*

*Q: What caused 9H to leave their tent on Kholat Syakhl on 1 February 1959?*

*A small group of men were outside their tent. The hikers did not think that they were friendly. As a result, they quickly exited the tent. (Two hikers fought men).*

*Ug: Was the small group of men spirits?*

*A: No. they were live humans.*

*Ug: Were they creatures who are similar to humans?*

*A: No.*

*Ug: Below is a top view.*

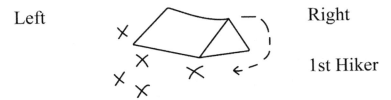

*There were 5 men (See x). One poked the side of the tent with a spear. A male hiker exited the tent. He exited right side. While the others took off through the other side. Luda came to the 1ˢᵀ hiker. She encountered a fight.*

*If you look at the men's faces, they are not young. Their faces have a sense of oldness.*

*Their faces appear taut. Their faces are a reddish-brown colour. This applies to all men.*

*One man was more brutal than the others. And, one man chased Luda (or equivalent).*

Ug: *What did they want?*

A: *Nothing. The 9H were enemies.*

*When the men left, 2 hikers laid in the snow. They were almost dead.*

U_G: *Who were the men?*

*Where did they come from?*

*What was their intent?*

NOTE: *One did have a dead animal. It hung from his right waist. This does not mean that they were hunters.*

*The men did follow some of the path of 9H.*

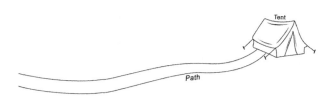

*However, if you retrace the men's path you obtain below*

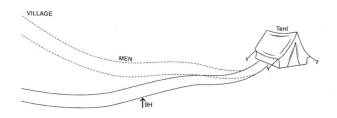

*The village is a small primitive village.*

*Comment: Ug will return with more after $S_6$, $S_7$, $S_8$, and $S_9$.*

*$S_6$: Alexander Kolevatov (=A)*

*Ug: A, will you please communicate with us?*

*A: Yes.*

*Ug: What happened on Kholat Syakhl on 1 February 1959? Will you help?*

*A: Yes.*

*Ug: Was everyone in the tent?*

*A: It is a vague question.*

> *But I suppose you mean the night that we ran for our lives.*

*Ug: Yes.*

*A: We all made it to the tent.*

*Ug: Did you fall asleep?*

*A: Yes.*

*Ug: What woke you?*

*A: The commotion. The others were getting up.*

    *Yury was yelling "Get out!"*

*Ug: What did you do?*

*A: I left. As I ran, I looked back.*

    *There was a fight. No need to return. The hiker hit the ground. I hesitated.*

    *But, I sensed that he could not be saved.*

*Ug: What else can you tell us?*

    *Did you get a look at the men?*

*A: I assume that they were men. I did not get a good look at them.*

*Ug: Thank you.*

*A: You're welcome. I wish that I knew more.*

*END*

*S₇: George Krivonischenko (=G)*

*Ug: G, will you please communicate with us?*

*G: Sure, I will.*

*Ug: What happened on Kholat Syakhl on 1 February 1959 at the tent? Will you help?*

*G: I'll try.*

*Ug: Thanks.*

    *Were all the hikers in the tent on the night of 1 February 1959?*

*G: Yes. We finished a short meal. We were tired. We needed sleep.*

    *I desperately wanted to curl up and sleep.*

*Ug: Did you fall asleep?*

*G: I sure did. I had no problem.*

*Ug: What woke you?*

*G: I was slapped by another hiker. I heard "Get up. Get out. Quickly."*

*I saw other hikers running from the tent.*

*Ug: What did your senses provide?*

*G: I was originally dazed. I'm a sound sleeper. But, I followed suit.*

*I did not hear another voice.*

*Ug: Were all 9H awake?*

*Did 9H listen quietly to voices outside of tent?*

*G: I'm not sure. They did not sit quietly awake listening to voices or equivalent.*

*Ug: What did you see when you left tent?*

*G: I did not take time.*

*Ug: Thanks.*

*G: You're welcome.*

*END*

*S₈: Rustem Slobodin (=R)*

*Ug: R, will you please communicate with us?*

*R: Sure, What do you want?*

*Ug: What happened on Kholat Syakhl on 1 February 1959 at the tent? We need your help?*

*R: We all need help. And, on that night we needed a lot of help (at least it seemed).*

*Ug: Did you fall asleep that night?*

*R: Yes.*

*Ug: What woke you?*

*R: It was the frantic hikers. I said "What the hell." I looked around the tent.*

*It was a mass exit. I got out. I saw the other hikers running. I stopped. I looked.*

*I saw a man with a spear. I took off. He threw the spear. But it landed far short. .*

*Ug: What did the man look like?*

*R: He was dressed in warm clothes, boots and so on (similar to Eskimo style).*

*Look at how Russians dress in winter and so on.*

*Even better look at Russian hunter. This is a better illustration.*

*Ug: Did you see guns?*

*R: No.*

*Ug: Did you hear a voice?*

*R: I heard "Yah." When I looked at him I took off. He threw spear. It landed far short.*

*Ug: What about the man's face?*

*R: It was old, taut, reddish-brown, and face narrows towards nose and mouth.*

*Ug: Thanks.*

*R: You're welcome. Sorry I don't know more.*

*END*

*S9: Nicolai Thibeaux-Brignolle (=N)*

*Ug: N, will you please communicate with us?*

*N: Why?*

*Ug: We want to know the reasons that you left the tent on Kholat Syakhl on 1 February 1959. N: You mean the disaster? I guess it can be called that.*

*Ug: Will you help?*

*N: Sure. I'll do my best. What difference does it make? There is no way to change these events. They are rooted in history.*

*Ug: Thanks.*

*Did you fall asleep?*

*N: I sure did. No doubt about it. But, I woke up too soon.*

*Ug: What woke you?*

*N: Other hikers were moving in tent. Yury yelled "Get Out"!*

*I looked to one side of the tent. I saw a slit.*

*A voice said "Yah Choi"*

*Ug: Please continue.*

*N: I got pushed. Which implied out. I exited opposite side where the tent was slashed.*

*Ug: What did you observe?*

*N: 1ˢᵗ I saw hikers running.*

*I looked right. I got a glimpse of a person. This person was dressed in light tan hide clothes. He had hood. There was fur around front of hood. He had laced boots.*

*His face was dark. It was not black or brown. It was like red clay. He had a knife hanging around his waist. The coat overlapped the upper part of his pants. He was medium to slightly medium height. This might be 5'7"or about. I only looked. I made no attempt to approach.*

Ug: *Did you see any hikers near him?*

N: *No. He stood only looking towards me.*

*I finally took off towards the hikers that I saw run.*

Ug: *Thanks.*

N: *I hope that this helps.*

Ug: *Sometimes the smallest piece of information tells a story.*

*Much thanks again N!*

*END*

Ug: Perspective

*They were in the tent at the same time. They said a prayer together. They were happy to make it this far. They looked forward to the next day. They thought that they would complete the trip. When they reached the top they would celebrate. They planned specific events when they reached the top.*

*9H went to sleep in the tent. The tent was poked. Eventually a slit was made. Hikers woke other hikers. One Hiker yelled "Get Out!" The tent was cut opposite the initial cut. Hikers exited in a rush. Some ran away from the tent. Two male hikers fought. $S_2$ did also. There were five men outside the tent. These men dressed in light tan colour clothes, the material looked like hide. They wore laced boots. They did not appear tall. Their faces were brown-reddish. Their faces appeared taut (face narrows as move toward nose). They spoke a language more like a native.*

*Indirectly 9H died because of 5 men (the men made no effort to save 9H).*

Ug: Questions and Comments

> Q: *Why did the men attack the tent?*
>
> > *IMAGE: A man stands in front of another man. The latter is Yury's description (See $S_1$). The former is tall, thin and dark hair with a complexion that is white (or almost white).*
>
> Q: *How do we interpret this?*
>
> A: *We are unsure at present.*
>
> Q: *Did the former ask the latter to follow the 9H?*
>
> A: *It is unknown at present.*
>
> Q: *Did the tall and thin man see the other man before or after 1 February 1959?*
>
> A: *Before.*
>
> Q: *Did the tall and thin man pay other man?*
>
> A: *No (was it a favour?).*
>
> Q: *After the 5 men attacked 5H on 1 February 1959, where did they go?*
>
> A: *They returned to their homes (They left 9H to die).*
>
> Q: *What did the man who was tall and thin, who had dark hair (black?) about 1" long and who wore light grey pants say to other man?*
>
> A: *It is unknown at present.*

FINAL COMMENTS

> *The nine hikers can be divided into two groups. The members of group 1 had wounds while defending themselves. The members of group 2 ran because they feared for their lives.*
>
> *The members of group 1 were too weak to help themselves. They died due to environmental conditions. The members of group*

two were too afraid to return to the tent. They died due to environmental conditions.

The camp of the nine hikers was attacked. And, the attackers are indirectly responsible for their deaths. That is, the five men indirectly murdered the hikers.

The above might be considered a cold case by some people. But the murder of a human on this planet is not really a cold case.

W. OHM

# Chapter 14

Many mysteries can have outlandish and exotic theories to explain what happened, but quite often they can turn out to have a fairly mundane explanation. The revelations in the two interviews with Deputy Prosecutor Okishev and the examination of the Dyatlov group negatives point to something happening at Kholat Syakhl on the night of 1/2 February 1959, and, without giving too much away, Okishev's comments point in the direction of something connected with the military.

Yakimenko's work with the thirty one frames on eight clippings are hard evidence that something was happening in the night sky above the group on that final night. He was keen to point out the nature of the documentary evidence to show that it was not just another take on a gimmick of a theory. So, if the group were indeed located on the side of Kholat Syakhl close to the ridge line and at least one (Zolotarev), and possibly one or two more (Thibo and one other, maybe Rustem) were outside the tent close to the end, then: What did they see? What could possibly have happened? Why did they move away from the tent and down to the tree line?

That there was something happening in the night sky is beyond dispute, as apart from the evidence of the film examined by Yakimenko, there are several separate eye witness statements confirming having seen lights in the sky over a period of time.

There were numerous sightings of lights/fireballs in the night sky in the northern Urals in early to mid-1959. This suggests something was already going on and had been going on at least since the night of 1/2 February on a fairly regular basis.

On the night the Dyatlov group died, Evgeny Okishev mentions sighting of lights in the area of the Pass:

> ....*Shortly before that we met with a worker of one of the prison camps in the North Urals. He described strange flashes of light which he and his wife saw late that evening on their way home from the cinema. The light came from the direction of the supposed accident with the tourists. We also received evidence from other local residents, and all of them spoke about a similar phenomenon, all testimonies were entered on our records of interrogation. We got a suspicion of existence of a military test field somewhere around...*

There is no guarantee, though, that just because these lights were seen in the sky, it necessarily proves that the lights were responsible for what happened to the group. However, the fact that four of the group were looking at the lights (the frame where the heads of three of the group are shown facing the light and in front of whoever was taking the picture, possibly Krivoy) shows the appearance of the lights must have been spectacular enough to draw their attention. It is also quite possible that all of the group were present outside the tent watching and that only three of them were caught by Krivoy's camera. If it is accepted that the lights were something to do, either directly or indirectly, with the group's deaths, then what were they?

Witnesses who observed the lights talk of parts falling from some of them which strongly suggests part of a rocket as the stages fall away after the launch. For this to happen, the actual launch site is probably not too far away as stages always fall away in the early part of a launch. Parts falling away could also have been caused by a hit on a drone type target by a missile. There have been a number of suggestions that the group were hit or were close to a rocket or missile or a part of one, coming down close to them on Kholat Syakhl. Also mentioned in these theories is the possibility of them being affected by highly toxic rocket propellant. Most of the suggestions have related to the R-7 ICBM which was being developed at the time and also the anti-aircraft S-75 missile. The R-7 is usually discounted because it followed missile lines far from the northern Urals and the S-75 had a very limited range and would have needed to be close to Kholat Syakhl to have come down there. This would be highly unlikely given the nature of the S-75 system which was quite cumbersome and difficult to set up in the mountainous taiga of the surrounding area where the group were. Difficult, but not necessarily impossible.

There were other missile contenders that could have caused the tragedy, however, and these are rarely mentioned. Among them are ABMs (Anti-Ballistic Missiles) and the *Burya* Cruise missile which were being developed at this time. One such ABM missile was the V-1000 which had a range of up to 300km (186 miles). The background to these missiles is that the Soviet Union was aware of the Allies lack of protection against German V-2s during the War and whilst development of their own ICBMs to be used offensively was a top priority, equal importance was given to defence against them. Development of the V-1000 started in 1956. It was a two-stage liquid fuelled interceptor that was 16.5 meters (54ft) long. The first successful Soviet interception of a test fired ICBM was made in 1957. When used against ICBMs they (the V-1000s) were fitted with small nuclear warheads, and when used against aircraft, they carried a high explosive warhead. They were being tested in the late 1950s prior to their full deployment in the early 1960s. Whilst the first main area of defence was Moscow, the Urals region had many sites of prime importance which would have been first strike targets in a nuclear attack. These included the plant known as Sverdlovsk-45 at Lesnoy / Nizhnyaya Tura which was used to produce highly enriched uranium (HEU) and in the late 1950s was being converted to assembly and disassembly of nuclear warheads. Further south, towards Sverdlovsk, other targets included the U-235 diffusion plant at Verkh Neyvinsk, along with tank factories, airfields and armaments factories in and north of Sverdlovsk. South of Sverdlovsk was the Atomic city of Chelyabinsk-40. Attacks on all these targets would come in the form of bombers and ICBMs from over the Polar ice cap and the job of the V-1000 would be to intercept them in the north of the Urals region.

The general view of Soviet ABM development is that there was not the money to develop a system which protected all the important targets across the USSR. Moscow was to be defended using these systems to start with, but it seems unlikely that no attempt would be made to protect the important nuclear and military facilities north of Sverdlovsk. As soon as US satellites came into use for spying purposes, one of the first things the CIA did was to target them on a region to the north of the Dyatlov Pass where building work was being carried out. This was assumed to be a new base for anti-aircraft missiles for US bombers coming in to attack the Urals region. However, this turned out to be a mining area with a rail link. The fact that the Americans were constantly carrying out surveillance in the region for missiles shows that they expected to meet missile defences in any attack on the Urals region.

Once initial tests had been carried out on the V-1000 or any other air defence missile, there is no reason why they could not have been moved up to the northern Urals to be tested there to protect the vital assets in that region. At the time of the Dyatlov deaths, there were two other Soviet ABM systems being developed and eventually not proceeded with. Due to the nature of the secrecy surrounding these ABMs, very little is known about them by Western intelligence analysts.

The direction of travel of the lights observed in the sky is also significant. A sighting of one of these meteors / lights by meteorologist Tokareva on 15 March 1959 mentions a comet travelling from the south to the north east. This sighting was at Ivdel and the sighting would make sense for an ABM situated north of Lesnoy to be launched in this same direction as this is the direction bombers and missiles would be coming from. The Dyatlov Pass is situated to the north from Lesnoy which is roughly where a launch would be made from. There was also a fighter base (Yugorsk) 160+ kilometres (100+ miles) east of the Dyatlov Pass, both of these locations would be within the range of a V-1000 missile fired from either place. With the 300km (186 miles) range of the missile, it is also possible it could be fired from the lowland area of the western side of the Urals.

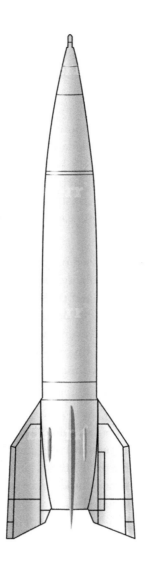

The Soviet A-1 Rocket which was an exact copy of the German V-1

The Soviet R-2 Missile

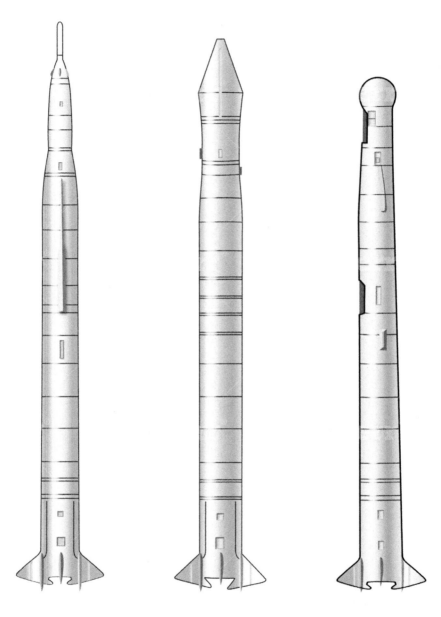

The Soviet R-5 group of missiles

Other missile contenders that could have been involved in the Dyatlov tragedy include the R-1, R-2 and R-5 (*see Appendix II*) for a superb analysis of the Dyatlov photos by Hungarian researcher SZTALKER). Of particular interest are the R-2 missiles which were fitted with experimental warheads including one warhead which was fitted with radiation in liquid form to see how it dispersed over a target area. Such a warhead could have been the reason for the testing of the levels of radiation on the clothes on some members of the group. The early R-5 missiles were used for experimental purposes from the mid-1950s until 1971.

Much about the lights in the sky suggests a rocket or missile with stages or boosters falling away or a target or drone of some kind being hit. A strong contender for the possibility of a drone or UAV (Unmanned Aerial Vehicle) is the Lavochkin La 17 which went into production in 1956, and one variant was used as a target drone for Soviet fighter pilots and anti-aircraft and ABM systems. The Lavochkin La 17s were launched from highly mobile wheeled-platforms and the boosters fell away after the launch.

A Lavochkin La 17 (Mikhail Petrov)

Compare this photo of Plane 2 with the angular shape of the Lavochkin La 17. It appears to show a similar shape breaking up (Valentin Yakimenko)

Apart from the V-1000 and similar ABM missile systems as well as a failed ICBM launch, there are a number of other military possibilities.

Firstly, is the possibility of an army ground exercise in the area including the use of Special Forces troops. The second possibility may have involved the dropping of explosives by military aircraft. The third possibility is Soviet interceptor aircraft attacking drone targets and balloon type targets fired by artillery up to heights of 25,000 metres (82,000ft) which descend and are attacked by interceptors using rockets and cannon as target practice. Lastly is the possibility of an early type of surveillance drone being involved. All of these can involve the use of flares. Some of the negatives examined by Yakimenko appear to show a flare falling to the ground. A military exercise could have involved explosions caused by the firing of artillery, mortars or army rockets, with the use of flares for illumination, which is common in night exercises. The rockets used by the army at this time would have had a much lower trajectory and relatively short ranges. The Soviet army was also testing small thermobaric weapons at this time, including rocket propelled grenades which had a thermobaric warhead with an explosive radius of only 9 metres (just under 30ft) and a grenade launcher which fired multiple thermobaric grenades with an explosive radius of 3 metres (just under

10ft). These weapons did not have fragmentation and relied on the power of the blast alone. These could have accounted for the tremendous localised damage caused to the chests of Luda and Zolotarev.

The second possibility mentioned above, relates to testimony from an anonymous source of two Tu 95M *Bear* bombers that flew over the region that night of 1/2 February from their base at Uzyn in the Ukraine. The first aircraft could have dropped either free fall bombs or parachute mines with tremendous blast power. The second aircraft could have carried out an analysis of the drop, using flares to illuminate the area and taking pictures with the new AFA-42/100 camera which the *Bears* had been fitted with for photo reconnaissance imagery and post-strike bomb damage analysis. At this time, prior to full deployment of the R7 ICBMs, the *Bears* were the vanguard of Soviet power and great secrecy was attached to anything connected with them, including training exercises. At this time, the Soviet Air Force, in line with the army, was also testing large and small thermobaric bombs and missiles with thermobaric warheads.

In all of the above possible military events, flares may have been fired to illuminate the area. This could have resulted in a possible scenario whereby the group became curious and came out of the tent. After watching some of the flares and possibly seeing targets descending, some of the group may have gone back into the tent as they were getting cold. After hearing the first explosions, the group may have become very frightened and slashed their way out of the tent to join up with those outside the tent. The highly alarmed group may have realised that with their deviation up out of the Auspiya valley, they had somehow ended up in the middle of a military exercise and come to an immediate decision that it would be safest to move down to the cover of the tree line. Another series of explosions coming closer may have made the group head immediately for the tree line without stopping to put on any footwear or take anything with them. Once at the tree line, they may have felt that with the cover there, they would be safer and would return to the tent later to salvage what they could when the danger had passed. A blast could then have occurred when they were getting closer to the tree line which could have killed all of them. A follow up team coming into the area by helicopter would have found the bodies and "tidied up" the scene as best they could. The helicopter could then have lifted the team up to the tent which was a kilometre and a half from the tree line. Alternatively, the group making their way down to the tree line may have spread out, with some moving faster than the others, and a blast could have hit Zolotarev, Luda and Thibo. The others may have helped them to safety and prepared the snow shelter for them. The location of the cedar tree would have been chosen so they could see what was happening on the mountain and at the tent, waiting for the end of the exercise. Once the snow shelter had been prepared and a fire started with Doroshenko and Krivoy attending to it, Igor Dyatlov may have decided it was safe enough to take Zina and Rustem with him to try and return to the tent to bring down what they needed to try and survive. However, without footwear and exposed to the severe conditions, they were unable to make it back to the tent and died where they were found.

It is quite likely the military realised what happened with daybreak. If they had been carrying out a ground exercise or shooting down Lavochkin La 17 drones or balloon targets or conducting any post-analysis of the area, the tent could have been spotted from some distance away and the realisation of what had probably happened became apparent.

The final suggestion of a surveillance drone is also a possibility. The nature of the military defences across the top of the Urals industrial region meant that an early warning system had to be in place and those systems had to be protected. The Cold War resembled the Great Patriotic War in that the main threat which faced the Soviet Union, came from the West overland. However, the USSR from the 1950s onwards, faced an air threat from the north as well, with bombers coming in over the North Pole and attacking the Ural industrial region directly. The Urals region was vital to the Soviet Union but the defences to the north were paltry compared to the defences facing NATO in Europe. In the late 1950s, the Soviets were trying to build their air defences in the northern Urals region as fast as they could. As part of this defence, a communications system was set up to coordinate air defences in 1957. The 82nd Radio-Technical Regiment, which had its headquarters in Serov, established a facility in Ivdel (located at 60 43 38N 60 24 43E). This communications facility was a vital part of the defence system and if it was knocked out early in a major attack, it left a big hole in the defences of the northern Urals. Whilst there would be no major invasion by land coming from the north of the Urals, a facility like this was wide open by attack by smaller units of special forces infiltrated from the north. Whether such special forces came in by sea from the north or were parachuted in, it would be extremely difficult to stop such a group as it would require large numbers of land forces to provide a proper defence and this was just not practical or possible in the huge northern expanses of the Soviet Union. Equally, vital parts of the northern air defences could not just be left open to assault without providing some kind of defence for those facilities.

It is assumed by some that the Soviet Union lagged behind NATO and the West in many areas of military research and technology. This was true, but it didn't apply to all areas. In some respects, the Eastern Bloc/Warsaw Pact was on a par with the West/NATO and ahead of the West in development of sensors, radar and imaging as well as experimentation with stable aerial platforms which have now developed into today's drones. One way to provide surveillance to cover a large area on the ground is to use an aerial platform to provide coverage using sensors, radar and searchlights. This could be done using helicopters or a platform using double rotors. The Soviet Union was well advanced in the use of double rotors as they provide a far more stable platform than a single rotor. It is a strong possibility that such an aerial platform may have detected the group and their campsite on the side of the mountain. While such an aerial surveillance platform would need to sort out "clutter" on the ground such as forestry workers and animals that were not hibernating, what may have drawn attention was the presence of a group of people in close proximity to each other on the mountainside. The presence of a large metallic object (the group's stove) could have activated the sensors to something suspicious on the ground. Whether or not a surveillance platform may have carried any weaponry is possible, but through its command and control system could have alerted its military controllers to the presence of suspicious activity. The controllers could bring in weaponry to eliminate the threat. Had the Dyatlov group become aware of danger in the air from a drone, or helicopter type platform, they may have decided to evacuate the tent quickly fearing for their lives. Where there was any kind of a security threat, the Soviet military had a tendency to shoot first and ask questions later, the downing of the Korean Boeing 747 in 1987 being a good example.

The one organisation that may have some answers in their archives is the KGB (now FSB). There is much speculation about members of the KGB being involved in the search for the missing ski tourists. Denials by FSB spokesmen continue to the present day. It is inconceivable that the KGB would not have taken an interest in this case with three of the dead Dyatlov group having being involved with secret atomic research or work linked to it. Both Krivoy and Rustem had worked in the closed city of Chelyabinsk 40 and Kolevatov had worked at a secret nuclear research institute in Moscow for three years prior to his move to Sverdlovsk.

The KGB interest would be all the more likely, considering the rumours of the group attempting to make their way to the West, but it is more than likely such a rumour could only have come from a KGB source. Moreover, they (the KGB) would have maintained their interest as guardians of state security until all the loose ends were tied up to the satisfaction of the authorities. Evidence of this KGB involvement in military/civilian "problems" was seen in the leak of Anthrax spores at military compound 19 in Sverdlovsk in 1979. Another example of KGB involvement in a military/civilian "problem" was the shooting down of the Korean Airlines Boeing 747 Flight No KAL007 in September 1983. The black boxes from KAL007 were held by the KGB for ten years until after the break-up of the USSR. The KGB involvement suggests support of the disinformation by the authorities at the least. It would be expected that the black boxes would have been kept by the Soviet Air Defence Forces (*PVO Strany*) or the Soviet civil aviation authorities as it was a civil aircraft.

Coming back to the Dyatlov incident, there is a suggestion by some theorists of the scene being staged by the KGB. If any type of missile or drone had come down to earth and exploded nearby, a clean-up team would have had a substantial amount of work to do, especially if a high explosive warhead had been fitted to a missile. All evidence and debris would need to be found and then taken away. The members of the Dyatlov group who would be all dead or close to death by this point would have had to be moved down to the tree line and put into their various locations.

This would require a number of people to carry out quickly. It is interesting to note that in all the locations where the bodies were found – two by the cedar tree, four near the snow shelter and the three on the slope going up to the tent, there were no traces of any footprints of the Dyatlov group or anyone else. The snow had covered everything. It seems almost inconceivable that a team of KGB troops would move the bodies of dead or dying students down to the treeline and then stage the scene at the tent. Inconceivable, but not impossible. However as stated above, a more likely scenario though is that the group may have realised too late that they were in the middle of a military exercise with live explosives being used and slashed their way out of the tent and then started moving quickly, walking fast but not running, down to the comparative safety of the tree line where they were hit by another blast, which came much closer than the earlier explosions.

The possibility of a military accident and radiation was mentioned by Okishev in his interview when he referred to the possible move of nuclear tests from the Caucasus to the northern Urals with one informant telling him that this may have happened, but they would not discuss it. When the radiation tests were carried out on the Dyatlov group, the clothes were noticed to have a purple hue about them which may have been rocket fuel.

The real problem with trying to dig to the bottom of any involvement by the military is that you can scrape the surface and then you hit a brick wall. The military in any country tends towards secrecy by the very nature of what they do and give as little information away to any potential enemy as possible. Security and secrets in the Soviet Union were, and still are, a national obsession. It is worth noting that the Russian/Soviet military archives in Podolsk have large segments of their archives from the Second World War (known in Russia as the Great Patriotic War 1941-45) which have never been opened up to outside researchers. So to follow or check out any theory which may involve the Soviet military (whether nuclear, missiles, army or air force) is extremely difficult.

Unfortunately, after a brief period of relative openness after the fall of the Berlin Wall and the break-up of the USSR, the obsession with security is back with a vengeance. A number of new laws have been passed in recent years including a new all-embracing law in 2012 which emphasises that state treason is a broad concept and that disclosure of state secrets is a form of it. It enables the state to prosecute anyone who openly discusses or disseminates any information related to military matters or security issues. Even before this law came into effect, two prior examples suffice to give an idea of how bad the situation could be for anyone who has gone too far over the mark.

In 1998 a book was published entitled *Russian Strategic Nuclear Forces*. There were six contributors, one of whom was Maxim Tarasenko. Whilst the book drew on sources and information that were freely available, it was the first detailed history of the development of Soviet nuclear weaponry and also detailed civilian use of nuclear explosions within the USSR. Shortly after publication, the FSB (formerly the KGB) ordered all copies of the book to be withdrawn and destroyed. The office of the publisher was raided and anything relating to the book, including DVD copies were confiscated and destroyed. There were no sanctions against any of the authors. In May 1999, 35 year old Maxim Tarasenko was out for a walk with his step-son in the town of Zelenograd where they lived. As they walked along, a car being driven at speed appeared and hit them. Maxim Tarasenko was killed and his step-son was injured. The car didn't stop. Of course, whilst the two incidents may be entirely unrelated, it is also possible for anyone contemplating a similar type of work to Tarasenko to draw their own conclusions, even if they are wrong, and opt for a quieter life.

The second example concerns a satellite engineer named Gennady Kravtsov. The rate of arrests for treason has gathered pace in recent years (15 arrests in 2014 and 20 in 2015). Gennady Kravtsov had worked for the GRU (*Glavnoye razvedyvatel'noye upravleniye*), Russian military intelligence on military satellites from 1990 to 2005. In 2010 it had been five years since he resigned from his job with the GRU and felt that enough time had elapsed to be able to apply for a job using his knowledge and skills outside Russia, so he sent his CV to a company in Sweden to see if they would consider employing him. This came to the attention of the FSB and he was arrested and eventually sentenced to 14 years in a maximum security penal colony. It seemed excessively harsh and was reduced to six years on appeal, but the guilty sentence still stood.

So, for anyone starting to make enquiries of people who had once served in the military, no matter how long ago, it can be well understood if they were reluctant to talk. This would be especially the case if the enquiry concerned a contentious issue.

A few years ago, I had managed to locate someone who had been posted to a Soviet military base that I thought may have had some relation to the Dyatlov story but whilst he was happy to discuss generalities, he made it clear he was not prepared to talk about specific military matters

It may seem that the military accident theory presented here is over-critical of the attitude of the authorities. What would seem to be a fairly clear cut case of an appalling accident in the West is viewed differently by some in Russia. It needs to be understood that the vast majority of Russians have a deep love for their country and all things Russian. Even though the Dyatlov Incident happened during the Soviet era, there are many Russians who would feel that there is no useful purpose in trying to blame the military for an accident that happened in the 1950s. Despite this, however, the attitude of some Russians I have spoken to is that the Dyatlov Incident is a long time ago and took place in the Soviet era and that if they (the authorities) are withholding information, then they should release that information and clear the mystery up once and for all. No blame is being attached to the current government.

Is it possible that an ABM like the V-1000 or the shooting down of a Lavochkin La 17 drone or an aerial surveillance platform or explosives dropped from a bomber or mortar/shells/rockets from an army exercise led to the deaths of the group? As conscientious law enforcement officials, Lev Ivanov, Evgeny Okishev and Nicolai Klinov, even if they had been told nothing, may have guessed what had happened to the group and wanted to get to the bottom of it. Unfortunately for them, initiative was never a highly sought after quality in the Soviet system and a stop was put on them going any further. It is quite likely that every step of the investigation was being closely monitored and everything happened very quickly at the end. The final four bodies were found on the 4 May 1959 and with Ivanov's and Okishev's hunch about what had probably happened, they must have known with Urakov's arrival from Moscow that the case was going to be halted in its tracks. The case was closed on 28 May 1959, less than four weeks after the final four bodies were found.

What seems to shine through in the summing up of Lev Ivanov and the commentary and interviews with Evgeny Okishev is a kind of very subtle evasion of getting to the real core of the problem. Ivanov talks about "Burn marks on trees and how disappointed he was at the eventual outcome when he was sure something was going on". Okishev mentions the same disappointment and how they are told to just shut the investigation down when the last bodies are found. Nobody actually comes straight to the point and says straight out that they think they were killed by military action of some kind. Okishev refers to military tests but is careful not to actually connect the deaths and the tests. It could be argued he did not have the hard evidence to come out and say it, but he had no problem exonerating the Mansi and does so, on the basis of discussions with one of the Mansi representatives. Okishev does, at least, refer to the almost definite involvement of the KGB.

There is no actual great conspiracy as such about the Dyatlov Incident. I believe it was a tragic accident and the simple truth is that nobody wants to own up to it as it will show certain players in a very bad light, even though over 60 years have now passed. It could be argued "Why should they hide it?" My response to that would be that secrecy is an ingrained habit. For instance, why should a large part of the military archives be closed off in Podolsk, even though many of those files are believed to show the Red Army's fighting abilities in a very positive light during the Great Patriotic War? Another example is Colonel-General Semyon Romanov, who in May 1983 was described in the press as "died suddenly in the performance of his duties". He was killed in a series of massive munitions explosions over four days in the closed city of Severomorsk. Half of the Northern Fleet's stocks of missiles were destroyed in the explosions. This was not mentioned.

The concluding statement of the investigation of attributing the deaths to "an unknown, compelling force" on Okishev's admission was written by Lev Ivanov and Okishev himself, and approved by Klinov. And again, on both Ivanov's and Okishev's admission, it was a totally unsatisfactory conclusion, but under the circumstances it was the best they could come up with. The deaths were certainly due to a compelling force, but unknown? It is highly unlikely. It is unknown in the sense that we don't know the exact cause but the real answer still lies with the authorities and the military.

# Chapter 15

In amongst the ongoing discussions of various theories and more recent events, one of the most interesting developments in the case was the opening up, in April 2018, of Semyon Zolotarev's grave in the Ivanovskoye (*St John the Baptist*) cemetery and examination of the remains. This was led by a team under the auspices of the *Komsomolskaya Pravda* who have done much good work in pursuing the truth behind the Dyatlov story. The account of the examination is well covered elsewhere but one useful exercise, if it could ever be done, would be to exhume the remains of the first five bodies (Doroshenko, Krivoy, Zina, Rustem and Igor Dyatlov) and compare their remains with the original autopsies. My own feeling is that it was strange that there appeared to be two different causes of death for the group. If any members of the first group were exhumed and found to have injuries similar to Zolotarev and Luda, then it would point to a cover up which again would point the finger of suspicion towards a military accident. It might be that such an exhumation showed nothing of the sort, but at least it would lay that theory to rest.

At the same time as the exhumation of Zolotarev's grave, and after discussions with Yury Kuntsevich, we decided to try a more formal approach to making an attempt to getting the case officially reopened. What it needed was finance. Yury K was able to provide some finance from the Foundation and I set up a GoFundMe campaign here in the West to raise the balance of funds to not only make the application to have the case formally reopened, but to also cover our lawyer's (Leonid Proshkin) fees and to cover travel costs to and from Moscow. We had a wonderful response and the petition was duly made on 19 September 2018, with sworn affidavits from the relatives of Yury Doroshenko and Rustem Slobodin.

The basis of the petition was the rights of the deceased Dyatlov group's surviving families and relatives to a satisfactory outcome in the investigation of their deaths. The result of the original investigation could hardly be described as giving closure to the families and relatives. An approach was also made to the Russian Office of the Human Rights Commission but their response was that they did not feel that the Dyatlov deaths was a matter that fell within their remit.

In any event, the petition was duly made to the Investigative Committee in Moscow, and listed in the petition was a number of anomalies which stood out from the original handling of the case. There was no response within the 30-day period for which an official response should be made to such a petition and the Foundation, through the lawyer duly protested and asked for a response to be made. When it finally came, in a letter dated 26 October 2018, the response from the Investigative Committee stated that it was the decision of the prosecuting authorities in the Sverdlovsk region to close the case on 28 May 1959 and that the case had never been transferred to the Investigative Committee in Moscow. It stated that without the original decision being overruled by the Prosecutor or the Court in line with articles 37 and 214 of the Criminal Procedure Code of the Russian Federation, they (the Investigating Committee) could not deal with it. Although it appeared to be a kind of "Don't call us, we'll call you" type response, it gave some hope because it suggested that the petition be made to the local prosecutor first to cancel the decision to close the original investigation in order to reopen the case for a fresh investigation. It also acknowledged that two of the relatives could only be treated as victims of the outcome of the original case if the original decision to terminate it was overturned and a new investigation opened.

As most Dyatlov followers will know, a new investigation was formally announced, fittingly I feel, to coincide with the 60th anniversary of the

Dyatlov group's deaths. There had been a somewhat scurrilous article written on the internet at the time which suggested that the fund raising was a waste of money and time because others had tried before and not got anywhere. However, we went through the correct channels and duly made the petitions to have the case formally and properly investigated. I should point out that on raising the balance of funds I was the second largest contributor to get it moving and the largest contributor was a businessman from Tennessee, USA (who wishes to remain anonymous) who offered us more funds if we needed it. So, the two biggest 'losers' would have been myself and the Tennessee businessman, but it was a chance we were more than prepared to take.

Whilst there was great excitement about the announcement of a new investigation of the case, the parameters that were set were more than a little disappointing. For me the biggest disappointment was not a mention of anything to do with the military. Nevertheless, it was a huge step forward and at the time of writing (end of May 2020) there has been no final outcome. This situation has not been helped by the worldwide Covid-19 crisis which has hit Russia hard.

So, we can only wait and see what the final outcome will be, but I have a feeling that whatever it is, the Dyatlov mystery and all its theories are going to be discussed for a long time to come.

# Appendix I

## Table of examination of negatives from Dyatlov group cameras (By Valentin Yakimenko)

- Photo in article: 1
- Object (Conditional Name):
- File format (jpg, tif, Preview):

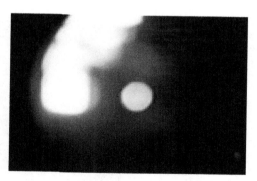

krivoy photo 1.jpg

- Photo in article: 2
- Object (Conditional Name):
- File format (jpg, tif, Preview):

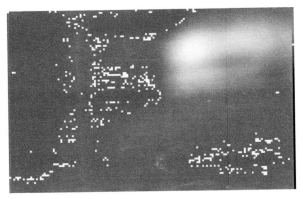

photo 2.tif

- Photo in article: 1a
- Object (Conditional Name):
- File format (jpg, tif, Preview):

3 heads new.jpg

226

- Photo in article: 3
- Object (Conditional Name): ZLT 1 shot
- File format (jpg, tif, Preview):

zlt 1-1_positive.jpg

- Photo in article: 3a
- Object (Conditional Name): Lynx
- File format (jpg, tif, Preview):

img_1800.jpg

Another image of same object:

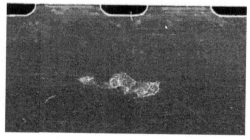

lynx.jpg (was used earlier in article)

227

- Photo in article: 4
- Object (Conditional Name): Horn
- File format (jpg, tif, Preview):

img_1803.jpg

Another image of same object:

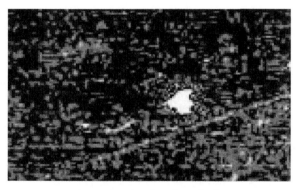

horn new.jpg (used earlier)

- Photo in article: 5
- Object (Conditional Name): Jaws
- File format (jpg, tif, Preview):

img_1765.jpg

- Photo in article: 6
- Object (Conditional Name): Lynx 2
- File format (jpg, tif, Preview):

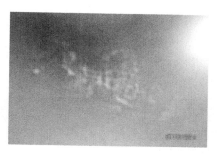

img_1805.jpg

Another image of same object:

img_1817.jpg

- Photo in article: 7
- Object (Conditional Name): Mushroom
- File format (jpg, tif, Preview):

img_1818.jpg

- Photo in article: 7a
- Object (Conditional Name): Mushroom, image enlarged
- File format (jpg, tif, Preview):

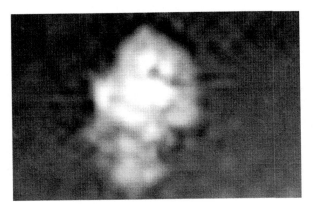

img_1818.jpg

- Photo in article: 8
- Object (Conditional Name): Eagle 1 dark
- File format (jpg, tif, Preview):

eagle 1-dark-175.jpg

- Photo in article: 8a
- Object (Conditional Name): Eagle 1 light
- File format (jpg, tif, Preview):

eagle 1- 175.jpg

- Photo in article: 9
- Object (Conditional Name): Eagle 2 dark
- File format (jpg, tif, Preview):

eagle 1- 175.jpg

Another image of same object:

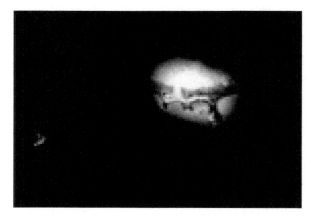

spot new with eagle 2b.jpg

- Photo in article: 9a
- Object (Conditional Name): Eagle 2 light
- File format (jpg, tif, Preview):

img_1714.jpg

Another image of same object:

spot new with eagle 21.jpg

- Photo in article: 10
- Object (Conditional Name): Chicken
- File format (jpg, tif, Preview):

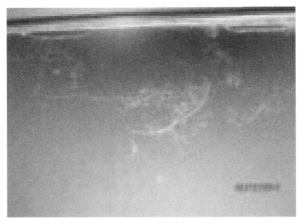

img_1764.jpg

Another image of same object:

chicken 1764 new 2

- Photo in article: 11
- Object (Conditional Name): Piece of lopwood
- File format (jpg, tif, Preview):

img_1778.jpg

- Photo in article: 12
- Object (Conditional Name): Figure-dummy
- File format (jpg, tif, Preview):

img_1767.jpg

Another image of same object:

figure-dummy new.jpg

- Photo in article: 13
- Object (Conditional Name): Wedge
- File format (jpg, tif, Preview):

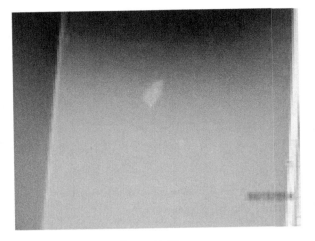

img_1776.jpg

Another image of same object:

wedge new.jpg

- Photo in article: 14
- Object (Conditional Name): Photo 14
- File format (jpg, tif, Preview):

photo 14 new.jpg

- Photo in article: 15
- Object (Conditional Name): Plane 1
- File format (jpg, tif, Preview):

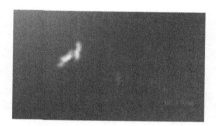

img_1729.jpg

Another image of same object:

plane 1 new.jpg

- Photo in article: 16
- Object (Conditional Name): Plane 3
- File format (jpg, tif, Preview):

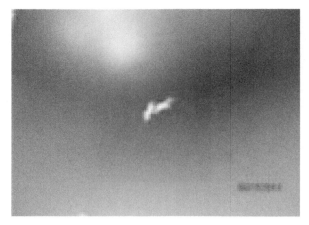

img_1782.jpg (image rotated)

Another image of same object:

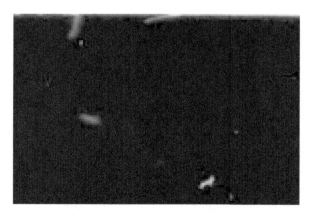

plane 3 new.jpg

- Photo in article: 17
- Object (Conditional Name): Plane 2
- File format (jpg, tif, Preview):

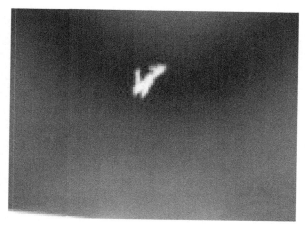

img_1717.jpg

Another image of same object:

plane 2 new.jpg

- Photo in article: 18
- Object (Conditional Name):
- File format (jpg, tif, Preview):

skan_10_029.jpg

*I apologise to the reader that in the book these will appear very small, although it should be possible in the Kindle version to expand them. The table is on my website for those who feel it is too small. www.dyatlov-pass-incident.com*

# Appendix II

Whether or not you agree with the rocket/missile theory, there is no shortage of people who support it or suspect a military rocket or missile may have played a part in the group deaths without directly saying it including Valentin Yakimenko, Evgeny Tamplon, Lev Ivanov, Evgeny Okishev among many others.

Part of the problem with Yakimenko's discovery of the various images on the group's negatives is that they do not appear to resemble anything that can be definitely identified as either a rocket or some kind of aerial object. There appears to be too many variations with criticism centred on the images being no more than flaws in the film itself which is quite understandable. Another criticism is that if these are aerial objects that have been caught by the group's cameras, then how have they managed to catch a falling rocket, or rockets, so close-up. The cameras were basic Soviet designs without the benefit of telephoto lenses. Again, this is fair criticism. When an aircraft or a rocket falls from the sky, the general assumption is that it retains its basic aeroplane or rocket shape. There is a well-known photograph taken of a Pacific Southwest Airlines Boeing 727 which collided with a light aircraft (a Cessna 172) over San Diego on 25 September 1978. The photograph clearly shows an airliner plunging to the ground in flames. What really helps the identification is that the photo was taken in daylight. Had the photo been taken at night, the flames would be clearly seen but the shape of the aircraft itself would be less clear. The objects in the Dyatlov negatives don't seem to have any pattern or shape to them that can be compared to an aerial object, other than the frames described in Appendix I as Plane 1, Plane 2 and Plane 3 which have distinct angular shapes.

So, the assumption that the most of the objects discovered in the negatives are unrecognisable, led a Hungarian Dyatlov researcher who prefers to go by the handle 'SZTALKER', to start a remarkable comparison of these shapes to see if they did in fact resemble an aerial object or objects of some kind. His research, which took a considerable amount of time, started from the premise that there was a relationship between the sheer number of photo frames taken of what appears to be strange shapes in the night sky and that these images bear some relation to the deaths of the whole Dyatlov group. He broke the images down into groups and then compared these groups of negatives to parts of a rocket breaking up. The shapes in the negatives various rocket parts consisting of the rocket stabilisers and the tail section, along with the fuel and oxidizer containers, engine parts as well as grid shapes from the frame of the rocket itself.

SZTALKER'S view is that the rocket captured in these negatives is either a Soviet R-1, A-1, R-2 or R-5. So far so good but this is where the discrepancies start. These rockets were developed from the Nazi V2 rockets and were built with the assistance of captured German scientists. They were also mainly used for ground to ground attack. Everything in this area of the northern Urals was directed towards air defence. The ranges of these rockets were from 270km (168 miles) in the case of the R-1 to 1,190km (730 miles) in the case of the much larger R-5.

By 1959, as SZTALKER himself says, these rockets were no longer in use except experimentally. The experimental version of the R-5 was the R-5A and the R-5 did go into service as the R-5M and was retired in 1983. There is the possibility though that if it was one of the outdated rockets, then it was being used in some experimental way. It is possible that it may have been used to collect weather data, act as an aerial target or to test new fuel.

Another question is where could such a rocket have been fired from? SZTALKER's view was that there were several locations in the Urals area and neither did it have to be a specific military location as all these experimental rockets and missiles could be transported by road to any suitable site. The R-5 for instance could be made ready to launch in one hour.

Whether or not you agree with his findings, it is a remarkable piece of research and with several of the sequences of breakdowns, it is hard to argue that they are not parts of a rocket, particularly the engine nozzle sequence.

What follows on the next few pages are some of his detailed analyses.

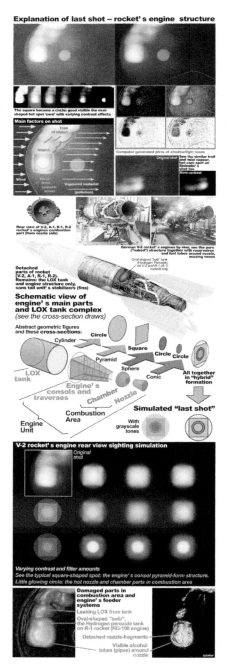

EXPLANATION of LAST SHOT -- ENGINE OF ROCKET

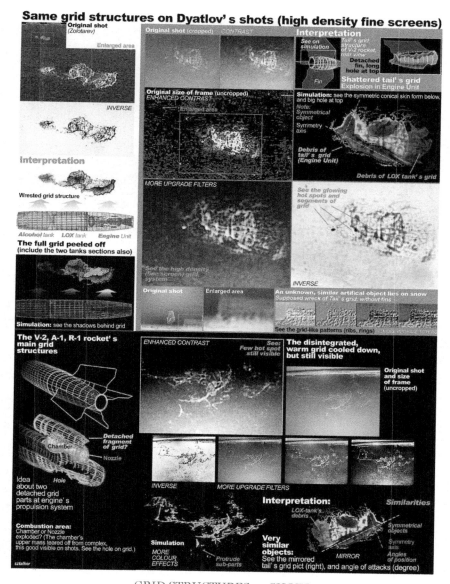

GRID STRUCTURES on SHOTS

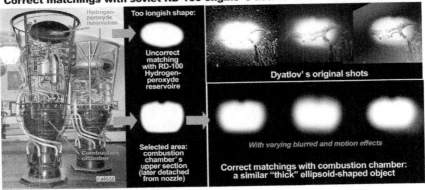

RD-100 and 101 with GLOWING CHAMBER simulation

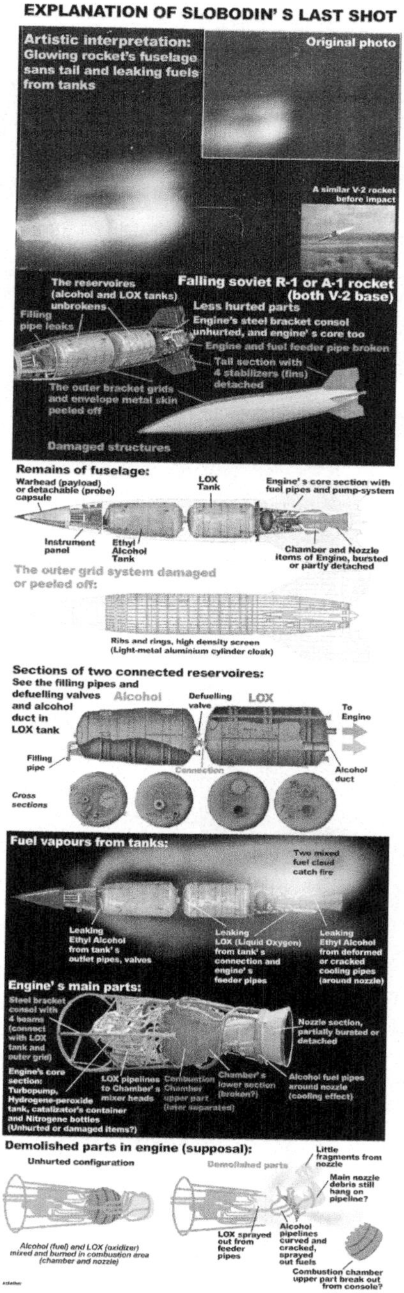


SLOBODINs SHOT INTERPRETATION

# Zolotarev's last shot (cropped frame)

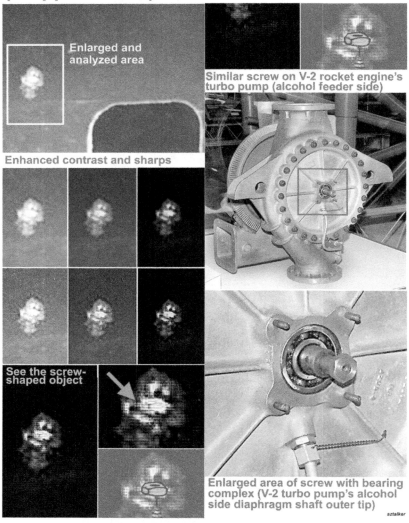

Enlarged and analyzed area

Similar screw on V-2 rocket engine's turbo pump (alcohol feeder side)

Enhanced contrast and sharps

See the screw-shaped object

Enlarged area of screw with bearing complex (V-2 turbo pump's alcohol side diaphragm shaft outer tip)

sztalker

SCREW-SHAPED OBJECT ON ZOLO LAST SHOT

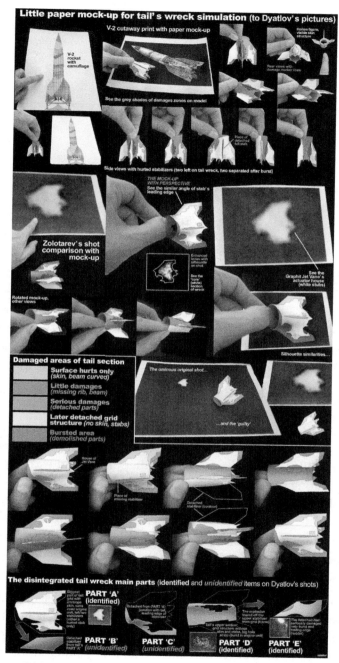

PAPER MOCK-UP for TAILs WRECK SIMULATION

# Appendix III

## Ultrasound & radio frequency signals

There are two similar areas whereby some type of soundwaves could help explain what made the Dyatlov group behave as they did – ultrasound and radio frequency signals, based on the WW II phenomenon known as "radar hearing".

The theory of ultrasound being in some way responsible for the Dyatlov deaths is one of the possibilities put forward from when the first books started appearing on the subject. Most of the early suggestions relate to the work of Vladimir Gavreaux and have been dealt with elsewhere. What the theory suggests is that ultrasound was responsible for disorienting the group to the extent that they left the tent in a deeply confused state and wandered down the mountain to their eventual deaths at the tree line. Whilst this is certainly a possibility, it does not explain the fractures and mechanical injuries suffered by Luda and Zolotarev and lesser mechanical injuries on some of the others. Ultrasound on its own does not cause mechanical-type injuries.

There are two ways that the group may have been affected. Ultrasound may have been used by the military testing a secret weapon and the other is that a vortex was created by the peak of nearby Kholat Syakhl, which created an ultrasound effect that affected all the members of the group.

In the case of the military there is no denying that research was carried out into the possibilities of using ultrasound or radio waves as a weapon of some kind and this was not restricted to the Soviet Union. One of the reasons I included this expansion of the ultrasound / radio waves theory is that I was contacted by a number of people who directed me to the use of this type of weapon in the first Gulf War (Operation *Desert Storm*) against Iraq. Allegedly, a Psychological Operations unit (PsyOps) had used mind-altering technology against Iraqi troops in Kuwait. Using what is known as *Silent Sound* techniques, this technology used standard radio frequency broadcasts to send the messages. After the destruction of the Iraqi Command and Control systems, they (the Iraqi military) had to use commercial FM radio stations to send communications in code and these were sent on the 100mhz frequency. The US team were able to send contradictory and confusing military disinformation as well subliminal messages on this same frequency from a base in Kuwait. The subliminal messages were intended to manipulate the EEG (electroencephalograph) patterns in the brain to induce very negative thought processes and feelings such as extreme anxiety and fear. The surrender of so many Iraqi troops without putting up a fight is pointed to by some as proof of the effectiveness of this form of warfare.

This technology is known as *Silent Sound Spread Spectrum* (SSSS which is also known as *S-quad* or *Squad*) and was developed by Dr Oliver Lowery of Norcross Georgia and a US Patent (No 5.159.703) was obtained for it on 27 October 1992 with the system being described as "Silent Subliminal Presentation System".

The system is described as a silent communication system in the very low or very high audio frequency range or adjacent ultrasonic frequency spectrum, which can be introduced into the brain by vibration or acoustically, using loudspeakers, earphones or piezoelectric transducers (piezoelectric transducers convert electric charges produced by some solid materials into energy). The system also uses supercomputers to analyse human emotional EEG patterns and store them and in turn these can be used to induce change in the emotional state of a human being using the above mentioned techniques of carrying the messages.

The problem with this is that these examples are all long after 1959 and this is a problem which occurs with many of the Dyatlov theories (the use of certain rockets and missiles for example). Had these techniques been around at that time, then they could have gone some way to explaining what happened to the group. The development of sound weapons, as well as certain types of missiles and rockets, were not advanced enough for the possibility of them to have been used in 1959. For instance, computers of the type required for the *S-quad* system previously mentioned would not have been around in 1959 although there is no reason to suppose that military research in the Soviet Union and the West was not going on into this type of system to be used as a weapon of some type. The KGB was known to have been trying to develop a system in the 1970s. The system was described as a Pyschotronic Influence System (PIS) which was used to turn soldiers into programmable human weapons using a combination of hypnosis and high-frequency radio waves. Although this may appear as a totally Soviet initiative, it was in response to similar research being carried out in the USA at that time. Although there is no real way of being certain, it is believed that the origins of this type of technology started as early as 1961; however this is still two years after the Dyatlov deaths.

One auditory effect that would have been available at the time of the Dyatlov deaths was what was known as the Microwave Auditory Effect. The study of this arose from military personnel who had been working in the vicinity of radar transponders during the Second World War. The effect consists of induced pulsed frequencies with a clicking or buzzing sensation generated directly inside a person's head without the need for them to have any kind of electronic receiving equipment. These auditory sensations were studied by American scientist Alan Frey in the early 1960s and there is little doubt that there was some kind of study carried out in the Soviet Union around the same time or even earlier. The effects on humans involved dizziness, pins and needles sensations and headaches. It is more than likely that the Soviet military would have had a presence in the area of the Dyatlov group and that their use of the Chistop Massif for radar and / or radio relay purposes could have some bearing on some type of weaponry being tested or developed using this technology.

The suggestion that a vortex was created by the two mountain peaks which caused an ultrasound effect is a possibility. The one thing I felt about it is that despite conditions having to be right for this vortex to take place, since the Dyatlov Pass area was opened up again in 1963, the Pass itself has become a very well visited area from that year onwards. On one afternoon, I sat by the memorial rock for several hours and in that time, half a dozen different groups of hikers passed by in different directions. It was like Piccadilly Circus or Times Square in the northern Urals. Also, many hikers both in the summer and winter, camp on the mountain and in the 50+ years since the tragedy, nobody has reported suffering any ill effects. I spent a night up there on my visit and whilst there was a very strong constant wind, I certainly didn't suffer any adverse effects.

# Appendix IV

## Dyatlov & animal mutilations

*Before I expand on this theory, the concept of which was recently sent to me, I wish to say to the reader that I neither endorse it nor oppose it. I mention it as a new theory on top of the numerous theories which are already out there. The reader does not have to agree with it and the reader does not have to read it if they don't wish to. Pretty straightforward. There are those, however, who will find something of interest here if this is a line of thinking they follow.*

I had never heard of animal mutilations until I was doing some film work in Lithuania with a crew on behalf of the Discovery Channel on the Dyatlov story. The crew were going on to the USA to film a story on animal mutilations for the *Unexplained* series on the Discovery Science Channel. I looked up a little bit about it and thought no more about the subject as it appeared to only involve animals, and strange though it all seemed because of the nature of the mutilations, I saw no possible connection to the Dyatlov story. In recent months when it was brought to my attention again, I did a little more research on the subject. In particular, I was referred to a series of six videos on YouTube which were concerned with human mutilations and which specifically mentioned the Dyatlov group deaths in one of the videos.

The nature of animal mutilations in many cases involve little or no blood and surgical type injuries which can include removal of internal organs, removal of ears, lips excised, the jaw stripped of flesh, removal of one or both eyes, teats either partially or wholly removed, genitals sliced off, limbs partly removed, removal of the rectal area (usually with sharp surgical precision), removal of the tongue from the back of the throat or midway and with no bleeding. In all cases the animal is left dead. The series of six videos I have mentioned was made by researcher Richard D Hall in conjunction with others and he interviews Animal Mutilations researcher David Cayton. David Cayton refers to the Dyatlov group deaths in the first video and a number of the well-known death photos of the group are shown, including the awful photo of poor Luda in the morgue. He (David Cayton) points out some of the similarities of animal mutilations with injuries in the Dyatlov group. These include the missing eyes, the missing tongue (in the case of Luda, although he does not mention her by name) and although organs were not removed, there was the terrible damage to the organs and bones in the chest area of two of them. David Cayton refers to the morgue photo of Luda and points out that her entire jawbone had been stripped of flesh, exposing her teeth. This is something which he says is common in animal mutilation cases. This series of videos goes on to outline human mutilations which appear to be an adjunct to cases of animal mutilation as the injuries in both seem to be the same. Richard D Hall, also outlines the work of a secret NATO unit run primarily by the USA and he makes contact with a man who had worked for this unit and interviews him.

The most obvious question is what is likely to cause such injuries and deaths? For this to happen to humans is a straightforward case of murder, however it was caused. The fact that these mutilations have occurred to animals is not disputed and there have been a few documented cases of similar injuries to humans, notably a case in Brazil in the late 1980s. The four possible explanations for these cases are; attacks by some kind of predatory animal; acts involving satanic cults; secret military projects and/or UFOs. Since the 1970s, many ufologists have linked these cases of animal mutilations to UFO and ET activity, because one common factor that links numerous cases is the presence of unknown lights in the sky at night. The presence of unexplained lights in the night sky, of course, is also a factor in the Dyatlov story as seen by observers on the night of 1/2 February 1959 and on other dates around that time. There is also the analysis by Valentin Yakimenko (in Chapter 7) of the negatives of some of the Dyatlov group cameras which appear to show them having taken pictures of lights in the sky on the night they died.

# Appendix V

## Balloons

It is assumed by many that the overflights of the USSR by NATO or Western spy balloons ended with *Project Genetrix,* which was before the Dyatlov Incident took place. For anyone who feels the balloon theory is a plausible one, there are some grounds for this theory because the balloon flights continued until well into the 1980s. This was despite the presence of spy flights and spy satellites. After Gary Powers' U-2 was shot down, such aircraft could no longer overfly the Soviet Union, so future spy aircraft were restricted to staying just outside Soviet airspace along almost all of its borders and using sensors and cameras to see as far as possible inside the USSR and to test electronic defences at the borders.

These reconnaissance balloons were known as ADAs (Automatic Drifting Aerostats) and although the USA was the main user, they were also used by a number of NATO countries, with the launches taking place mainly in Scandinavia, principally Norway, and would drift from there, over the Soviet Union at heights between 10,000mt (32,800ft) and 25,000mt (82,000ft) carrying a reconnaissance pod underneath the balloon weighing 1,000kg (2,200lbs). The majority of these flights, once released from Norway would travel towards Yakutia, over the northern Ural Mountains where the Dyatlov deaths took place. The balloons' ultimate destination would be Japan where they could be retrieved.

The balloon flights were regular enough for the head of the PVO (Air Defence Forces) to later produce a manual on how to deal with them. The manual's title was *Instruktsiya po unichtozheniyu ADA* (*Instructions on how to destroy ADAs*).

The Soviet government and air defence forces viewed these balloons as a major irritation. They had managed to bring the U-2 overflights to a stop and spy satellites were way beyond reach, and it was accepted nothing could be done about them. However, the balloons were violating Soviet airspace and, being fairly low-tech, there was no easy cost effective method to stop them. To add to the irritation of the Soviet authorities, many of the earlier balloons carried propaganda material which was released over the USSR. An S-75 Dvina missile (SAM 2 *Guideline*) was too expensive to use to just bring down a balloon. Similarly, later interceptors such as the Tupolev Tu 128 *Fiddler*, which patrolled the northern and Polar regions of the USSR, did not want to use expensive air-to-air missiles against such a low cost target. The expression used by the pilots was "Using a cannon to shoot down a Sparrow". The cannon in this sense meaning the old cannon ball type, rather than the actual large calibre guns used by aircraft to shoot the balloons down. At the time of the Dyatlov tragedy, the Yak 25 and MiG 17s at Yugorsk Air Base just over 160 kilometres (100 miles) away from Kholat Syakhl would have been used to intercept these balloons and shoot them down using cannon fire. Nor was it as easy as it might seem for a jet fighter or interceptor to shoot down a slow moving balloon. The balloons were equipped with sensors to detect radar emissions from aircraft and missiles and at a certain point to release ballast causing the balloon to suddenly shoot up higher at the last minute.

One innovative approach by the Soviet Regular Frontal Aviation and PVO fighter units was to adapt some Antonov An 2s. The old An 2 was a biplane, and one was used to assist in providing equipment in the search for the Dyatlov hikers. These old biplanes were fitted with turbochargers and propeller reduction gearing to enable them to reach the then record breaking height (for a Russian single engine piston aircraft) of 11,000mt (36,000ft) to intercept the balloons. They were equipped with a powerful searchlight and remote control 23mm cannon. Unfortunately, even with this approach, some balloons were beyond reach.

For the followers of the balloon theory, it could be a possibility that one or more balloons may have been in the night sky in the area of Kholat Syakhl on the night of 1/2 February 1959. Zolotarev, Luda and Thibo may have been watching and photographing an attempted interception of what appeared to be light orbs. One may have been shot down and the balloon descended with the helium escaping rapidly down onto the slope of Kholat Syakhl. As the balloon came down Zolotarev, Luda and Thibo may have made their way towards it and as it reached a certain height not far from the ground, explosives triggered by barometric pressure may have been set off to destroy all the equipment. The pressure from the blast could have caused the injuries to the three members of the Dyatlov group on the ground. Hearing the loud blast and the screams of the three, the others in the tent may have become highly alarmed and cut their way out and made their way down to the slope with some caution as they approached the injured. Not knowing what was going on, they may have sought shelter within the tree line to wait and see what happened.

This theory does not tick all the boxes but it is certainly plausible in parts.

# Appendix VI

## Luda's tongue

Luda's missing tongue is probably the single item which is most discussed and speculated about. I don't believe the story of the missing tongue and I give my reasons in chapter 9. There will, of course, be people who do not agree with me. However, there are those too that consider it to be almost central to the story of what happened.

There are three scenarios involving the loss of her tongue. With that in mind, I wanted to look deeper into the medical aspects of what can happen with the loss of someone's tongue. I was surprised to find that it is not quite as life threatening as it may sound. Some people have their tongues split down the middle for aesthetic reasons seemingly without suffering any ill effects once it has healed up. To bite your own tongue and cut through the Ranine artery would require very sharp teeth and the tongue clots extremely quickly. For death to occur, the person would most likely need to be lying on their back and more than likely unconscious in which case they could die from asphyxiation from the blood or the tongue itself blocking the air passage. One point worth noting is that to bite through your own tongue would involve absolutely agonising pain.

The scenarios for the missing tongue and root area are; that she bit her tongue off in shock; her tongue was removed by a third party/parties (a torture scenario); the tongue and root area were eaten away by micro-organisms in the stream she was lying in (she was found face down on a large rock in the stream). Another suggestion is that a larger animal may have been responsible for the removal of the tongue, being soft tissue, it may have attracted a smaller predator which wasn't hibernating. However there were no indications on any of the bodies of some animal eating other flesh or tissue.

In the autopsy report, Luda's tongue and the entire root area was noted as "missing", so the likelihood of her having bitten through it in a kind of shock is unlikely as there would have been some portion of the tongue remaining as well as the root area which would have been impossible for her to bite off. It is possible that she could have bitten through the tongue and that the remaining part of the tongue and root area was all eaten away by micro-organisms while she was lying on the rock in the stream with the melting snow and ice (a variation of the theory that the whole tongue and the root area disappeared in this manner).

The surgical way to remove the tongue is comparatively easy but would require someone who knew what they were doing, whether it was a surgeon operating for benign purposes or a malevolent torturer carrying out the removal as an act of sadism.

To benignly carry out surgery in hospital to remove a tongue or part of a tongue is usually done in cases of severe infection or cancer using radium needles, where no other options are available.

The procedure would involve gagging the mouth open, and inserting two silk slings. One sling would go through the anterior part of the tongue and the other sling would go just in front of the epiglottis (a flap of cartilage behind the root of the tongue). The mucous membrane on the floor of the mouth is then incised on either side and the muscles attached to the genial tubercles (a small bone that serves as an attachment for two muscles related to tongue movement) are divided. By doing this, the tongue is considerably loosened and it can be drawn up well out of the mouth so as to enable the section to be made across it with scissors at any point. Any other way of crudely trying to remove the tongue such as cutting through it without preparation and trying to tear it out in some way would leave visible signs of damage. A careful removal of Luda's tongue would have been extremely difficult in the dark, and if she was alive, she would not have been willing, which then begs the question: Why would anyone go to all that trouble? Considering the circumstances, she was close to death and even if her tongue was forcibly removed nearer the time she had just left the tent, what would be the point unless it was some kind of sadistic display over powerless prisoners, but would have been next to impossible to carry out if she was alive and conscious. Even if the tongue was removed after she had died, once again it is not an easy operation to undertake and seems utterly pointless.

A number of people have pointed to the fact that both Zolotarev and Thibo were found just a few feet up from where Luda was found, both of them were lying in the same stream. As no mention was made of the tongues of Zolotarev or Thibo being missing, the question is asked as to why the micro-organisms in the water had only affected one person and not all three of them? They have drawn the conclusion that Luda's tongue must have been removed before she reached her final resting place. Kolevatov was a member of this group of four bodies found in the area of the snow shelter in the ravine, but his body was on the bank just out of the running stream water.

The two main possibilities are that she may have bitten her tongue off in shock and the micro-organisms in the water removed all the remaining traces or it is a complete red herring placed in the autopsy report making the injuries and the case even more confusing than it already is.

# Appendix VII

## Date of opening of the criminal case

The long held belief has been that the Dyatlov group were not expected to arrive back at Vizhay until around 11/12 February 1959 when Igor Dyatlov was to send a telegram back to the Sports Club at UPI saying they were on their way back.

Nothing was suspected that something may have gone seriously wrong until after half to three quarters of the way into the month of February 1959. What came to the attention of people who suspected a cover up or conspiracy of some kind was the date on the cover of the criminal case file. The date the file was opened and had been written on the cover was 6 February 1959. This was almost a week after the group had all died but a week before Igor Dyatlov was due to send the telegram to say they were on their way back. So the question was: How could anyone have known that they were all dead a full week before they were due to make contact? The formal search did not start to look for the missing hikers until 20 February 1959.

One explanation put forward was the use of a dual calendar system in the USSR. The change from the Julian to the Gregorian calendar ("old style" to "new style") was decreed by the Soviet Government in 1918. This means that by 1959, more than a generation had grown up with the "new style". The "old style" remained (and is still used today) in church calendars. For instance, Russia celebrates Orthodox Christmas on 7th January (which is a state holiday). The New Year is celebrated officially on the 1st January and unofficially on the 13th January (the so-called "Old New Year"). Atheism was official government policy, so young people grew up with little or no knowledge of, nor respect towards church and religious holidays. People who occupied senior positions in Soviet government bodies and in law enforcement had to be communists, and this automatically implied atheism. However it was (and currently still is) the practice to give double dates in some historical documents. The generally adopted format is: *The main is date indicated in the new style followed by (date in brackets in old style)*. Thus the date on the Dyatlov case file cover, if put down in this format, may have looked like this: *19 (06) / II 1959*. However what appears is this: *06 / II 1959*. On first appearance this could be a clerical mistake.

Once again, due to some excellent research by Valentin Yakimenko we may have an answer to this discrepancy. He examined the following documents:

1.   Cover of binder with dates (case opening and closure)

2.   Order on the institution of criminal proceedings and case opening, with the date in the first line.

3.   Hard cover of the case with dates of opening and closure.

The originals of these documents are kept in the Sverdlovsk Oblast archives and unfortunately, the Dyatlov Foundation only has scanned copies to work with. A close inspection was made by Yakimenko and revealed the following more or less in his own words;

*Cover of the Binder (No Image)* The year is written in large bold letters neatly and clearly on the line, but the day (Arabic figure of six) and month (Roman figure of two) are inscribed above the line. It would appear that these have definitely been added later, in a different hand and with different ink. Could the date have been *19 (06) / II 1959?* There do not appear to be any erasures. Is it possible the ink could have faded?

*Order on Case Institution* It is logical to assume that the 'Order on Case Institution' was the first to appear, and only after this came the date of the case opening itself, which was inscribed on the cover. The date of the order itself looks odd: *96.* Not zero-six, but nine-six. Had the date been corrected? Or could it be that a bend in the paper itself make the figures merge visually? What looks like a figure of nine in this sheet has a tail that makes it a figure of two. It is possible that this could be a feature of the person's handwriting. This was compared with the way the same figure is written further along on the same page: "1959" in the same line, and "1079" (*elevation*) a few lines below. The way the figure "2" is written, begins from a dot, the pen then scrolls from this dot in a clockwise direction: down-left-up-right-down, continuing as a smooth curve down to the left and ending in a left-to-right tail. Could a bend in the paper be responsible for the "awkward" tail? Note also that this is the beginning of the order form, and the awkward letter might be a slip of pen as sometimes happens when someone starts writing. The pen stroke in the figure "9" goes in the opposite direction, the stroke begins from the top, making an open circle in an anti-clockwise direction: up-left-down-right-up, and short of closing the circle, it abruptly breaks into a down stroke and ends with a small curve turned from right-to-left. It was concluded from these observations of the writing that the date of the document must be "26 February 1959".

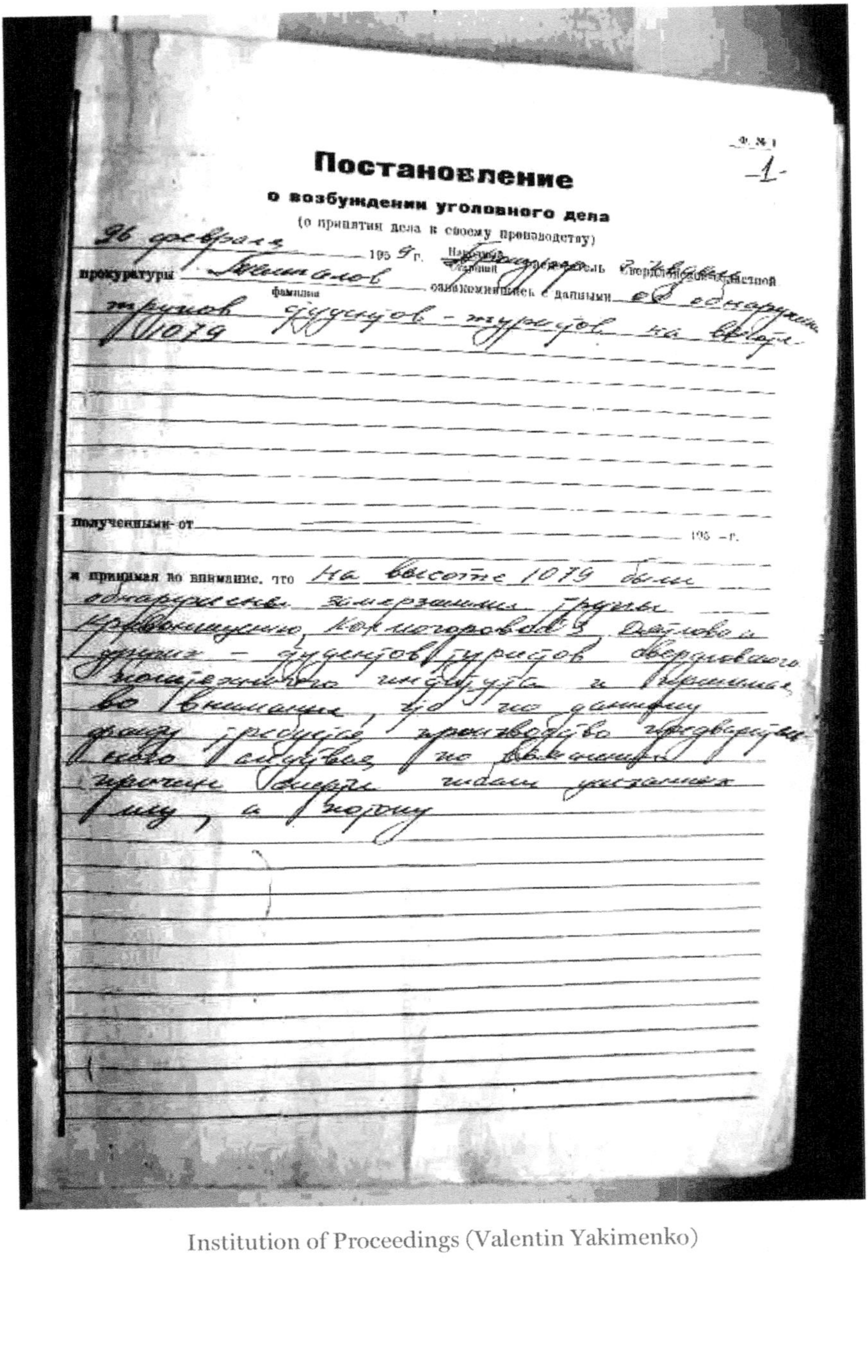

Ф. № 1

-1-

# Постановление

**о возбуждении уголовного дела**

(о принятии дела к своему производству)

26 февраля 1959 г. Прокурор г. Ивделя юрист 3 класса Свердловской областной прокуратуры Темпалов ознакомившись с данными об обнаружении трупов студентов-туристов на высоте 1079

полученными от 195 г.

и принимая во внимание, что на высоте 1079 были обнаружены замерзшими трупы Кривонищенко, Колмогоровой, Дятлова и других — студентов-туристов Свердловского политехнического института и принимая во внимание, что по данному факту следует произвести предварительное следствие по выяснению причин смерти указанных лиц, а потому

Institution of Proceedings (Valentin Yakimenko)

*Case copy* The hard cover was added much later, after the case had been closed. All document pages are numbered and laced: inside there are transcripts of interrogations, diaries, medical examination reports, photographs. The hard cover bears stamps and inscriptions saying that it is an archive item. When exactly did it appear? It bears clearly written dates in Arabic figures which give no doubt as to the dates of opening and closure. However, the date of Opening could have been borrowed from the old cover or a document inside.

Hard cover of the case with dates of opening and closure
(Valentin Yakimenko)

What Yakimenko found (and presented at the annual Dyatlov Conference in 2016) was that the original front cover was very badly worn, with the ink letters badly faded and the date of its opening partly erased. At some stage this cover was placed in a new binder for safety, and it was at that point that someone had carelessly rewritten the date as 6 Feb 1959. Whether by carelessness or inattention, it has been done because they failed to properly read the half-erased figures. However, the true date appears in the first document under the case cover which is the Order on Institution of Criminal Proceedings (*Image above*). Yakimenko was only able to work with the scanned image of the old cover. All he could do was

267

to try to prove that the true date of 26/II 1959 had been present on the old cover. He has shown that part of the figure "2" is there, but visible as a slight semicircular shade – but nevertheless it is still there.

Yakimenko's conclusion was that he was convinced the date on the front cover is 26 February 1959, and that is the true date of the case opening.

It is a strong argument but not everyone will agree with it. It could be argued that on 26 February only the tent was found. The first bodies were not found until the following day (27 February); so why open a criminal investigation before any bodies were found? Many of the searchers were from UPI and knew the Dyatlov group members well. Most of the searchers fully expected to find their friends alive and had assumed they had only gone down to the tree line to seek shelter. It should also be pointed out that Yakimenko's superb work here shows the police work was more in line with the chronology of events; it does not follow that others did not have previous knowledge of what had happened.

# Appendix VIII

## Work of the Dyatlov Foundation

Yury Konstantinovich Kuntsevich was at the funerals of the Dyatlov group in 1959 and the events of that time made a deep and lasting impression on him. In due course he became a firm and lifelong friend of survivor Yury Yudin until his death in 2013. Yury Konstantinovich also established the Dyatlov Foundation, which is based in Ekaterinburg and was set up to:

- Perpetuate the memory of the Dyatlov group.

- Act as a centre to educate and provide assistance to those interested in researching the story of the hikers.

- Provide paid guides to those wishing to travel to the Dyatlov Pass and the surrounding area connected with the journey of the Dyatlov group.

- Undertake the care and maintenance of the Dyatlov memorial and graves in Mikhailovskoye (*St. Michael the Archangel*) cemetery and the two graves in Ivanovskoye (*St John the Baptist*) cemetery in Ekaterinburg.

- Establish the truth of what happened to the hikers on the night of 1/2 February 1959.

The Dyatlov Foundation is a non-profit organization and asks for small donations to help with the above work. The Foundation was instrumental in getting the authorities to reopen the Dyatlov Case in 2019 through a fund raising campaign. Even with the help given through the fund raising, a significant portion of the costs was borne by the Foundation and recently (in early 2019), the services of a second lawyer have been engaged who has agreed to work without charge for a short period to assist.

In addition to the above, the memorial at the Mikhailovskoye (*St. Michael the Archangel*) cemetery will require cleaning due to reconstruction and quotes are being obtained for this work. In the longer term, a memorial to the Dyatlov group in Ekaterinburg is being considered and more news on this will be given in due course.

# Appendix IX

FOI request to the CIA

Central Intelligence Agency

Washington, D.C. 20505

11 December 2019

Dr. John Curcio

Reference: F-2019-01160

Dear Dr. Curcio:

This is a final response to your 20 February 2019 Freedom of Information Act (FOIA) request for **any and all information relating to the following incident or individuals [identified in your 20 February 2019 letter]: between 1 and 2 February 1959, nine ski-hikers lost their lives under unclear circumstances in the northern Ural Mountains in Sverdlovsk Oblast, Soviet Union.** We processed your request in accordance with the FOIA, 5 U.S.C. § 552, as amended, and the CIA Information Act, 50 U.S.C. § 3141, as amended.

We did not locate any records responsive to the portion of your request for records on the 1959 incident in which nine ski-hikers lost their lives under unclear circumstances. Although our searches were reasonably calculated to uncover all relevant documents, and it is highly unlikely that repeating those searches would change the result, you nevertheless have the legal right to appeal the finding of no records responsive to your request.

With respect to the remainder of your request for records on the individuals identified in your request, in accordance with Section 3.6(a) of Executive Order 13526, the CIA can neither confirm nor deny the existence or nonexistence of records responsive to your request. The fact of the existence or nonexistence of such records is itself currently and properly classified and is intelligence sources and methods information protected from disclosure by Section 6 of the CIA Act of 1949, as amended, and Section 102A(i)(l) of the National Security Act of 1947, as amended. Therefore, your request is denied pursuant to FOIA exemptions (b)(1) and (b)(3).

As the CIA Information and Privacy Coordinator, I am the CIA official responsible for this determination. You have the right to appeal this response to the Agency Release Panel, in my care, within 90 days from the date of this letter. Please include the basis of your appeal.

Please be advised that you may seek dispute resolution services from the CIA's FOIA Public Liaison or from the Office of Government Information Services (OGIS) of the National Archives and Records Administration. OGIS offers mediation services to help resolve disputes between FOIA requesters and Federal agencies. Please note, contacting CIA's FOIA Public Liaison or OGIS does not affect your right to pursue an administrative appeal.

| To contact **CIA** directly or to appeal the CIA's response to the Agency Release Panel: | To contact the Office of **Government Information Services (OGIS)** for mediation or with questions: |
|---|---|
| Central Intelligence Agency Washington, DC 20505 Information and Privacy Coordinator (703) 613-3007 (Fax) (703) 613-1287 (CIA FOIA Public Liaison / FOIA Hotline) | Office of Government Information Services National Archives and Records Administration 8601 Adelphi Road – OGIS College Park, MD 20740-6001 (202) 741-5770 (877) 864-6448 (202) 741-5769 (Fax) ogis@nara.gov |

If you have any questions regarding our response, you may contact the CIA's FOIA Hotline at (703) 613-1287.

Sincerely,

*Mark Lilly*

Mark Lilly
Information and Privacy Coordinator

# Acknowledgements

Once again I would like to thank my good friend Yury Kuntsevich (referred to in the text as Yury K) and the Dyatlov Foundation. Also, my dear friend Marina Yurevna Yakhontova for all her help which goes way beyond translating, Yury Yakimov for seeing me and explaining his story in detail, Valeria Nikolayevna Gamatina for the details and photo of her late husband and treating us so well on our visit, Natalia Napolskikh and Danil (and Anatole, Uncle Mischa, Slava, Sasha, Mischa, Igor, Sergey) for their kindness and hospitality plus additional photos for my website.

Plus I want to thank (in no particular order):- Alexey Martin of RUFORS, Shamil Shabirov (a man who proves Russians have a sense of humour!), photo journalist Mikhail Petrov for his help and also use of photos – his excellent work can be seen on the link below, the *Spirit of the Forest* Lisa Kuzmina, Nastya Golovachova, Rashid (Privet Brataan!), Sergey Fadeev, Alexander Alekseenkov, Elnara & Sasha & Svetlana Zeitullaeva, Olga Skorikov, Dr Gabor Szekely, SZTALKER for allowing the use of his excellent research, Zoltan Komor for his kind help and translations with SZTALKER, Dr John Curcio for sharing his efforts regarding information which might be held by the CIA, Natalia Zayatc for Illustration work, BHARDWAZ for illustration work, Triona McCloskey for proofreading, Catherine Baduin for putting it all together and Jane Korunoski for the superb cover work.

I would like to give a very special mention and thank you to Valentin Gerasimovich Yakimenko for allowing me to use the results of his superb research on the Dyatlov negatives and the date on the original case file.

I am also very grateful to certain people I regularly correspond with, who are a great help for discussing ideas and various theories. In this group, I would like to mention Irina Hood, Ronald Cyr, Hendrik Pustow for useful suggestions on calendar dates, Norene Yarbrough, Bill Haymes, Ken Watson, John Wantling, Andre Van Meulebrock, Professor Bill Ohm (both Bill Ohm & Norene Yarbrough had interesting views on the night sky lights). Bill is a medium/Intuitive Communicator and can be contacted on *professorohm@outlook.com*, Steve Smith for many helpful suggestions and e mail discussions, Sean O' Connor for some excellent background and technical advice.

Another person I wish to mention is 'M' the Canadian Pathologist who gave me some very useful advice about deaths in extremely cold conditions. On the subject of medical matters I also want to thank Dr John Brewster & his lovely wife Lillian whom I constantly pester for medical information.

Last and definitely not least, I want to mention the two men who came to my rescue at the Dyatlov Pass and drove me from the Dyatlov Memorial Rock all the way back through the mountains 600km to my hotel doorstep in Ekaterinburg – Artem and Zack. I cannot thank them enough to have done all that and refused payment of any kind to the extent they would not let me pay for the meal on the way back. May God give them both a good life.

# Bibliography & Sources

I am very grateful to Valentin Gerasimovich Yakimenko for permission to reproduce his ground breaking research on the Dyatlov negatives and his work on the case file date.

As always, I am very grateful to Yury Kuntsevich to be able to use the resources of the Dyatlov Foundation plus the organisation of the trip to the Dyatlov Pass.

The two interviews with Evgeny Okishev and Leonid Proshkin in Chapter 11 by Nikolai Varsegov, Natalia Varsegova are courtesy of *Komsomolskaya Pravda* and appeared on 13 August 2013

Lev Ivanov's article in chapter 10 appeared in two parts on 22 and 24 November 1990 in the newspaper *Leninsky Put'* and are courtesy of *Leninsky Put'*

I am extremely grateful to Professor 'W' from a Continental university who gave me substantial help on the background to the Mansi way of life. Professor 'W' has asked to remain anonymous for the simple reason that 'they' do not wish to be inundated with enquiries related to the Mansi and the Dyatlov Incident.

I am also very grateful to Professor Art Leete, Professor of Ethnology at the University of Tartu for clarification on the Polina Shnaider story

275

and how it relates to the story of the Mansi murdering a female geologist in Dyatlov accounts.

The dreadful, complete story involving the death of a child in the introduction is in an excellent book *Cops: Their Lives in Their Own Words* by Mark Baker, 2007 Abacus Books. I highly recommend it.

For anyone wanting to find out more about the Soviet's methods of dealing with ADA balloons, read pp 329-334 of *The Tu 128 Fiddler* by Alan Dawes, Sergey Burdin & Nikolai Popov, published by Fonthill Media. An absolutely superb book, but definitely one for the serious Soviet military aviation enthusiast.

I have mentioned Moscow-based photo journalist Mikhail Petrov's help with photographs. His website and excellent work can be seen at *http://www.mikhailpetrov.ru.*

Alexey Martin is the main contact in the Urals region for paranormal activities. His website is *http://www.russia-paranormal.org.*

For details of Soviet nuclear rocket and missile development as well as details of underground nuclear explosions and tests, look no further than: *Russian Strategic Nuclear Forces.* This cannot now be bought in Russia, but copies are available in the West and it is published by MIT (Massachusetts Institute of Technology) and edited by Pavel Podvig. This is a book for the serious Soviet nuclear researcher

## The Mansi & Shamans

- *The Struggle against "Shamanism". Soviet religious policy towards the indigenous religions of Siberia and Northern Russia* (Studies on Inter-Religious Relations 40) by O. Sundstrom. 2007, Uppsala: Swedish Science Press

- *Repression of Shamans and Shamanism in Khabarovsk Krai, 1920s to the early 1950s.* By Tatania Bulgakova and Olle Sundstrom

AND

- *The Cultural Bases in the North. Sovietisation and Indigenous Resistance.* By Eva Toulouze, Laur Vallikivi & Art Leete are both published in: *Ethnic & Religious Minroities in Stalin's Soviet Union, New Dimensions of Research* (Edited by Andrej Kotljarchuk & Olle Sundstrom, 2017, Södertörns högskola (Södertörn University) Library SE-141 89 Huddinge)

- *The Kazym War. The decline of Shamanic culture in Western Siberia.* By A Leete, Tartu University Press (2002)

- *Shamanism.* By Piers Vitebsky, University of Oklahoma Press (1995)

For the period 1928 up to the start of the War for a description of how the northern tribes (particularly the Khanty) were treated, a good grounding is given in:

- *The Tenacity of Ethnicity: A Siberian Saga in Global Perspective.* By Marjorie Mandelstam Balzer (Princeton University Press 1999)

## Alakit River Story

Very little can be found and it is in connection with the Dyatlov Incident. I am grateful to Irina Hood for the sources:

- https://odynokiy.livejournal.com/147754.html

- https://iknigi.net/avtor-mihail-gershteyn/11954-tayny-nlo-i-prishelcev-mihail-gershteyn/read/page-3.html

## Gennady Kizilov

I always felt that journalist Gennady Kizilov was one of the few people to really tear the official story to shreds. I don't agree with everything he concluded, but he had the right approach.

- http://www.samlib.ru/k/kizilow_g_i/150308-1.shtml

Aerial Surveillance

Since the first publication of this book, I met up with a long time acquaintance, a Physics and Engineering graduate, who has asked not to be identified. I will call him Shuggy.

He is now retired from a career spent working on US and UK Defence Programs with a major Defence Systems Contractor. He explained to me the evolution and development of Radar and Electro-Optical systems used for Navigation, Reconnaissance and Weapons Targeting and encouraged me to believe that the Russian capability of these systems would have been in no way inferior to Western systems at that time. In his post-graduate work he had come across several advanced materials research papers from the Eastern Bloc that supported that view. He had read my original book "Mountain of the Dead " and it was he who put forward the suggestion of the Dyatlov group coming under surveillance and possible attack by an aerial platform of some kind.

After reading the second edition of this book he contacted me again giving more advice to help identify the possible type of aerial platform involved. He re-interpreted a number of Photographs in Appendix 1 by considering the probable exposure time of the Photos to conclude that an object emitting pulses of light had crossed the frame, consistent with a Drone with Pulse jet boosters or main engine having overflown the group. He suggested that this could have been a developmental variant of the Lavochkin Reconnaissance Drone. I am most grateful for his input.

GoFundMe Campaign for Raising Funds

I would like to give a special mention and thank you to all the people who kindly donated towards getting the case re-investigated: The Tennessee, USA businessman who made a substantial donation and who I will call 'S', plus (in no particular order); Michael Seaborn, Ian Estes, Christopher Jeffery, Sandra & John Fountain, Zoltan Komor, Lisa Ashby, Ron Cyr, Scott Philbrook, Joe Segovia, Jonas Osinkis, Warren Parsons, Laurent Jayr, Coral Hull, John Wantling, David Cayton, Steven Hall, 'Diane/Deena', 'Luther (Luder23 – Walking Breading)', Allan Kristensen, Wolfgang Bierbach, Teodora Peshava, Bill Ohm.

# Other Mystery Books
# by the Author

Non-fiction

- Mountain of the Dead: The Dyatlov Pass Incident
- The Lighthouse: The Mystery of the Eilean Mor Lighthouse Keepers
- Unsolved Aviation Mysteries: Five Strange Tales of Sea and Air

Author's Websites

For additional theories and for photos of the trip I made to the Dyatlov Pass in 2015 please check out my website here:

*www.dyatlov-pass-incident.com*

My general Author's website here;

*www.keithmccloskey.com*

Printed in Great Britain
by Amazon

29812995R00162